Thinking Rationally
about
Christian Theology

A Handbook on Polemics

Thinking Rationally
about
Christian Theology

A Handbook on Polemics

Timothy B. Chrisman

BENNINGTON, VT

This book is dedicated to Keri,
My soulmate in our walk with the Lord.

Table of Contents

Foreword
by
Dr. Jerry Sutton

Several years ago, it was my honor to supervise Tim Chrisman as he prepared his PhD Dissertation. As a serious minded pastor, he was (and is), in my estimation a sound example of a Pastor-Theologian. He has accomplished a commendable work in his Thinking Rationally about Christian Theology: A Handbook on Polemics. Polemics, or the discipline of countering heretical beliefs, goes back to the Patristic period in the works of scholars like Irenaeus and Cyprian. Sad to say, it is a discipline needed in every generation because of the constant unfolding nuances of unbelief.

In my estimation, this volume deserves your attention. Why do I commend it? First, from his example as a pastor, he knows first-hand that heretics abound. He is keenly aware of the necessity to provide sound, biblical answers to unbiblical beliefs, half-truths, and malicious distortions of orthodox Christianity. Second, he is addressing issues that are prevalent in our postmodern culture. In a day when doctrine is downplayed and the notion of absolute truth is questioned, here is help for those who want to respond but are not sure how. Thirdly, his thoughts are well organized following the classical organization of the study of theology. And finally, his work is an apologetic in the finest meaning of the term. He is both commending and defending the essence of the Christian faith. Here is a ready defense.

Tim, thanks for a job well done! I commend your book warmly with the hope that it will help many to defend their faith with confidence.

- Dr. Jerry Sutton,
Washington DC

Preface

During my first pastorate, I encountered visitors who attended the morning worship service of our small congregation. At the end of the service, the visitors, a married couple, informed me that Jesus is the Son of God, but not God, and that belief in Jesus as God and Savior would result in God the Father's eternal rejection. This belief, a variation of the heresy called Arianism, was the message that this couple proclaimed in churches throughout the region, spreading confusion among many communities of believers. I showed them several Scripture passages that proved their convictions to be unbiblical, but they left, continuing to hold their heretical beliefs.

Doctrinal confusion exists to an excessive degree within the Church today—so much so, that in the twenty-first century in the West, a Christian who holds to a completely biblical theology is a rare find. A majority of self-proclaimed Christians have within their doctrinal system one or more unbiblical beliefs. Two reasons are the cause of this travesty. First, the errant beliefs from competing world religions, postmodern philosophies, cultic movements, and popular misconceptions have negatively influenced the Church. Secondly, the majority of pulpits have been silent in the area of doctrine, making the average church attender woefully unprepared to distinguish sound theology from heresy. Due to these two challenges, the Church in the West has distanced itself from its original orthodoxy that was grounded in the Word of God. Polemics, as the discipline that counters heretical beliefs, must return to the Church. True believers must recover this often-ignored art to defend the biblical faith and correct the errors which are embraced by so many who claim to identify as Jesus' disciples and even attend Christian worship services.

Thinking Rationally About Christian Theology
A Handbook on Polemics

This text is an effort to help pastors, church leaders, seminary students, and believers who are actively participating in the Great Commission to address unbiblical beliefs as they arise and provide a defense of the major tenets of the faith.

As polemics is a discipline that is practiced by a believing community, this work is the result of the support and effort of many believers. This book would not have been a reality if not for Mark Ballard, Jared August, Ralph Slater, and the editorial team of Northeastern Baptist Press, to which I owe my appreciation. To the congregations of Tsena Commocko Baptist Church and Little River Baptist Church, I would also offer my thanks for their constant encouragement and demonstration of Christlike love during my twenty-three years of pastoral ministry. For my wife, Keri, and my two daughters, Kaylee and Emily, I am grateful for their belief in me and their love for me; despite all of my eccentricities. To my Lord and Savior, Jesus Christ, I am most of all thankful for the eternal salvation granted solely by grace and provided by His sacrificial death and His victorious resurrection.

- Timothy B. Chrisman

Introduction

Historical Background:

They called him a "dumb ox." He rarely spoke, and so his fellow students thought him mentally deficient. However, his mentor declared "We may call this lad a dumb ox, but I tell you that the whole world is going to hear his bellowing."[1] Albertus Magnus, his mentor, was certainly right: The "dumb ox" was none other than Thomas Aquinas (1225-1274). During his 59 years, Aquinas published two great masterpieces: Summa Theologica *and* Summa Contra Gentiles. Summa Contra Gentiles *consisted of his apologetic of Christianity in response to Islam and* Summa Theologica *represented Aquinas' unfinished but detailed synopsis of Christian doctrine.[2] Aquinas' brilliant synthesis of Augustinian theological method with Aristotelian logic began to impact the Church and Western thought during the High Middle Ages; still today his is the official teaching philosophy of the Roman Catholic Church, which acknowledges him as one of the Doctors of the Church.*

M any Christians, ridiculed for their seeming lack of intelligence, find themselves in a situation similar to that of the young Aquinas. Secularism continues to dominate, and atheism, agnosticism, and those who

---

1   Roger E. Olson, *The Story of Christian Theology* (Downers Grove: InterVarsity, 1999), 333.

2   Aidan Nichols, *Discovering Aquinas* (Grand Rapids: Eerdmans, 2002), 7–12.

Thinking Rationally About Christian Theology
A Handbook on Polemics

self-designate as non-religious continue to mock the tenets of Christianity. Its teachings are increasingly unpopular and even regarded as ludicrous. In such an environment, Christians may find it hard to respond to intellectual attacks from skeptics who denigrate the doctrines of the faith. Facing our skeptics, Christ-followers find ourselves in an uncomfortable position: Somewhat embarrassed about our own beliefs due to the popular misconception that the doctrines of Christianity have no basis in rationality, some Christian teachers have tragically asked Christians to accept on blind faith doctrines such as the Trinity and the existence of hell, and that such beliefs are not rational or not to be questioned.

To compound our difficulties, within the Church, Christians are also confronted with unbiblical beliefs. Those assuming the roles of teacher, popular speaker, and (sadly) even pastor present concepts that stray far from biblical Christianity. Unbiblical concepts, often directly in line with historical heresies, are falsely recognized as orthodox beliefs. Although false teaching or heresy has plagued the Church almost from its birth (Gal 1:6-7; 1 John 4:1-3; Rev. 2:14-15), more recently Church leaders have allowed the world's ideologies to shape her doctrines, but pointedly in stark contrast with biblical faith.

Several notable theologians, apologists, and church leaders are sounding alarms concerning these developments, but much distortion of Christian theology has gone unchecked. With the situation so dire, believers must be reintroduced to the doctrines and discipline that the apostles and the writers of the Early Church used to combat false teaching. Rarely spoken within some Christian circles, and only mentioned in seminaries but seldom taught as a discipline, "polemics" is the field of study that exposes heresy and unbiblical ideologies, differentiating biblical orthodoxy from popular opinion. Polemics may be described as the discipline that defends against attacks within the Church, whereas apologetics defends against attacks from without.

Scripture attests to the value of polemics. In Paul's letter to Titus, the apostle writes to his protégé that the churches' teaching elders on the island of Crete were firmly to fix their minds on the apostolic teachings so that they could preach sound doctrine and contest those who contradicted it (Titus 1:9). Jude exhorted the first-century "beloved" who acknowledge "our only Master and Lord Jesus Christ" to defend the faith against those who deny Christ; certain teachers claimed to be believers, but introduced ungodly behavior and unbiblical doctrines (Jude 3-4). A significant part

Introduction

of the apostolic ministry to the early Christians was to address heretical teachings that had infiltrated local congregations (Acts 15:1-29; Gal 1:6-10; 2 Cor 11:1-4; 2 Pet 2:1-22; Rev 2:14-16, 20-29). When the Apostolic Age ended, the polemical ministry of the Church continued through theologians including Irenaeus of Lyons (c. 130 – 202), Tertullian (c. 160 – 220), Athanasius of Alexandria (296 – 373), Augustine of Hippo (354 – 430), and Dominic (1170 – 1221). Much later, Joseph Butler (1692 – 1752), J. Gresham Machen (1881 – 1937), and Harold O. J. Brown (1933 – 2007) corrected the heresies that arose during their lifetime.

Christians of the twenty-first century find ourselves in a world that increasingly embraces creeds that stand opposed to the faith. As we present the tenets of the faith, much of the world and even many within the Church find a reason to take offense in our beliefs or consider them ludicrous and irrational. Quite to the contrary, our orthodox Christian beliefs are rational, defensible, and biblical; by them Christians grasp the world and all that God made. Sincere Christians stood at the forefront of the disciplines of science and mathematics with an unblinking recognition of a nature ordered by its maker. To get a grasp of the soundness of the doctrines of the faith, even Christians today must rationally examine them in light provided by their original teachers and defenders and the contexts provided by history. This resource is an attempt to accomplish that task. So let us embark on a journey that has the potential to equip believers for the apologetic tasks and polemical battles that we wage to contend for our faith.

Chapter 1

Prolegomena

> *Zeus's father and mother were Cronos, a titan, and Rhea. Cronos, the son of Uranus, is the god of the sky and ruler of the gods, and Gaea (sometimes spelled "Gaia"), is the goddess known as "Mother Earth." Discontent with the rule of his father, Cronos overthrew Uranus and, to prevent his children from overthrowing him, swallowed them each a moment after their birth. Due to Rhea's deception, Zeus was able to escape. After reaching adulthood, Zeus returned and poisoned his father's drink, causing Cronos to vomit the children he had consumed. These children were Demeter, Hades, Hera, Hestia, and Poseidon. Upon freeing his siblings, Zeus allied with them and went to war with Cronos and his fellow Titans. This war, which nearly destroyed the universe, ended with Zeus' victory, partly due to the assistance of Prometheus the Titan, the hundred-handed Hecatoncheires, and the Cyclopes. Victorious Zeus and his fellow gods, the Olympians, ruled supreme from atop Mt. Olympus.*[3]

This synopsis comes from Greek mythology, which tells the story of the origins of the pantheon of gods and their subsequent exploits. For centuries, many Greeks accepted the stories of the gods as true. Yet today, such stories are regarded as myths, containing no element of truth whatsoever. Ancient myths of this sort are today regarded as completely fictional stories used to explain varied natural phenomena, such as weather patterns, geological formations, natural disasters, and the births of na-

---

3   Edith Hamilton, *Mythology* (New York: Warner, 1942), 66–9.

tions. Once mankind has grown in its understanding of science and other academic fields, so the claim goes, such myths are no longer necessary, despite their usefulness in transmitting cultural folkways and societal values.[4] Therefore, today's thinking goes, no one needs to believe them any longer. Some have grouped Christian beliefs in the same classification.

To group Christian theology with Greek mythology, however, would be an ignorant dismissal of the factual evidence that supports its truth claims. Secondly, and even more fundamentally, such classification denies the radical differences between theology and mythology. The mythology of the Greco-Roman pantheon consists mainly of stories of a deity, or usually deities, interacting with natural or supernatural forces or other deities and, on occasion, communicating and guiding human beings. In essence, such narratives, though very exciting and the subject of extensive studies,[5] are now taken to have no factual basis to them whatsoever. Such myths, then, are the result of human speculation. Theology, on the other hand, may be defined as the result of Divine communication as to the nature of God, His will for mankind, and His ultimate plan for all of creation. The origins of theology come not from human speculation, but from Divine disclosure. As Christians study their beliefs and communicate them with fellow believers and also with unbelievers, they must remember that they are participating in a factual exercise. Theology stands alongside other academic disciplines such as philosophy, science, medicine, literature, and history. That is why an introduction to theology, before the actual study of the doctrines that make up theology, is so important.

When one begins a study in theology, the natural impulse is to begin with the actual doctrines of the faith. Rushing headlong into the doctrinal study without understanding the very nature of theology can lead to difficult issues further down the road for the believer. That is why responsible theologians who produce systematic theologies devote the first chapter of their studies to "prolegomena." Prolegomena or "first words" refers to the subsection of theology that involves defining

---

4   From Greek, mythos (μύθος) is "...any thing delivered by word of mouth... in its widest sense, word, speech..." [H. G. Liddell and R. Scott, A Greek-English Lexicon (New York: Harper, 1867), 953, assoc. w/ Homer].

5   Cf., e.g., Jörg Rüpke, *Pantheon: A New History of Roman Religion* (Princeton: Princeton Univ., 2018).

theology,[6] the nature of its study, a discussion of why studying theology is essential, a listing of various categories and sub-categories of theology, and theological method or the process of how one develops one's theology. Such topics hardly sound controversial, but, in all actuality, the truth and facts of such an approach have been the subject of debate over the years.

Historical Background:

In 381 A.D., Roman Emperor Theodosius I (r. 379-395), declared Christianity the national religion of the empire. From that point, through the Middle Ages and even into the Early Modern Era, Christianity, or at least the Christian worldview, dominated in the West. A dramatic change occurred when the Age of Enlightenment with its accompanying or even underlying skepticism dawned in the seventeenth and eighteenth centuries.[7] Skepticism reject-

---

6   See for example, Petrus van Mastricht, *Prolegomena*, vol. 1 of *Theoretical-Practical Theology* (Grand Rapids: Reformation Heritage, 2018, trans. T. M. Rester, ed. J. R. Beeke). Many theologians who accept divine communication as the basis of biblical theology study the Bible's statements as a series of facts to be cataloged and considered in the broader context of revealed truth. On the Bible's words as "facts" or data to which theological "science" may be applied, see Charles Hodge, *Systematic Theology* (Grand Rapids: Eerdmans, 1973 rprnt.), 1:1–19. See, generally, the early chapters of Millard J. Erickson, *Christian Theology* (Grand Rapids: Baker, 2013), 3–117. For Hodge and Erickson, such use of direct biblical data viz. its logical and metaphysical implications, probable inferences we may draw from Scripture, allows Scripture to give us "inductive conclusions" (66), conclusions from general revelation, and finally speculative hypothesis are to be considered in arriving at theories of biblical meaning "adduced" with creativity and readjustment. See also: Henry C. Thiessen, *Lectures in Systematic Theology* (Grand Rapids: Eerdmans, 1989, rev. Vernon D. Doerksen; available online at several URLs, who holds that "theology rests upon a solid objective basis" (3), "The Bible is to the theologian what nature is to the scientist, a body of unorganized or only partly organized facts" (5); Robert Letham, *Systematic Theology* (Wheaton: Crossway, 2019).

7   Descartes' method of doubt (despite his rationalism), and Bacon's, Locke's, and Hume's empiricism with Spinoza's philosophical monism all tended to moderate or even eradicate religious authority in the Age of Reason.

ed the Bible as the ultimate authority for matters of doctrine and ethics, ushering in a reliance on philosophical and theological movements to reinterpret, deride, or altogether dismiss many of the tenets and truth claims of Christian orthodoxy. With the changing attitude towards Scripture and Christian doctrines, theology suffered a demotion in stature as an academic discipline. By promoting free and independent self-determination as to how, what and why to believe, mottos such as "I think, therefore I am" undermined the authoritative proclamations of various church authority and opened wide the doors for any person to draw any conclusion he wanted about God, creation, salvation, eternal life, etc. Heresies and unbiblical teachings, then, no longer came from obscure academics or fringe radicals, but developed into a regular practice, to the point that many heresies are confused as being the biblical doctrines of historic Christianity. Christians, and not just academic Christians, need to recognize theology as a worthy pursuit, and an essential one to expose and reject unbiblical beliefs from the Church. The first section of this book will then be an attempt to present theology in that light.

Christian Theology as a Rational Pursuit

Theology has always been a fascinating subject, even for those who do not care to admit it. Children ask their parents what God is like. Individuals in the waning years wonder what happens after death. Those who deny God's existence often discuss why they believe God does not exist, which is, in itself, a theological (as well as a philosophical) discussion. Generally, most people during their lifetimes will turn their thoughts to theological subjects. Just as individuals use math daily for all sorts of tasks, people should regularly reflect on their Creator and His purpose and will for them.[8]

Three ideologies work against understanding theology as a serious, rational pursuit. One is pluralism. Pluralism asserts that multiple faiths possess equal validity. This turns the objective search for truth into a subjective one because there are multiple truths of equal soundness

---

8   See R. C. Sproul, *Everyone's a Theologian: An Introduction to Systematic Theology* (Sanford, FL: Ligonier, 2014)

that address the same reality, in this case the real being of God. If the pluralistic conception is warranted, then a person's preference dictates his beliefs, rather than carefully examining a source of authority such as the Bible. Another harmful ideology is individualism when it is taken to an extreme. Such individualism recognizes the absolute authority of the autonomous person. Arguing from the perspective of individualism, one could claim that her doctrine may contradict Scripture, but because it is her personal belief and for that reason alone, it is a seen as a legitimate belief. The most dangerous of these ideologies is relativism, which simply states that absolutes do not exist; such absolutes include truths about God, self, identity, and morality. With the acceptance of these popular perspectives, the result is the view that the study of doctrine relies more on speculation rather than rigorous examination. Later, the attitude of personal skepticism can take hold. Much about widespread conceptions of God, the nature of Christ, and eternal salvation that results from pluralism, individualism, and relativism is, when presented in media, espoused by celebrities. Such views are even declared from many pulpits, the tragic end product of speculation.

Applying pluralism, individualism, and relativism to other scenarios reveals their absurdity. It becomes evident that no driver would cross a bridge designed by engineers who held that the structure's design might represent multiple and contradicting calculations. No patient would want to be operated on in a procedure based solely on the surgeon's personal opinion. Nor would a passenger want to fly in a plane whose pilot believes that the measurement of the distance between the ground and the plane that he is flying is relative to the pilot's estimation and not based on the altimeter. And such absurdity does not merely pertain to the measurable or that which is calculated: speculation without critical examination often produces disastrous results when applied to theology and ethics, two fields generally regarded as non-empirical in nature. If skeptics protest that an individual's personal beliefs concerning God could do little harm, the believer must respond that having the wrong beliefs could produce eternally disastrous results. The Bible consistently warns about such results throughout the canon. Before he died, Moses issued a warning to the Israelites before they crossed over the Jordan to invade the lands of Canaan. If they failed to obey the LORD and His commandments, judgment would come in the form of a host of curses that included pestilence, persecution from enemies, and exile (Deut. 28:15-68). Jesus warned that drastic measures to turn from sin were preferable to being cast away from God into the everlasting torment of hell (Matt. 5:28–30; 18:8–9; Mark 9:45–47).

Contrasting the warnings against rash speculation, the Bible puts forth examples of thoughtful insight concerning God's nature, His astounding works, and other doctrinal themes. The psalmist was amazed at God's eternal existence (Ps. 90:1–4). David's Psalm reflected on the LORD's omniscience and omnipresence (Ps. 139:1–24). Isaiah illustrates the idiocy of idolatry by explaining how the sacred images are the product of human hands and cannot compare to the unsurpassable God (Isa. 40:18–26). John expounded on the amazing truth that the eternal Person of God the Son came into the world as a man to save the world (John 1:1–14). Peter acknowledged that, to God, a thousand years are like a day to human beings (2 Pet. 3:8). Each of these passages discloses a deep reflection on beliefs about God that Christians believe is God's self-disclosure. The pursuit of studying doctrine is a profound undertaking.

Theologians of yesteryear understood this. Augustus Hopkins Strong (1836 – 1921) classified theology as a science for two main reasons. For the first and obvious reason, for believers, theology deals with objective facts, facts revealed to man by God. However, Strong adds that theology does not involve the collecting of facts alone. The facts of theology must be examined in how they relate to one another, which is the second reason for describing theology as a science.[9] Because of the effects of scientism, or the belief that the physical sciences are the only means to gain facts, most in the contemporary culture would cringe at the association of the word, "science" placed beside "theology." Yet, even if "science" is not used in its definition, theology as a discipline requires critical thinking and deep reflection. A mathematician must make sure that his calculations are precise when solving an equation. Just a slight deviation would result in a wrong answer, to which carelessness also often may lead. The same may be said of theology: careless approaches have led to many an aberrant doctrinal system, leading thousands or even millions astray. Mathematics and theology represent two different fields, but those who study the things of God would be wise to put forth their best mental effort and proceed with a joyful spirit and humble caution.

---

9   Augustus Hopkins Strong, *Systematic Theology*, vol. 1 (Philadelphia: Judson, 1907), 1:11.

Prolegomena

Systematic Theology

The placing of truths of the doctrine of the Christian faith into a coherent and rational format so that it is recognized as a consistent, logical belief system is what is called systematic theology. Whether in single-volume summaries or large, multivolume tomes, systematic theology divides Christian doctrine into major categories and divides those categories into minor ones. It then recognizes how the subjects relate to the passages of Scripture in correlation with each other to present one consistent belief system. Responsible theologians understand that a rigorous method is necessary, one which acknowledges the ultimate authority of God's Word to judge how Christians in the past as well as in various traditions and perspectives should be applied in constructing a theology.

Should Christianity have a systematic theology? Some would answer in the negative; they hold that organizing beliefs with appropriate Scripture passages into categories and subcategories would violently distort the message of the Bible. Systematizing doctrine is also seen as a means to impose dogma. Harsh images are conjured of the past ages of the Church, such as when, in the Middle Ages and in reaction to the Protestant Reformation, doctrines were simply declared true by the authority of the Church and her leaders, and any deviation from officially recognized doctrine brought swift and severe punishment. Such dogmatism, it is claimed, is not the main emphasis of Christianity. Jesus' ethical teachings should be emphasized over dogmatic statements.

Others believe a specific narrative theology as a better alternative than systematic theology. Narrative theology, as its name suggests, emphasizes the stories in the Bible and their themes instead of direct propositional statements about God. Therefore, the narrative theologian's "system" prefers stories that illustrate belief instead of direct statements about belief; narrative theology celebrates "the ambiguity of reference" over unambiguity.[10] Such are the results of the devastating impact of deconstructionism on the theology of the late twentieth century and early into the twenty-first.

---

10   Maarten Wisse, "Narrative Theology and the Use of the Bible in Systematic Theology" in *Ars Disputandi* (URL http://www.ArsDisputandi.org [5(2005):1.3.3], accessed January 6, 2023).

Thinking Rationally About Christian Theology
A Handbook on Polemics

Before believers completely succumb to the deconstructionism in theology, they should look to their doctrinal heritage. Christian theologians have long recognized the necessity of placing the doctrines of the faith in a format that clarifies their logical agreement. Charles Hodge (1797 – 1878) submitted four reasons why Christianity needs a systematic theology. 1) The human mind is constructed in a way that systematizing and integrating the doctrinal facts found in Scripture comes naturally to us. 2) Humans cannot know how the separate truths found in the Bible relate to one another unless some system is used, similar to the arrangement of facts in relation to one another in other scientific disciplines. 3) A systematic theology is the only means to logically defend Christian doctrine against skeptics and detractors. 4) Systematic theology is the result of God's will since it was God who revealed Himself through the Bible, and the Bible contains the systematic, theological works known as the epistles or New Testament letters.[11]

Despite varying objections to developing a systematic theology, it is a Scriptural concept. The psalmist (in Psalm 119:1-176) composed a lengthy discourse of 176 acrostically-arranged meditations on the Word of God, explaining its qualities and value. Reflecting on the creation of the Earth and the early history of the nation of Israel, the psalmist of Psalm 136 determined that God demonstrated His compassion on behalf of His people through miraculous intervention (Ps. 136:1-26). Jesus refuted the Sadducees, who challenged the belief in life after death, by applying God's announcement to Moses at the burning bush to a statement about the continued post-mortem existence of Abraham, Isaac, and Jacob (Matt. 22:23-33). Luke's record of Peter's sermon at Pentecost revealed an application of the prophecies of Joel 2:28-32 and Psalm 16:8-11, as well as the miracles and resurrection of Jesus, to provide support for Jesus' identity as the Messiah (Acts 2:14-36).

Paul's letter to the Roman Christians explains mankind's sinful predicament (Rom. 1:18-3:23) and our need for salvation through Christ (Rom. 6:17-23; 10:1-13). In response to a rejection of the resurrection of the dead at the church in Corinth, Paul reasoned with the congregation to persuade them of the truth of resurrection; starting with the resurrection of Jesus as the basis of the defeat of death, stressing his argument's very logical nature, Paul then provided a detailed synopsis of how the

---

11   Charles Hodge, *Systematic Theology*, vol. 1 (Grand Rapids: William B. Eerdmans, 1981), 1:2-3.

resurrection of believers would be accomplished (1 Cor. 15:1–58). To the Ephesian Christians, Paul devoted a significant portion of his letter to discussing the doctrine of grace (Eph. 2:1–10). With the description of faith, the writer of Hebrews submits a precursor to later summaries of Christian belief by first defining the doctrine and then drawing support by listing a host of examples from the Old Testament (Heb. 11:1–40).

Lengthy discussions about particular attributes of God and detailed explanations of various beliefs in the Bible provide strong support for the systemization of theology. Scripture perfectly portrays how doctrine should be discussed and shared. The joy that the writers of Scripture convey when they express theological beliefs demonstrates that theology does not have to be communicated harshly or used as a weapon, as systematic theology's detractors sometimes claim. Systematic theology requires reflection on the things of God, which, if done in humility and reverence, can be a form of worship. The systematizing of doctrine does not exist to abuse people or as a power play, but to draw people closer to God. David exemplifies this as he exults in the majesty and power of God and gives thanks for all that the LORD has given mankind (Ps. 8:1–9). Much of what opponents charge as reasons for discarding the idea of systematic theology is the historical abuse and misuse of theology.

As Hodge and Scripture itself attest, it is natural to develop a structure for one's beliefs and provide summaries to communicate them. For those who stress the use of narrative over systematic theology, it should be pointed out that biblical narratives do help to illustrate and bring life to theological concepts, but the framework of Christian doctrine does not consist solely of stories that vaguely communicate its truths. Rather, Christian doctrine is based on statements from among the testimonies of Scripture that communicate, as clearly as possible, the convictions of our faith. Other academic fields operate in the same manner. Consider the following statements:

- The Earth orbits around the sun.
- The Byzantine Empire fell with the capture of Constantinople in 1453.
- An adjective is a word that describes or modifies a noun.

All of these are statements that communicate propositional truths concerning aspects of various disciplines. Biology depends on the classification system that categorizes every life form on Earth. Literary experts rely on the qualification and description of the different types, or genres, of literature. Scholars should not object when theologians do the same with the myriad of biblical beliefs, which would include, "Jesus is both fully God and fully man" and "Humans are created in the image of God." The human mind is clearly fashioned to understand propositional truths, and such truths would include theological truths as they are formulated in the biblical record.

The biblical narratives are essential in that they present historical records of God's interaction with human history, but that is not their only purpose. Biblical narratives, just as with biblical discourse and the Bible's histories, wisdom literature, visionary accounts, and full-on prophecies, submit themes that cover the truth of God's nature, the nature of mankind, and ethical principles by which human beings should live. They correspond with other propositional statements about facts, which are also prevalent in the Bible, and biblical accounts cohere with each other and with what we learn from other special sciences and sound philosophical positions that are biblically-based and logically sound.

Systematic theology, in sum, is not a misrepresentation of the message of the Bible; it faithfully communicates the doctrinal message of the Bible. For that reason, it holds a necessary and crucial place in ordinary Christian life. Systematic theology should, therefore, be consistently and regularly utilized by the Church, especially but not exclusively in service to its educational ministries.

Chapter 2

Commonly Held Doctrines of Systematic Theology

Historical Background:

During the Protestant Reformation, in the year 1527, the imperial city of Rottenburg witnessed a scene of prolonged and grotesque execution. In the marketplace square, the condemned first had a piece of his tongue cut out. Afterward, portions of flesh were ripped from his body with hot metal tongs a total of seven times. Finally, the victim was tied to a ladder by ropes and pushed into a fire.[12] The executed was named Michael Sattler, a former prior in St. Peter's monastery, who had become an Anabaptist.[13] Sattler's rejection of infant baptism, his insistence on the believer's baptism, his refusal to worship Mary the Mother of Jesus, and his pacifism were among the reasons for this gruesome execution.[14]

As the flames began to engulf his body, Sattler was still able to speak and urgently declared to the mayor, the judges, and the general populace the need for repentance and conversion. Following this, the Anabaptist reformer prayed, "Almighty, eternal God, Thou art the way and the truth: because I have not been shown to be in error, I will with thy help to this day testify to the truth and seal it with my blood." His final words were, "Father, I commend my spirit into Thy hands."[15]

---

12   William R. Estep, *The Anabaptist Story*, 3d. ed. (Grand Rapids: William B. Eerdmans, 1996), 57.

13   Ibid., 58.

14   Ibid., 68–69.

15   Ibid., 72.

> *Michael Sattler's martyrdom signifies a conflict over truth. The Catholic Church believed that they possessed the truth about their cherished doctrines and practices of infant baptism and Mary's exalted status. Yet, conversely, Michael Sattler regarded believer's baptism and pacifism to represent true Christian beliefs. Both parties were firmly convinced, even, in Sattler's case, at the point of death, that they held valid convictions. Since Satan tempted Eve in the Garden of Eden, the world has experienced an ongoing truth crisis, a crisis that ultimately pits God's truth against the lies of Satan and of the world. How does one know the truth? The Bible has a lot to say on the subject, and God's communication of the truth, which theologians call, "revelation," is an essential part of Christian doctrine.*

Doctrine of Revelation: General Revelation

Through His creation, God reveals His existence. Some have confused general revelation with natural theology, but the two are distinctly different. Natural theology is the effort to build a doctrinal system on the basis of general revelation. Christians, who may disagree about the usefulness of natural theology, understand that some aspects of the nature of God can be determined by observing creation, but to build an entire credo by doing so is impossible. Humans are limited in their capacity to fully understand God.

Opposition to general revelation comes primarily from atheism and agnosticism. Atheists naturally deny God's existence: Nothing in the world indicates that it is designed by God, because they assert that God does not exist and that also, due to the plurality of claims of special revelation from the various world religions, all claims as to God's existence are suspect.[16] Agnostics claim that there is no scientifically verifiable evidence in the universe that demonstrates there is a God.[17] Most Christians accept general revelation, but some have dismissed it in favor of God communicating

---

16 C.M. Lorkowski, *Atheism Considered* (Basingstoke: Palgrave MacMillan, 2021), 121–27.

17 Julian Huxley, *Religion Without Revelation* (New York: Harper and Brothers, 1957), 5–7.

solely through special revelation. Karl Barth famously rejected natural theology and deemphasized general revelation. He claimed that the possibility of knowing God came solely through special revelation, specifically through the Word of God and Jesus Christ.[18] Barth, however, has remained in the minority; a majority of Christians appreciate the use of general revelation and specifically seek to build arguments for God's existence on it, such as William Paley's (1743 – 1805) argument of design which is perhaps best known.[19]

Does the natural world reveal that God exists? David certainly thought so. He stated that the very stars in the sky and the sky itself point to the existence and greatness of their Creator (Ps. 19:1). Luke's written account of Paul's sermon at Lystra explains that God revealed Himself to all of His creation through providing all of the goodness that nature had to offer (Acts 14:17). In his opening to his letters to the church in Rome, Paul declares that the world, as part of creation, declares the existence of the Creator (Rom. 1:18–20). Just a few verses later, Paul adds that human nature, e.g., in the area of the conscience, because of its awareness of right and wrong, also demonstrates the handiwork of a Divine Creator (Rom. 2:14–15). As the result of the Lord's direct creative activity, the world and the entire universe, according to the Bible, reveals the existence of God.

Masterpieces, whether they be creations of artists, composers, or writers, all bear one common trait: they did not come to exist on their own. They have been created by a master. When one admires the masterpiece, one admires the master even more, because the master is greater than the masterpiece. As a masterpiece of such magnitude that humans have yet to fully comprehend it, the universe can only have been created by a Master who far exceeds the magnitude of His creation.

---

18   Karl Barth, *Church Dogmatics*, 2.1, T. H. L Parker, W. B. Johnston, Harold Knight, and J. L. M. Haire, trans., G.W. Bromiley and T.F. Torrance, eds. (Peabody: Hendrickson, 1957), 168–72. Barth considered natural theology misleading to the unsaved in that it gave them no knowledge of sin, judgment, and salvation through Christ; it is up to the Church to share the good news of the special revelation of the life, death, and resurrection of Jesus to the unbelieving world.

19   Charles Tallaferro, "William Paley: Apologetics of Design and for Culture," in *The History of Apologetics*, eds. Benjamin K. Forrest, Joshua D. Chatraw, and Alister E. McGrath, (Grand Rapids: Zondervan, 2020), 347-351.

More recently, advances in science during the past few decades have indicated that the Universe exists because of the hand of a Grand Designer. Scientists have discovered what is now termed "cosmic fine-tuning." Demonstrated in mathematical expression, the physical laws of the universe have within them certain constants that never vary—the smallest variation of any of them would alter the universe so dramatically that it could not sustain life. Examples of fine-tuning include the law of gravity in which the gravitational force of two objects is determined by their respective masses, the distance between them, and the quality that is constant irrespective of mass and distance. Another constant is found in the atom, where the ratio of protons and electrons for every atom is always the same.[20] This evidence, along with many other similar constants, suggests the existence of an omnipotent and omniscient Designer who created the universe and all that is contained within it, as Dr. Craig suggests.

The fact of general revelation is exciting, but believers must remember that it has limitations. Such facts testify to God's existence and declare His all-powerful and all-knowing nature. However, one cannot know by them God's miraculous and providential interventions throughout Israel's history. Nor can one learn about Jesus' miraculous conception, earthly ministry, crucifixion, resurrection, ascension, and imminent return. With this information beyond the reach of general revelation, one cannot attain knowledge concerning personal salvation through it. General revelation fails to disclose everything the individual needs to have a relationship with his Creator. Another mode of revelation is needed.

Doctrine of Revelation:
Special Revelation

General revelation demonstrates the reality of God, but, as noted, it cannot communicate God's will for mankind nor can it be our only source for the many aspects of the multifaceted nature of God. Special revelation is God's self-disclosure to specific individuals or groups of people at specific times to reveal Himself. This type of revelation communicates truth about God and His will for mankind and His purpose for those who believe in Him.

---

20   William Lane Craig, *Reasonable Faith*, 3d ed. (Wheaton: Crossway, 2008), 158. Craig's discussion of such constants and their extremely fine-tuned character is well worth studying in detail.

Commonly Held Doctrines of Systematic Theology

The testimony of the Bible declares that, at times, God has communicated to individuals. At times, God spoke directly (Gen 4:6-7, 10-12; Ex. 3:4-4:17; 1 Sam. 3:2-14; Isa. 6:9-13; Ezek. 2:1-8) and often He spoke through His messengers, the prophets (e.g., 1 Sam. 10:18-19; 2 Sam. 7:4-16; 1 Kgs. 11:29-39; 2 Kgs. 22:15-20; Isa. 28:16-29; 42:5-20; Jer. 1:7-10; 7:1-27; 23:1-40; Ezek. 5:5-17; 14:2-23; 34:1-31; Amos 1:3-3:15; Heb. 1:1). There are three major means by which God has revealed Himself. Manifestations were God's miraculous interventions in history that disclosed an aspect of His nature not previously made known. God's call of Abraham (Gen. 12:1-3), of Moses through the burning bush (Ex. 3:2-6), the encounter of the Israelites with the LORD at Mt. Sinai (Ex. 19:1-19), and the Incarnation of the Son of God (Luke 1:30-37) all may be classified as manifestations. "Inspiration" concerns the Holy Spirit's work in directing the prophets, chroniclers, apostles, and their associates (e.g., Mark) to write the Old and New Testaments (2 Tim. 3:16-17; 2 Pet. 1:20-21). Illumination is God's work for His people to understand and apply His Word, to enable them to edify the Church and proclaim the Gospel to the unsaved (Ps. 119:18; Eph. 1:17-18; 1 Cor. 2:12; 1 Pet. 1:12). Thus, God has communicated to humanity throughout the history of the world and continues to do so, specifically through His Word.

Special revelation, as a tenet, had a long history of opposition. Opponents came from among those philosophers and intellectuals who argued against any concept of theism in which God as a Person interacted with His creation and intervened in the world's history. Among the earliest such opponents was Epicurus (341 - 270 BC.), who posited that the pantheon of Greek gods existed in an entirely separate sphere from human beings and did not communicate with humans at all.[21] The sixteenth and seventeenth centuries saw the rise of philosophical Deism to preeminence in Britain and France. (Deism argues for the existence of God and His creation of the world but denies His intervention in the world's history after its creation. God merely created the world and stood back and observed.[22]) Logical positivism, an early twentieth-century

---

21 Epicurus, *Letter to Menoeceus* in *Greek and Roman Philosophy After Aristotle*, ed. Jason L. Saunders (New York: The Free Press, 1966), 52. Such an early deism removed the gods from human ethical decisions.

22 James W. Sire, *The Universe Next Door*, 5th ed. (Downers Grove: Inter-Varsity, 2009), 50-62.

development from the early writings of Ludwig Wittgenstein (1889-1951) and from A.J. Ayer (1910-1989) and the Vienna Circle, holds that no fact can be verified unless empirically, i.e., positively, by the methods of science. So, positivism disregards any notion of supernatural revelation, specifically, direct divine revelation.[23] Although its own principle of positive verification was attacked as unverifiable by thinkers such as Karl Popper, the views of Ayer, *et al*, held sway in popular culture long past their intellectual primacy and their possible abandonment by their own proponents (such as Ayer himself in the area of the ethics of non-cognitive emotivism).[24]

For Christians, the extra-philosophical denial of revelation is not the main issue, for who today will grant that the principle of empirical verification is itself verifiable? But for committed Christian believers, the extension of divine revelation beyond its biblical parameters has challenged the meaning Christians give to the concept of revelation. Some, such as those within the New Apostolic Reformation and the Latter-Day Saints, hold to *continuous* revelation, which argues that God continues to reveal Himself in ways that add to mankind's understanding of God as declared in the Old and New Testament. The Latter-Day Saints continue to hold to the position that revelation is open to new inspirations from God, especially through the "President of the Church."[25]

---

23   Robert C. Solomon and Kathleen M. Higgins, *A Short History of Philosophy* (New York: Oxford University Press, 1996), 274–6.

24   Cf. under the head of "Ethics" the entries in the *Stanford Encyclopedia of Philosophy*, retrieved 6/10/23, at URL https://plato.stanford.edu/entries/ayer/ ("Emotivism was thought by some to be the *reductio ad absurdum* of the verificationist theory of meaning, and indeed it was not the preferred meta-ethical position of other positivists...") and https://plato.stanford.edu/entries/ethics-virtue/ ("This is not to say that only virtue ethicists attend to virtues, any more than it is to say that only consequentialists attend to consequences or only deontologists to rules. Each of the above-mentioned approaches can make room for virtues, consequences, *and* rules. Indeed, any plausible normative ethical theory will have something to say about all three.") If virtues and consequences are mere emotions, as the early Ayer believed but may later have rejected as overly reductionist, no actual rules may be said to pertain to normative ethics, and such a positive assertion may indeed reduce Ayer's emotivism to noncognitive absurdity.

25   Christopher B. Cone, "Kingdom Through Culture: The New Apos-

Commonly Held Doctrines of Systematic Theology

Essentially, the Bible is itself a form of special revelation, as discussed below, but it is also a record of God's special revelation to mankind. From the beginning, God revealed Himself. He called Abraham to travel to Canaan and sire a nation (Gen. 12:1–3; 15:4–21). Through the burning bush, He called Moses to lead the Israelites out of Egypt (Ex 3:1–10). In judgment, the LORD revealed Himself to the Israelites and the Egyptians through the ten plagues to free His people from slavery (Ex. 7:14–21; 8:1–6, 16–17, 20–24; 9:1–6, 8–11, 13–26; 10:19, 12–15, 21–23; 12:29–30). After leaving Egypt, the Israelites made a covenant with Yahweh at Mt. Sinai, where He displayed His majesty through a thick cloud, lightning, and thunder and gave His people the Law (Ex. 19:16–18; 20:1–17). After His people conquered and settled in the Land of Canaan, God continued to reveal Himself and His will to Israel through His judges (Judges 4:4–15; 7:1–22; 13:2–25) and His prophets (1 Sam. 8:10–18; 2 Sam. 12:1–12; 18:21–39; Isa. 7:3–25; Jer. 7:1–27; Amos 2:6–16; Hag. 1:1–11). As rich a history of God's revelation as is contained in the Old Testament, God's ultimate revelation comes in the Person of Jesus Christ, who embodied the character and nature of God and secured salvation for mankind (Matt. 1:18–23; John 1:1–14; Col. 1:15). Upon Jesus' death, resurrection, and ascension, the Lord continued and still continues to reveal Himself to His people and the world through the work of the Holy Spirit (Acts 1:8; 2:1–4; 4:31; 7:5–56; 13:1–3; 16:6–10). Though the Age of the Apostles' authority ended at the close of the first century, the Lord promises that He speaks through His Word and in the context of prayer and worship (Phil. 4:4–7; Jas. 5:13–18; 2 Pet. 1:19–21).

To demonstrate the reasonableness of special revelation, the believer should recognize that it is connected first to God's existence and then to

---

tolic Reformation and Its Cultural Appeal in *Journal of Dispensational Theology* 24:68 (Spring 2020)) Cone-Christopher-kingdom_through_culture__the_new_apostolic_reformation_and_its_cultural_appeal.pdf (agathonlibrary.com) (accessed May 16, 2024) RoseAnn Benson, "The Articles of Faith: Answering the Doctrinal Questions of the Second Great Awakening" in *Joseph Smith and the Doctrinal Restoration*, ed. W. Jeffrey Marsh (Provo: Brigham Young Univ., 2005) at URL https://rsc.byu.edu/book/joseph-smith-doctrinal-restoration (accessed May 16, , 2024) "Prophets and Revelation" in *New Testament Seminary Teacher Manual of the Church of Jesus Christ of Latter-Day Saints* https:www.churchofjesuschrist.org/study/manual/new-testament-seminary-teacher-manual/appendix/basic Doctrines (churchofjesuschrist.org) (accessed May 16, 2024).

His own nature and to the nature of man. If God exists, then it is safe to assume He is the One who created human beings, since He reveals that we are made in God's image. A God who created human beings, who are relational in nature, would desire to reveal Himself to His creation with the purpose of entering into relationships with them. It is also logical to assume the necessity of divine special revelation. Human beings, in their limited capacity, cannot gain much knowledge about God and His will for them unless He reveals it to them.

Even though humans have limited capacity, we are designed to receive and process information. Reading, solving mathematical equations, and figuring out puzzles would be impossible if humans could not do so. This ability, of course, is necessary for survival. It also suggests God's desire to communicate with His creation. God created human beings to receive and accept messages from Him. The veritably universal ability of human beings to gain knowledge, learn, discern, and apply knowledge implies this. Throughout recorded history, the human mind has always been able to collect and process information. It takes intelligence to bring an intelligence gatherer into existence and the superior intelligence gatherer that is the human mind must have, as Genesis insists, originated from a vastly Superior Intelligence. The universe was constructed through the use of a vast amount of intelligence as well. Intelligence is also needed to sustain the universe and operate within it. Planes are designed, bridges are constructed, and surgeries are all performed with the most information available. Partial information fails to enable human beings to capably function in the universe. General revelation provides only partial information concerning God as Creator and Sustainer. Special revelation is needed to have an accurate understanding of God, His nature, and His will for mankind. A God who created and sustains the universe with knowledge far above human understanding would logically desire to give a large amount of information about Himself to His creation in order for His creation to make well-informed decisions to accept Him and become His servants.

Special revelation additionally comes under attack from another sector. Some cults typically contend that new revelations are ongoing to give credence to their own movement against biblical orthodoxy. According to the Church of Jesus Christ of Latter-day Saints, Joseph Smith (1805 – 1844) received revelation from the angel Moroni about the existence of the Golden Tablets, i.e., the Book of Mormon. Contentions of revelation from cults present a problem in relation to the importance and authority of the Bible. If God continues revealing Himself in new ways, then the canon of Scripture is no longer a complete record of God's manifestations, which lessens its importance and subtracts from its authority. Of even greater concern is that if God is still manifesting Himself in new ways, then anyone can claim that they have received a new revelation. Such is the origin of and foundation of many cult-like religious movements, some of which have proven fatal to their adherents.

How can orthodox Christianity distinguish itself from cults and movements that are claiming to be new manifestations of God? The sufficiency of Scripture, as a guide for faith and practice, demonstrates that the modes of revelation, manifestation, and inspiration, have been completed. As the Apostle John penned the last words of the book of Revelation, he warned that any who added words to the book would suffer from plagues recorded in Revelation sent by God Himself (Rev. 22:18). Cults and other utopian movements that have come out of orthodox Christianity (e.g., Latter-day Saints, Jehovah's Witnesses, Christian Science, the Brook Farm and other utopian universalists) have typically claimed that revelations proclaimed by leaders, such as Joseph Smith, Mary Baker Eddy, and Charles Taze Russell (and their own so-called "scriptural" writings) should be regarded as containing some level of divine inspiration. Often, these teachings and these scriptures directly contradict the Bible, particularly in relation to the nature of God and the plan of salvation. Is God's total revelation incoherent?

Arguing from the perspective that the Bible is a trustworthy revelation requires a demonstration of its accuracy, but not in a way that appeals to the inherently unverifiable principle of verifiability, in which Hume and A. J. Ayer believed without warrant. Numerous archeological and historical studies and extra-biblical sources such as non-Christian Roman historians and more contemporary skeptics have established the historical and geographical accuracy of the Bible with regard to rulers, major events, and descriptions of cities. No other documents, religious or secular, can compete with the accuracy of the Bible with regard to essential textual agreement and multiple early copies and references to the same sources. The Bible, then, is to be trusted as a source of information. If other sources of information claim equal or superior inspiration to the Bible yet contradict it, then it is safe to conclude that they are unreliable and therefore, cannot be trusted as revelations from God.

Special revelation is not only a theological term and a defensible principle, but the disclosure of the Creator of the Universe revealing Himself for the purpose of eternal salvation of mankind. Christianity is founded upon this understanding. Any distortion or denial of it twists the entire faith.

Doctrine of Revelation: Inspiration of Scripture

God's inspiration of Scripture entails the understanding that the Holy Spirit directed prophets, psalmists, apostles, and associates of the apostles to write the very words which make up the sixty-six books of God's Word, the Bible. Within orthodoxy, the verbal plenary view, holding that every word is fully inspired by God best fits the biblical understanding of the doctrine of inspiration.

The divine inspiration of Scripture faces an attack on two major fronts. Skepticism denies any supernatural inspiration, though some who fall under the designation of atheist, agnostic, or of no religious affiliation find that the Bible may have some value as representing the beliefs of Christians.[26] But even as such, skeptics deny the complete inspiration of Scripture. However, the denial of biblical inspiration also comes from within the Church. Theological liberalism, which began in Europe in the early nineteenth century and was pioneered by (among others) F. D. E. Schleiermacher (1768–1834), exchanged the traditional doctrine of Scripture as God's direct revelation to man for the Bible as a record of religious experience that functions as a helpful guide for Christians after the first century, but that is not, strictly speaking, the inspired Word of God.[27] Beginning in the late twentieth century, with the advent of postmodernism and the widespread acceptance of relativism, the Bible in contemporary theology became valued not for what it is, but for what it does. When reading the Bible, many Christians believe today, one receives the message of God only as the Spirit speaks through it to personal experience. The inspiration, then, is not in the text, but in the reader who receives the text.[28]

---

26 Huxley, *Religion*, 16.

27 John Douglas Morrison, *Has God Said?* (Eugene: Pickwick, 2006), 46–47.

28 Stanley J. Grenz and John R. Franke, *Beyond Foundationalism* (Lou-

Commonly Held Doctrines of Systematic Theology

Pertaining to the witness of God's Word, Scripture self-attests to its own inspiration by God Himself. Two passages immediately come to mind for believers familiar with the contents of the Bible. Paul declared that all Scripture was inspired by God (2 Tim. 3:16), and Peter explained that the writers of Scripture were moved by the Holy Spirit (2 Pet. 1:20–21). These two passages do not exhaust the discussion of this subject in the Bible. In Psalm 119:1–176, the psalmist consistently refers to Scripture as originating from the Lord and being His Word. In certain instances, the Lord commands prophets and apostles to write the words that He speaks to them; indicating that the passages following are inspired by God (Ex. 34:27–28; Jer. 36:1–8; Ezek. 24:1–14; Hab. 2:2–20; Rev. 21:5). Paul indicated to the congregation in Corinth that the instructions in the letter he was writing to them were God's commandments (1 Cor. 14:37). Echoing this sentiment, Peter acknowledged that Paul's letters were to be regarded in the same way and on the same level of inspiration as the other books of Scripture (2 Pet. 3:15–16).

Every major religion and cult in the world have religious scriptures that followers refer to as the source of authority for their beliefs and instruction for worship and ethical conduct. A few religions, such as Islam and Orthodox Judaism regard their Scriptures on a similar level of inspiration and accuracy as biblically orthodox Christians view the Bible. The Latter-Day Saints accept the inspiration and full reliability of the King James translation of the Bible, the Book of Mormon, the Pearl of Great Price, and the Doctrines and Covenants. Other religions, such as Hinduism, claim that their Scriptures, the Vedas, have some degree of inspiration for the purpose of communicating spiritual truth, but persons of Hindu faith do not consider the stories transcribed in their scriptures as actual historical and factual truth. Therefore, there are a variety of perspectives concerning scriptures across the religious spectrum. Devout followers of these religions and belief systems claim some form of inspiration for their scriptures as a main reason that their movements should be considered valid. If such is the case, as many skeptics point out, how can Christians claim that their Scriptures alone are inspired by God and valid?

---

isville: Westminster John Knox, 2001), 90-92. Cf., generally, Kevin J. Vanhoozer, *Is There a Meaning in this Text?: The Bible, the Reader, and the Morality of Literary Knowledge* (Grand Rapids: Zondervan, 1998).

The starkest difference between the Bible and other writings claiming divine inspiration is that the contents of the Bible are factual, whereas the contents of the other writings are not warranted by factual evidence. Archeological discoveries in the twentieth and twenty-first centuries have confirmed the historicity of the record of events, names, and places of the Old and New Testaments. The Book of Mormon bears a similar assertion of inspiration, but archeologists and historians have yet to find a shred of evidence verifying any truth to its contents. Furthermore, the contents of the Bible must be literally true and completely factual for Christianity to be meaningful, and without meaning it cannot survive. For other faiths, such as Hinduism, the stories contained in the Scriptures do not necessarily have to be true. However, the foundational beliefs of Christianity are based on facts; facts that include God's creation of the universe and humanity, God's continual intervention in the history of Israel, the fulfillment of prophesied factual events, and witnesses to the life, death, and resurrection of Jesus Christ.

Since the earliest days of the Church, the Bible has been read in the context of corporate worship (Col. 4:16; 1 Thess. 5:27). This practice has been an essential part of worship in the Church, because Christians understood that they were reading and hearing words that came from God. Christians do not hold such views on grounds of mere sentimentality, but they accept and practice the teachings of the Bible because the Bible itself has indicated that it comes from God and historical facts on record attest to it by furnishing external evidence as to its accuracy. Internally, its main statements are stable and coherent.

Doctrine of Revelation:
Inerrancy of Scripture

According to the doctrine of the inerrancy of Scripture, the Bible, comprising the sixty-six books of the Old and New Testament, is completely free from error in every genre and every subject matter to which it refers. Inerrancy is possible because God, while inspiring the writers of Scripture, prevented them from writing errors into the original manuscripts, also known as "the autographs."

Testimony of inerrancy can be found in the pages of the Bible. The most direct support for inerrancy is John 17:17, where Jesus declared that all of God's Word was true. Proverbs 30:5 confirms this statement by saying that each word from God is true. David implies something similar by writing that the law of God is perfect, without corruption, and that it always provides sound counsel (Ps. 19:7-9). Elsewhere David states that the words of the LORD are pure (Ps. 12:6). Another Psalm proclaims that God's word in its entirety is true (Ps. 119:151, 160). Matthew reports Jesus' Sermon on the Mount as declaring that all of God's Word would be fulfilled, from which we infer its truthfulness (Matt. 5:17-18). Consistently, the Bible claims for itself that not only is it inspired by God, but free from error.

Inerrancy's detractors hail from many different perspectives. Muslims have long claimed that both the Old and New Testaments were corrupted over time, which is the reason why the Bible differs so much from the Qur'an.[29] Skeptics, who range from atheists to agnostics or to liberal or progressive Protestants, do not necessarily go as far as Muslims, though some do, asserting that Scripture contains errors. Often, they point to omissions, repetitions, and apparent contradictions as items they take as solid proof of the Scripture's errancy. The result of skepticism's sway over the intellectual life of many parts of the world has led many, even within Christian denominations, to discard the belief in biblical inerrancy.

Old and New Testament scholars who accept biblical inerrancy generally agree that most of the "errors" posited by skeptics can be explained by copyists' mistakes or poor textual transmission practices. Many errors have occurred over the centuries by scribes who have made common mistakes (e.g., repeating a prior word) when reproducing biblical manuscripts. These occurrences have been common knowledge for centuries and do not in any way impact the inerrancy of autographs or primary biblical doctrines based on the multiple textual variants we possess in the thousands. More problematic are supposed contradictions found in the Bible. Candidate passages in this category include Matthew 8:28-34, which records two demoniacs in Gadarenes instead of the one reported in Mark 5:1-17 and Luke 8:26-37, and the various accounts of the disciples at the empty tomb of Jesus in the four Gospels.

Several biblical scholars, theologians, and apologists have tackled the issue of problem passages. The most famous effort is that of Gleason Archer's

---

29 Anis A. Shorrosh, *Islam Revealed: A Christian Arab's View of Islam* (Nashville: Thomas Nelson, 1988), 222.

(1916 – 2004) *Encyclopedia of Bible Difficulties.*[30] A more recent work is Norman Geisler's (1932 – 2019) and Thomas Howe's *Big Book of Bible Difficulties.*[31] Though Archer's and Geisler's well-researched and helpful explanations will not convince the hardened skeptic, they will encourage Christians trying to reconcile Bible passages, and help discouraged Christians and perhaps lead open-minded critics to take a second look at the message of the Bible. The primary theme one finds in studying difficult passages is that careful study of context and historical and cultural background often resolves the issue. After such study, relatively few passages fall into the category of truly difficult. One should also keep in mind that believers have known about and studied such passages for centuries, and yet Christianity has weathered the existence of such passages.

Difficult passages in the Bible can be categorized by types of responses: 1) The reader seeks to find the reason behind the difficulty, believing that a solution exists. 2) The reader recognizes the difficulty to be an error within the manuscripts of transmitted texts, but one that does not have a major effect on the message or on the overall reliability of the Bible. 3) The reader finds in the difficulty a reason justifying his having serious suspicions as to the reliability of the Bible. Of the three responses, the first falls within the parameters of those who believe in full inerrancy, while the second can be described as a position among Evangelicals who accept some form of limited inerrancy or may reject the term inerrancy altogether. It should be no surprise that the third response falls outside of normative Christian belief. Any denial of the truthfulness and the reliability of God's Word also, on its face, issues a denial of the truth of the Gospel or its supporting witnesses, e.g., in Paul's letters or in Jesus' own affirmations of old covenant truth.

Inerrancy's enemies exist both within and without the Church. Enemies outside the Church have the obvious motive of discrediting the entire faith of Christianity. Those who historically or currently reject biblical Christianity for some deviant form of belief have the clear motive of attempting to prove that biblical Christianity is not the true form of the faith. There is also a third motive for dismissing inerrancy, by those who

---

30 Gleason L. Archer, *Encyclopedia of Bible Difficulties* (Grand Rapids: Zondervan, 1982).

31 Norman L. Geisler and Thomas Howe, *The Big Book of Bible Difficulties* (Grand Rapids: Baker, 1992).

take the doctrine's very concept as unbiblical and thus fail to represent true Christianity and in fact oppose part or all of its doctrines, as, for example, did the so-called Gnostic Gospels.

Part of the charge against the doctrine stems from the belief that inerrancy was an invention of the nineteenth-century Princeton Theological Seminary theologians Charles Hodge (1797-1878), A.A. Hodge (1823 - 1886), and B.B. Warfield (1851 - 1921), as these men were under the influence of Francis Turretin's (1623 - 1687) rigid reformed Protestant tradition. Before the Princeton divines came on the scene, these opponents claim, Christians accepted biblical inspiration and biblical reliability as sufficient for support of the trustworthiness of the Bible.[32] Yet, an examination of the writings of several Early Church Fathers, medieval theologians, and Protestant Reformers, beginning with Clement of Rome (30 - 100), demonstrates that Christians for millennia have believed in an error-free Bible.[33]

Another argument against inerrancy views the doctrine as an unnecessary platform for the infallibility of Scripture. Inspiration and reliability, according to this argument, are enough to present the Bible as God's Word for the Church. However, inerrancy hinges upon the nature of God Himself, for if Scripture is inspired by an inerrant God, it must itself be inerrant. If the Bible contains errors, then God Himself makes errors or God has somehow failed to enable the writers of the Bible to communicate God's perfect message perfectly. Neither is God deceitful. For Scripture declares that God does not lie (Heb. 6:18). Therefore, God's Word as the inspired product of a fully trustworthy God can be trusted.

Inerrancy makes perfect sense when connected to a perfect God. God Himself is free from error, and all of His works are perfect. Upon completing the creation of the Earth and the universe, God stated that all He had made was "good" (Gen. 1:31). The salvation through God, the Son, Jesus Christ, is complete, eternal, and leads to the perfection of every believer. Believers long to see the day that Scripture has prophesied, when there will be perfected a new heaven and a new earth (Rev. 21:1). With a long list of such amazing accomplishments and promises, it is

---

32 Jack Rogers, "The Church Doctrine of Biblical Authority," in *Biblical Authority*, ed. Jack Rogers (Waco: Word Books, 1977), 35–40.

33 Carl F. H. Henry, *God, Revelation, and Authority* (Waco: Word Books, 1979), 4:370–78.

fairly safe to assume that God's Bible would inspire a perfect revelation to communicate a description of His nature, His will, His ultimate plan, and His means of salvation for humanity. Without a perfect, written revelation, can mankind put their trust in books that are but a somewhat reliable collection of religious writings?

The Bible is quoted more than any other source in the world because it is true. Its words explain the origins of the Universe by the hand of a Divine Creator, that Divine Creator's love for His creation, His Son's sacrificial death and resurrection for their behalf, and the wonderful eternity that awaits those who believe and trust in Him. Inerrancy, then, is not the invention of dogmatic minds that were full of pride, but the perfect and complete result of inspiration by an infallible God who desires to communicate the only means of salvation to an unbelieving world.

Doctrine of Revelation:
The Infallibility and Authority of the Bible

Tied to and often used as a synonym of inerrancy, infallibility (a separate word) refers to the faithfulness in Scripture in that it always guides the reader correctly to the truth. If Scripture is infallible, then it is authoritative. When the Church speaks of the authority of the Bible, it refers to the belief that the Bible is the guide to what all believers must believe: we must hold to its narratives, accept its doctrines, heed its warnings, and obey its ethics. The Protestant Reformers held to *sola Scriptura* or "Scripture alone." They viewed the Bible as the sole authority for their beliefs and practices.

Naturally, those outside the faith disregard the authority of the Bible. This would include atheism, agnosticism, and Islam, all of which discount the Bible's authority due to its content. The Latter-Day Saints accept Scripture (Authorized Version—KJV) as an infallible and authoritative guide for living in obedience to God, but present their own writings (i.e. the Book of Mormon, Doctrines and Covenants, Pearl of Great Price) as carrying the same weight. However, even persons within historic Christianity take issue with the Bible's authority. Roman Catholicism considers not only Scripture as infallible and authoritative but also the apostolic tradition passed down through the centuries of Church tradition; papal and bishop share the status of biblical authority and are equally infallible and authoritative.[34] A growing number of Protestants claim to value the Bible as a collection of spiritual writings, but no longer accept its authority for moral living. Much of the leadership of mainline Protestant denominations accepts a form of deconstructionism that leads to an ongoing reinterpretation of Scripture, being committed to the idea that Christianity in this way can stay relevant in the twenty-first century. Along with progressive Christianity, mainline Protestants and even some more progressive evangelicals consider the Bible a helpful guide to historic Christian belief, but not prescriptive for modern readers.[35] For this reason, they deem certain passages that support biblical marriage, condemn homosexuality, and present evidence that life begins at conception as faithful to the beliefs at the time of writing, but no longer applicable for today.

Throughout the Old and New Testament, passages indicate that the words of Scripture always counsel correctly and are to be taken seriously and obeyed. Moses' instructions to the Israelites before their entry into Canaan stipulated that when a king ruled over them that he should copy the Book of the Law, read it, and obey it closely so that he would have a long life and prosperous reign (Deut. 17:18–20). In his closing remarks to the Israelites, Moses stressed the importance of obeying God's commands so that they could receive His blessings and not suffer from the consequences of disobedience (Deut. 28:1–68). After the Israelites conquered and settled into the land of Canaan, the LORD sent prophets to declare the Word of the LORD, which was considered binding; the LORD visited with disastrous results those who rejected it (1 Sam. 15:1–3; 1 Kgs. 13:1–32; 2 Kgs. 15:12; 24:1–3; 2 Chron. 11:1–4; Isa. 9:8–21; 28:14–22; Jer. 2:1–37; 7:1–10:25; 30:1–31:40; Hos. 4:1–14:9; Amos 3:1–6:14; Hag. 1:2–11; Zech. 4:6–10). Even the psalmists reflected on the authority of the Word of God. David testified that God's Word led its readers through a perfect path (Ps. 18:30). One psalmist wrote that those who rebel against God's Word live in darkness and experience suffering (Ps. 107:10–11). When discussing the book of Psalms' view of Scripture, it is necessary again to mention Psalm 119, which is completely devoted to describing God's Word. According to this psalmist, those who follow

---

34   Avery Dulles, *Models of Revelation* (Maryknoll: Orbis, 1992), 44.

35   Brian D. McLaren, *A New Kind of Christianity* (New York: Harper, 2010), 92.

God's Law walk in righteousness and away from wickedness (Ps. 119:1–4). The psalmist also beseeches the LORD to teach the principles of His Word so that he can live uprightly and not fall into sin (Ps. 119:33–37, 66–68, 73, 108). He testifies that he has kept God's Law, proving himself to be an example of obedience (Ps. 119:55–56, 60, 109–110, 168). Above all, he stresses the tremendous wisdom and value of God's Word as a guide to godly living and away from the disastrous path of sin (Ps. 119:39, 72, 75, 105, 111, 129–130).

As with the Old Testament, the New Testament affirms the efficacy and wisdom of Scripture and the necessity of following it. In the Gospels, Jesus rebuked Satan by saying that food alone is not enough for people to live by, because they also need God's Word (Matt. 4:4; Luke 4:4). Jesus also informed a woman in the crowd that those who obey God's Word are blessed (Luke 11:27–28). In His Sermon on the Mount, Jesus declared that He had not come to destroy the Law but to fulfill it (Matt. 5:17). He emphasized that not even the smallest letter of the Hebrew alphabet (Yod) or the tiniest extension on the letters of Hebrew letters (tittle) would be overlooked and instead would be fulfilled (Matt. 5:18). These statements represent God's attitude towards the significance of His law and the necessity of obedience to it. The writer of Hebrews acknowledged the extreme value of God's Word as a powerful discerner of human thoughts and motives (Heb. 4:12). John too explained the importance of obeying God's commands in that only those who obey are truly believers (1 John 2:3–6). With so many verses indicating the value of Scripture as a guide to living and the necessity of obeying it, the assurance of the Bible's infallibility and authority is unmistakable.

Because there is strong evidence that the Bible is inspired by God and inerrant, it is reasonable to regard it as infallible and authoritative. This reasoning and Christ's own acceptance of its infallibility and authority over all of human life (e.g., Matt. 5:17–20) should convince all who call themselves followers of Jesus Christ. When arguing for its infallibility and authority to the culture at large, it should be pointed out that the Bible has had tremendous success as a guide for academia, society, and for everyday living for centuries. Scientifically, the Bible, through its vivid description of an organized universe, encouraged the empirical method, which has led to numerous discoveries and advancements during the last four centuries. On a financial basis, capitalism was developed with the biblical concept of human depravity in mind. Humans, beset by their sinful nature, are greedy, and so the financial system that works best in the world would be one based on competition. Capitalistic nations, by and large, have produced the most wealth in the world and freed many from human suffering, exploitation, and impossibly low standards of living. The ethical teachings of the Bible have served as the basis for law codes of many different governments and civilizations including the constitutions of many western nations. With regard to family, several studies have shown that children are far more inclined to have a successful adulthood if they are raised with both biological parents; this is the biblical ideal (Gen. 2:24; Ex. 20:12; Prov. 1:8; Eph. 6:2).

The infallibility and authority of Scripture are an integral part of the life of the believer. A believer may be defined as one who trusts God's Word and obeys it. The secular culture at large and those who identify with the progressive Christian movement find devotion to the Word of God obsolete and unnecessary, but true Christians desperately depend upon Scripture as their divinely-inspired guide.

Doctrine of Revelation: The Canon of Scripture

Sixty-six books, thirty-nine in the Old Testament and twenty-seven in the New Testament, make up the entire Canon of Scripture. By "canon" is meant that the Bible, regarded as a limited number of books, is the rule of authority for the Church. Protestant Evangelicalism has historically re-garded all sixty-six books as the Word of God.

While there is no statement in the Bible that lists all of the books of the Old and New Testament and designates them as part of the recognized canon, there are verses that indicate that God communicated to believers how to determine what consisted of His Scripture and what did not. Paul indicated to Timothy that Scripture functioned proficiently for educating, convicting, and training believers for the purpose of leading them to spiritual maturity (2 Tim. 3:16–17). Also, several verses reveal that the Early Church regarded the books of the Old Testament as Scripture (Matt. 7:12; 11:13; 22:40; Luke 16:16; 24:44; John 1:45; Acts 13:15; 24:14; 28:23; Rom. 3:21; 2 Tim. 3:15). As to the books of the New Testament, some passages reveal the writings of the apostles and their associates were already beginning to be regarded as Scripture. Peter acknowledged the content of Paul's letters as Scripture and, by doing so, he was including them in the biblical canon (2 Pet. 3:15–16). The concluding verses of the book of Revelation have been viewed by some as a concluding summary for the entire Bible, warning against both adding to or taking away from the contents of Scripture (Rev. 22:18–20). Therefore, the accusation that the biblical canon was developed long after the first century and the actual writing of the New Testament is unfounded.

Over the centuries, there have been disagreements as to which books should or should not be included in the Bible. Early on, the Christian canon faced opposition from Marcion (ca. 110 – 160) who believed that the God of the Old Testament represented not the true God, but an evil demiurge. Therefore, Marcion edited the Bible by removing the entire Old Testament and any quote or reference to the Old Testament in the New Testament; he established a Bible consisting of Paul's letters, with the exception of the Pastorals, and a very abbreviated version of Luke. Tatian (110 – 180) edited the Gospels from four down to one synthesized biography of Jesus, called the *Diatesseron*.[36]

Although canonicity has been an issue since the Early Church, debate over the canonicity of Scripture continues apace. Some have rejected the traditional canon and have supplied alternatives. In some denominations, additional books are included in the canon. A majority of Protestants regard only the sixty-six books of the Bible as Scripture. Yet Roman Catholicism as well as the Coptic church, the Greek Orthodox church, and the Russian Orthodox church include Baruch, Judith, 1 & 2 Maccabees, Sirach, Tobit, and the Wisdom of Solomon in inspired Scripture or as wisdom literature that provides historical background and thus as "deuterocanonical" or part of a secondary canon. (The Roman Catholic Council of Trent declared them canonical, but rejected 1 & 2 Esdras and the Prayer of Manasseh. The Eastern Orthodox also accept as canonical those with 3 & 4 Maccabees, and Psalm 151. Even some Anglicans maintain that the Apocryphal books are part of the Bible and are to be read with respect and used in liturgy.) The late twentieth century saw the beginnings of a fascination with pseudonymous works claiming to be written by the apostles and various associates of the apostles in the New Testament. The Pseudepigrapha (or works falsely attributed to writers such as King Solomon), as this collection

---

36 Luke T. Johnson, *The Writings of the New Testament* (Philadelphia: Fortress, 1986), 536–7.

of books is termed, have been translated and are accessible to anyone wanting to read them. These books have been popularized as representing an alternative source of information about Jesus and as supplementing the valid canon of the traditional New Testament. Furthermore, a number of cults, such as the Latter-Day Saints, declare other books to be considered inspired. Are the books of the Bible the right ones? Should other ancient documents be included?

To address issues over the biblical canon, one must have a substantial grasp of church history. Due to early controversies, the early Church and its councils took a strong stand to declare which books were to be regarded as inspired and which were not. In addition to the understanding that books of the New Testament were to be regarded as Scripture during their writing, further developments in the second century occurred that revealed the Church's understanding of certain writings as having the same value as the books of the Old Testament. The Muratorian Canon document, written in the middle of the second century, recognized twenty of the New Testament books as inspired. Near the end of the second century, Tertullian (c. 155 – c. 220) considered twenty-three books to be Scripture. In the early third century, Origen (c. 185 – c. 253) acknowledged the twenty-seven books that today are recognized as the New Testament to be part of the canon, well before the Council of Nicaea in 325. Thus, the idea that this council subjectively recognized certain books to be included in the New Testament and summarily rejected other documents on the basis of political expediency is completely false.[37]

The status of the Apocrypha has been a contentious issue among Christians. Few who support their inclusion even know that devout Jews never regarded them inspired on the same level as the thirty-nine books of the Hebrew Bible. As for the Church, the books of the Apocrypha were never officially recognized by the Catholic Church as canonical until 1546, during the Council of Trent. The major motivation behind this acceptance was the rejection of their inspiration by Protestant reformers such as Martin Luther. Luther was one of the first post-Medieval theologians to regard the Apocrypha as not divinely inspired, placing all apocryphal books between the Old and New Testaments as supplementary "intertestamental" reading. Various Protestant translations included the

---

37 Craig L. Blomberg, *The Historical Reliability of the New Testament* (Nashville: Broadman & Holman, 2016), 651–4.

Apocrypha, but by the close of the nineteenth century, most Protestant Bibles no longer contained them.[38]

To recognize the Apocryphal books as part of Scripture presents a problem for devout Christians who regard God's Word as inerrant. The Book of Judith, for example, erroneously refers to Nebuchadnezzar as the "king of the Assyrians" and places him in a post-Exilic time frame after the actual Nebuchadnezzar, the real king of the Neo-Babylonian Empire, was long dead (Judith 1:1–10). Tobit is recorded as being alive during the Assyrian conquest of Israel in 722 BC, and two hundred and nine years earlier at Jeroboam's revolt against Judah in 931 BC (Tobit 1:3–5), but was said to be only one hundred and twelve years old (Tobit 14:1). Several of the Apocryphal stories in Bel and the Dragon, the Additions to Esther, Prayer of Azariah, and Susanna have legendary accounts that certainly cannot be historical.[39] Furthermore, never did the Jewish community universally recognize the Apocrypha on the same level as Scripture. Neither did Jesus or His apostles show any consideration of the value of those books as having the same value as the books of the Hebrew Bible.[40] This fact alone should give Christians pause in elevating the Apocrypha to inspired status. Furthermore, there is no recorded instance of a book or passage from that collection having drawn any person to faith in Christ. The Apocrypha remains a fascinating resource of ancient Jewish history, folktales, and wisdom literature, but it is only that.

Those who argue that the Pseudepigrapha should be regarded as Scriptural are hardly contending from an objective position. Several books, such as the Gospel of Thomas, are heretical, teaching unbiblical doctrines. They have never represented orthodox Christian doctrine, nor did the

---

38 Norman L. Geisler and William E. Nix, *A General Introduction to the Bible* (Chicago: Moody, 1968), 170–76.

39 Ibid., 173–4 Here are just a few examples: Bel and the Dragon portrays Daniel as mocking Cyrus the Great for worshipping the idol Bel, which was made of clay and bronze and unable to consume any offerings given to it (1:7). The Additions to Esther in the Greek version have Esther comparing King Artaxerxes to an angel of the Lord and fainting in the king's presence (15:12-15). In Susanna, a pre-exilic and quite young Daniel intervenes on behalf of the title character, who was falsely accused by two wicked elders (1:44-59).

40 F.F. Bruce, *The Books and the Parchments*, rev. ed. (Westwood: Fleming M. Revell, 1963), 171.

Pseudepigrapha have widespread acceptance in the Church. Currently, there are 5,800 ancient manuscripts of the New Testament in Greek and 19,000 ancient manuscripts in Latin, Slavic, Ethiopic, Armenian and other additional languages.[41] The fact that so many ancient manuscripts of the New Testament exist today reveals how much it was circulated in the ancient world. Though the number has expanded dramatically in the last two centuries, the Church has had access to ancient copies of Scripture throughout its history. Much of the Pseudepigrapha written by Gnostics have only single copies available. Non-Gnostic texts have a larger number of copies available, but their numbers are still, when compared to the canonical New Testament, very small.[42] This suggests the obscure nature of the Pseudepigrapha in the years following their composition. If these books were considered obscure then, no one should see them now as the equivalent of the canonical Scriptures. When reading the Pseudepigrapha, the objective reader will notice that the quality of writing is nothing like the beauty of the various genres within the sixty-six books that make up the writings of the Bible. Nor is there often a coherent message within each of the Pseudepigrapha. The often-touted *Gospel of Thomas* is supposedly a list of sayings of Jesus. However, while there is some overlap with verses similar to some found in the Gospels, the book has little organization and a plain reading of several of these sayings reveals them to be nonsensical.[43]

Looking at the evidence, the Pseudepigraphal books do not represent first-century Christian teaching, due to the late dates of their composition. They also fail to produce a coherent message, unlike the New Testament. Only radical scholars who have an underlying agenda to usurp biblical Christianity see any sort of canonical value in these writings.

As for additional documents claiming inspiration such as the *Book of Mormon*, no such document has the same accuracy that the Bible has demonstrated. Considering the *Book of Mormon*, not one piece of archeological evidence has validated any of the historical claims found

---

41   Norman L. Geisler, *Christian Apologetics*, 2d ed. (Grand Rapids: Baker Academic, 2013), 344–7.

42   Blomberg, *Historical Reliability*, 604–5.

43   *Gospel of Thomas* 2, 114, in *The Nag Hammadi Library*, 3d ed., ed. James M. Robinson (San Francisco: Harpers, 1988), 138: "Jesus said...'For every woman who will make herself male will enter the kingdom of heaven.'"

within its text.[44] Any such writings claiming to be additions to God's written revelation should be met with suspicion.

One additional issue concerning the Bible needs to be addressed, and that is the common heresy of believing either that certain books of the Bible may intentionally be rejected as part of Scripture or that designated books are to be avoided as authoritative texts for doctrine and instruction. The idea is that there is a "Canon Within the Canon." Reasons for accepting this practice include a dislike for particular beliefs or commandments found in certain books, a conviction that some books no longer apply to Christians (the Old Testament), or disinterest in specific genres. This dangerous practice diminishes the authority of Scripture and places the believer in a position of false supremacy over God's Word—if the Canon Within the Canon is a correct guide to approaching the Bible, then each believer has the right to practice arbitrary authority to accept or disregard whatever portions of Scripture he pleases. Such an attitude flies in the face of Scripture's own instructions on its importance and the application of its contents (Deut. 28:58–59; 2 Tim. 2:15; 3:16–17). Also a concern is the fact that if certain books can be ignored, then one cannot really call the books of the Bible a "Canon," because it is not a rule of faith for God's people. Additionally, if portions of God's Word can be discarded or their authority diminished, then God's authority matters little, because His Word is rejected. Any who reject God's Word make a difficult case for claiming that they are His servants, especially in light of the degree of widespread citations of the Old Testament made by Jesus and by the apostles and their associates who led the churches in the Acts of the Apostles and proclaimed the Gospel to other cities and cultures as a matter of historical record. Jesus' true servants affirm his teaching and that of his apostolic contemporaries, and favor its clear and coherent authority far above other ancient literatures of various genres.

The list of books found at the front of most copies of Scripture is more than a suggested list of readings. It represents the officially recognized and inspired Canon of Scripture that proved itself over millennia to be

---

44 Walter Martin, *The Kingdom of the Cults*, 6th ed. (Minneapolis: Bethany House, 2019), 245–9. Martin recorded that neither the Department of Archeology at Columbia University nor the Smithsonian Institution found absolutely any historical or archeological value in the Book of Mormon or in the claims as to its origin.

the factual and ever-truthful guide for upright and godly living. Every book, every chapter, every verse, and every word should be read, believed, obeyed, and cherished.

Doctrine of Revelation: Interpreting Scripture

It is the responsibility of every believer to correctly interpret God's Word and apply it to the matters of life and death personally as he or she reads it. A significant ingredient of interpreting the Bible is to accept it as inspired by God and understand that God communicates through His Word as believers read it. Studying the Bible is a serious task, and several passages explain that there is a right and wrong way to interpret God's inspired Word. When Ezra read God's Law to the Judeans gathered in Jerusalem, he had several Levites assist the people in understanding what was read (Ezra 8:1–8). Paul instructed Timothy to interpret God's Word correctly without distorting it (2 Tim. 2:15). Conversely, the Bible condemns the distorting of the true meaning of its verses (2 Pet. 3:16).

A first major distortion of a more traditional, grammatical method of interpreting Scripture was the allegorical method championed by Clement of Alexandria (c. 150 – c. 215) and Origen of Alexandria (c. 185 – c. 253). Applying Philo of Alexandria's (c. 20 – c. 50 A.D.) exegesis, Clement understood the meaning behind the words of Scripture to be taken as not the most obvious meaning of a given passage. He believed that any text of Scripture had at least two meanings, or possibly more, including a historical meaning, a doctrinal meaning, a prophetic meaning, a philosophical meaning, and a mystical meaning. The philosophical and mystical present the most danger of misinterpretation of biblical passages. For example, Clement wrote that Sarah and Hagar represented true wisdom and pagan philosophy. Mystically, Lot's wife symbolized attachment to the trappings of this world and rank impiety.[45] Origen continued Clement's work to promote this method; medieval theology by and large embraced it. The system of interpretation in this era would apply four different meanings to each text and sometimes as many as seven were applied.[46] Interpreting

---

45 Robert M. Grant and David Tracy, *A Short History of the Interpretation of the Bible*, 2d ed. (Minneapolis: Fortress, 1984), 55–6.

46 Ibid., 85.

biblical passages through the allegorical method places symbolism over historical context and the original intent of the writers. Allegorical interpretations have continued to work their way into popular writings and Sunday sermons, producing a damaging impact on those exposed to them by confusing interpretation with application of a text to the lives of those in the audience.

As the world entered the Modern era, the Bible came to be regarded as any other book. Baruch Spinoza (1632 – 1677) argued for the freedom of any reader of the Bible to interpret it according to his or her desires.[47] Spinoza's subjectivism continues today to impact the approach of many Bible readers, who declare that there is no right or wrong way to interpret Scripture, although many such interpreters have no idea of the beginnings of such an approach. Deconstructionism, advocated by Jacques Derrida (1930 – 2004) at a 1966 literary conference at Johns Hopkins University, subverts the importance of the author's original intent of the text.[48] Words, according to deconstructionism, represent fictions, and therefore, the one receiving words, particularly in written text, has the autonomy to interpret them as he sees fit.[49] This obviously has disastrous consequences for the objectivity of philosophy, but also for biblical studies and theology as well. Because of deconstructionism's influence, some Bible passages have, in the late twentieth century and into the twenty-first, become subject to radical reinterpretation and are now unrecognizable to any earlier reader. Such an approach is unstable and highly subjective.

Despite the popularity of the allegorical method, subjective interpretation, and radical deconstructionism, these avenues of interpreting Scripture cannot be recognized as acceptable because they cannot be applied in a logical and coherent way to the reality of the biblical universe. Communication, generally, must use comprehensible language and be interpreted in a coherent way so that individuals can understand one another and, when the need arises, make contractual arrangements and binding agreements as to meaning. It would be impossible to live in a world where its inhabitants typically spoke allegorically. Worse still, if everyone wrote and spoke and the original intent of their words were disregarded and

---

47 Gregg R. Allison, *Historical Theology* (Grand Rapids: Zondervan, 2011), 179–80.

48 Kevin J. Vanhoozer, *Is There Meaning in This Text*, 49.

49 Ibid., 21.

subsequently reworded, then no one could have meaningful conversation or discourse through written or electronic correspondence. Why then should using these methods to approach the Bible, God's communication to His people and all humanity, make any sense?

One of the reasons the Bible has readers from cultures all over the world is because of its clarity. Several passages signify God's use of His Word as a clear means of communication. God often commanded His prophets to write down the words which He spoke to them to preserve His message for future audiences (Isa. 8:1-2; 30:8-11; Jer. 30:1-3; 36:1-3, 11-15, 28; Ezek. 43:11; Hab. 2:2-3). The implication is that God's Word effectively imparts information in a comprehensible, stable way to human readers. Understanding the Bible as a clear communication from God resists subjectivism. A subjective interpretation of the Bible denies the importance of the Source of communication. In everyday life, the original communicator typically finds offense if the receiver of his message distorts it beyond recognition. God certainly finds offense in those who reinterpret His communication (Job 38:1-2; Mark 7:10-13). Throughout the centuries, individuals from all walks of life and various backgrounds and interests have found encouragement and comfort and gathered information concerning the nature of God and eternal salvation. To suggest radical reinterpretation of the Bible in the twenty-first century belies the millennia of clear comprehension of the Scriptures by millions of readers in hundreds of cultures.

A common objection to accepting the clarity of the Bible is that it is hard to understand. Admittedly, certain portions have cultural idioms and historical background that the average reader finds difficult. However, Old and New Testament scholars have provided explanations for such passages through their research in ancient languages, ancient cultures, and history. While such explanations for cultural passages cannot be acquired by a plain reading, the meaning behind them is accessible through proper study, and the results of these studies are provided in commentaries and study Bibles. The Bible is not a thirty-second video commercial that requires merely a quick view to understand its meaning. Rather, it is God's written revelation to mankind that requires careful examination and study, including some attention to genre and history which, when practiced, rewards the student with an understanding of the meaning of Scripture.

In times past, one would often find the Bible in a family home in a place of prominence because it was treasured. The Bible was treasured because the words within it were considered true, and the reader could understand its contents as clearly accessible given even a basic education. Scripture is not a collection of esoteric sayings, but God's communication to the world concerning who He is and His will for the beings created in His image. Scripture is capable of being understood by layperson and professional alike.

Chapter 3

Doctrine of God

Historical Background

Heraclius, Emperor of the Byzantine Empire (r. 610 – 641), had an extraordinary career as the sovereign over the surviving Eastern half of the Roman Empire. Leading his armies to victory, Heraclius defeated the Sassanid Empire at the Battle of Nineveh in 627, ending a war that lasted for over two and a half decades and a series of conflicts with the Persians that had extended for four hundred years. Additionally, the victory over the Sassanids enabled the Church to regain the True Cross on which Jesus supposedly was crucified. Although much of the territory gained in the war with the Sassanids was lost in a later conflict with the Islamic Arabs, Heraclius is remembered as one of the great emperors of the Byzantine Empire, along with Justinian (r. 527 – 565) and Basil II (r. 976 – 1025).[50] Tragically, at the close of his reign, Heraclius confessed that he never actually believed in monotheism.[51] For the Christian Empire, this confession created a scandal and tainted the image of the beloved emperor. Had such a confession occurred in the twenty-first century, it would have hardly concerned the general public. In the seventh century, however, Byzantine subjects had a different expectation of their Emperor. A heretical view of God reflected poorly on the head of state of a Christian nation. With regard to the Church, a heretical

---

50 Lars Brownworth, *Lost to the West: The Forgotten Byzantine Empire that Rescued Western Civilization* (New York: Crown, 2009), 120–26.

51 John Julius Norwich, *A Short History of Byzantium* (New York: Vintage Books, 1997), 97.

> *view of God has even more disastrous consequences because it is foundational to Christian theology and it can lead to the distortion of the Church in its beliefs and practices.*

In matters of doctrine, understanding who God is remains a fundamental feature of Christian belief. Theology proper is the study of God. Also known as the Doctrine of God, it encompasses God's existence, His attributes, His triune nature, and His works. Many Christians find the Doctrine of God beyond the reach of their comprehension but, while a full understanding of God and His nature is impossible, God created humans with the ability to know Him. Humans can learn about God and will face a sense of fear as sinful creatures in the presence of their Holy Creator and a sense of amazement as limited creatures becoming aware of the Unlimited Ruler of the Universe. As a believer learns more of what Scripture declares about God, he will be drawn closer to God and gain a greater glimpse of the Being whose might created galaxies with His words and whose unbounded love is demonstrated in His constant provision for His creation and His people. Thus, the Doctrine of God should not ultimately be a forbidding subject, but an inviting one that increases in fascination as one continues to examine it.

Doctrine of God:
The Personhood of God

God possesses personality, meaning that God exhibits emotion. More importantly, He is a personal Being. He thinks; He communicates; He determines what is pleasing and displeasing to Him, and He has the ability to have relationships with humans. When believers pray to the Lord, they are speaking with a God who knows their needs, listens to them, and has a genuine concern for their needs. But such personal categories and relational attributes as God possesses and exhibits are not possessed and exhibited as if God were made in our human image! Quite the opposite, God made us in His image (Gen. 1:27 ESV):

> So God created man in his own image,
> in the image of God he created him
> male and female he created them.

Doctrine of God

Two unbiblical beliefs in relation to God's personhood have misconstrued the proper understanding of God's personal nature. The first is the polytheistic misconception. Statements of belief in multiple gods tend to portray divine beings as completely parallel with human personality. Along with emotions and the ability to reason and communicate, these beings are portrayed as committing the same flaws that human beings exhibit: arrogance, jealousy, fits of rage, capriciousness, and disloyalty. Some, especially in media, have found a preference for depicting God in a fashion similar to ancient polytheistic conceptions, in which God consistently displays very human characteristics without transcendence, holiness, or even wisdom. These sins and character flaws can never be attributed to God, because He is sinless (2 Cor. 5:21; 1 Pet. 2:22; 1 John 3:5). A second misconception comes from pantheism. According to its advocates, the God of pantheism ultimately is impersonal and does not possess attributes. Pantheism has gained a wide influence in Western culture since the second half of the twentieth century, as is seen by common popular portrayals of God as emotionless and excruciatingly passive. At the extreme of pantheism, God is an impersonal force. Hardly does such a representation inspire devotion; neither is it accurate.

Scripture provides a far different picture of the Creator and Sustainer of the Universe. In fact, a wide range of emotions is attributed to God. When the LORD established His covenant with Israel and instituted the sacrificial system, He informed His people that He would enjoy the aroma of the sacrifices that they offered to Him (Ex. 29:18, 25, 41; Lev. 1:9, 13, 17; 3:5, 16; 8:21, 28; 17:6, Num. 15:7, 10, 13, 14). Psalms 147:11 and 149:4 declare that the LORD enjoys being in the presence of those who believe and trust in Him. David wrote that the LORD laughs at the plans of the wicked (Ps. 37:12-13). In contrast, He displays anger over sin and disobedience (Num. 22:22; Deut. 4:25; 6:15; 1 Kgs. 16:7, 13, 33; Jer. 7:20; 32:29) and even emotional pain over man's rebellion (Gen. 6:6; Isa. 54:6; 63:10). During Jesus' ministry, the Son of God expressed a wide range of emotions. Seeing that God the Father hides truths from the wise of the world and reveals it to His disciples, Jesus rejoiced (Luke 10:21). But Jesus wept over Jerusalem's rejection and future fate and over the lack of faith that Lazarus' mourners had (Luke 19:41; John 11:35). In anger over corruption and rigid exclusivism practiced in the Temple, Jesus overturned the tables and chairs of the money changers and threw them out (Matt. 21:12; Mark 11:15; Luke 19:45-46; John 2:14-16). Above all, Jesus showed compassion for the sick, the hungry, the suffering, and the spiritually lost (Matt. 14:14; 15:32; 20:34; Mark 1:41; 5:19; 6:34). With so many examples in Scripture, one cannot ignore the fact that the Bible depicts God as an emotional being who displays personal characteristics. Even in God's incarnation as "fully man," Jesus remained "fully God," and so His emotions such as compassion for humans and outrage at their heartless hypocrisies are divine also.

When examining the universe, one can clearly conclude that a Person Created it. The universe is intricately designed and finely tuned. Not only must we conclude that a Being with vast power created the universe, but that this Being also must have possessed a vast amount of intelligence to conceive of the universe prior to its existence, and must have possessed the means and information to know how to create a universe. Intelligence is a trait of a person and not an impersonal force or entity. An impersonal entity does not think, but simply reacts. If God was impersonal, the universe would not exist.

With regard to a specific part of God's creation, the humans made in His image also, likewise, have a wide range of emotions. If God is impersonal, without emotions, how would He know enough about emotions to create humans with emotions? Created beings, in one sense or another, reflect their Creator. The fact that human beings are emotional creatures suggests that their Creator also has emotions and expresses them.

God is a personal being. The Bible describes Him in words that statements of faith summarize as the infinitely intelligent, perfectly holy, immeasurably compassionate Creator and Sustainer of the Universe. The Universe that exists because of Him cannot possibly have originated from an impersonal force or a whimsical being whose emotions are outside His control. When believers call upon the Lord to answer their prayers, they should have every confidence that He is sincerely concerned about their needs and that He desires to answer their prayers. They are, in fact, conversing with a Person.

Doctrine of God:
The Trinity

There is only One God, but He is three Persons: God the Father, God the Son, and God the Spirit. Each Person has separate roles, but they are all equally God, having existed eternally without beginning, and they will never cease to exist. When a person encounters any one of the three Persons of the Trinity, he encounters God—not a part of God or a separate god, but God. Therefore, the three Persons are distinct, but they are unified as One Being.

Historically, the Trinity is one of the most assailed tenets of Christianity. Islam condemns the doctrine as tri-theism, declaring that Christians believe in three separate gods. Nearly every major cult and heretical deviation of Christianity, including Unitarianism, Mormonism, Jehovah's Witnesses, Christian Science, Unificationism, and Armstrongism reject the Trinity in some form or fashion. One of the first heresies to attempt an alteration of the doctrine of the Trinity, Modalism, denies the Three Persons of the Trinity by stating that a single Person acts in the roles of Father, Son, and Holy Spirit[52] through the different names, operations, or modes.[53] Although considering itself a Christian denomination, Oneness Pentecostalism embraces a form of modalism by claiming that Jesus alone is the true God.[54] Another second-century heresy that arose was subordinationism, initiated by Origen of Alexandria (c. 185 – c. 253) and promoted by Dionysius of Alexandria (d. 264). Subordinationism tended to emphasize the distinction between the Persons of the Godhead, and it emphasizes that the Son, as the "first-begotten" is subordinate to God the Father as the "unbegotten."[55]

Arianism provided a different alternative to earlier heretical views through the development of a mythology of the Son of God being created by the Father.[56] Emerging out of the Renaissance era, Unitarianism completely denies the Trinity, considering Jesus to simply be a man who lived an extraordinary life with a high ethical standard. This uniqueness

---

52 Tertullian, *Against Praxeas*, 11 (https://www.newadvent.org/fathers/0317.htm accessed Jan., 21, 2023).

53 J. N. D. Kelly, *Early Christian Doctrines*, 5th ed. (New York: Continuum, 1977), 119–123.

54 Richard Kyle, *The Religious Fringe: A History of Alternative Religions in America* (Downers Grove: InterVarsity, 1993), 164–165.

55 Harold O. J. Brown, *Heresies: Heresy and Orthodoxy in the History of the Church* (Peabody: Hendrickson, 1998), 109–110.

56 Arius et. al, *The Confession of the Arians, Addressed to Alexander of Alexandria* in *Christology of the Later Fathers*, ed. Edward R. Hardy (Louisville: Westminster John Knox, 1954), 332–334.

which Jesus possessed came from God's special adoption of Him, but nothing else distinguished Jesus from any other human.[57] Regarding the Trinity as polytheism, Christian Science accepts only God as One God and One Person.[58] Jehovah's Witnesses claim that God the Father created the Son who exists as "a god" whose purpose allows God to execute His will.[59] Sun Myung Moon (1920-2012), founder of the Unification Church, completely rejected the decisions of the Early Church councils and rejected the trinitarian conception of God.[60]

The Trinity's significance cannot be overestimated. An attack on the Trinity is an attack on Christianity itself. Any deviation from Trinitarian belief results in heresy and cannot be considered orthodoxy. Robert Letham has observed that the immanent interrelation among the Persons of the Trinity corresponds to the compassion of God. As Three Persons, God possesses the ability to relate to His creation, unlike the Allah of Islamic theology, which depicts Allah as distant. For that reason, Letham has theorized that the Islamic worldview has only produced authoritarian governments.[61] If there are no persons of the Trinity, it cannot be part of the highest good (God) to practice compassion to those under his sovereign rule; hence, a non-Trinitarian God cannot be said to practice divine love as a Person.

A common inclination to defend the Trinity would be to use analogies; many such analogies have been used over the years. Attempts to explain the Trinity in this manner are certainly noble, but can lead to additional confusion. The best starting point to discuss the Trinity is Scripture. Four passages in particular refer to the triune godhead directly. Matthew 3:16–17; Mark 1:10–11; and Luke 3:21–22 describe the moment after John the Baptist baptized Jesus. When Jesus emerged from the water, the Holy Spirit came down in the form of a dove to rest on Jesus, and a voice, which came from God the Father in heaven, declared that Jesus was His Son. In this historic

---

57 Brown, *Heresies*, 331.

58 Jan Karel Van Baalen, *The Chaos of the Cults: A Study in Present-Day Isms*, 4th ed. (Grand Rapids: Eerdmans, 1962), 99.

59 Ibid., 268–9.

60 James Beverly, "Unification Church" in *A Guide to New Religious Movements* ed. Ronald Enroth (Downers Grove: InterVarsity, 2005), 65.

61 Robert Letham, *The Holy Trinity* (Phillipsburg: P&R Publishing, 2004), 10–11.

inauguration of Jesus' ministry, all three Persons (Father, Son, and Spirit) were present. Beyond this event, Acts 7:55-56 chronicles the closing words of Stephen before the Sanhedrin (the ruling elite of the day). Being filled with the Holy Spirit, Stephen is given a glimpse of Heaven, and he sees Jesus standing at the right hand of God the Father. As in the baptism of Jesus, each of the three Persons is present.

In addition to passages that show the Trinity at work, some verses list the members of the Trinity in a single sentence or group. Prominent among those is Jesus' Great Commission, where He instructs His disciples to baptize in the name of each of the trinitarian Persons of the godhead (Matt. 28:19). Another such instance occurs in Peter's Pentecost Sermon, where the apostle briefly describes the roles of the Father, Son, and Spirit in the salvation of humanity (Acts 2:32-36). These Trinity passages provide a solid foundation for numerous other passages that refer to two divine Persons acting together (Matt. 4:1; Mark 1:12; Luke 4:1; John 1:1-3; 10:25-30; 12:27-29; Col. 1:15-20; Phil. 2:5-11; 2 John 1:3; Jude 1:1; Rev. 5:1-14). The unity of the Trinity, then, should be regarded as a thoroughly biblical doctrine.

Although some correctly charge that the word "Trinity" is not found in Scripture, the concept is present. Indeed, the term was originally applied by Tertullian (c.155 – c.220) to God. The second century apologist and theologian used the Latin *trinitas* (which simply means, "triad") to refer to the Godhead. Although the word itself was first used for this purpose a century after the completion of the New Testament, it describes a biblical concept. According to the testimony of Scripture, the Trinity has always existed ("you [the Father] loved me before the foundation of the world" John 17:23-25), even though the three "Persons" were not always so designated. By comparison, ancient civilizations called the stars by various names and described them in different ways, even regarding them simply as points of light. We now know them to be composites of hydrogen and helium. Since their creation it was so, yet now we call them stars or in astrophysics refer to their physical properties. The Trinity, as the stars have existed since the dawn of creation, has always existed and is now what is known to be.

A large portion of the world's population, the peoples of Islam, dismiss the Trinity as tritheism . Many believers who have not spent time studying the doctrine may strongly object, but have little insight as to how to counter this accusation. In all concept, purpose, and in actuality, the

Trinity is completely different from tritheism, a belief in the existence of three separate gods. Separate beings are completely distinct from each other, having separate existence, agenda, and inclination. The Trinity consists of One Being who exists in Three Persons who are distinct but work in perfect harmony with one another and have exactly the same agenda. Most importantly, the Three Persons equally exist in the same nature, essence, and being as God. Tritheism is also polytheism, which typically presents deities that are very much like human beings in nature. The Greco-Roman gods and the Scandinavian pantheon consist of mythical beings who are controlled by the same flawed urges and compulsions humans possess, which disqualifies them from deserving worship or obedience. Another problem emerging from a belief in tritheism is that three gods cannot possess the noncommunicable attributes of God (rf. the later discussion of omnipotence, omniscience, omnibenevolence, omnipresence, and eternality), because they are three separate beings. Noncommunicable attributes are only plausible if we can attribute them to one Being, because it is irrational to think that three different beings would equally have the same superlative qualities if they are completely distinct from one another; two entities cannot *both* be the most perfect being. If each being has equally the same attributes, then how are they distinct from one another; indeed, how can they be separate gods? With omnipotence there is the further problem that three separate beings cannot equally be omnipotent because if they are, then they cannot have power over each other. Therefore, more than one entity cannot be all-powerful along with others.

Despite strong Scriptural support, the Trinity is often dismissed by the simple declaration that it does not make sense or is "illogical." While difficult to comprehend, the full doctrine of the Trinity does not operate outside of logic.[62] In point of fact, the concept of the Trinity logically fits in the existence of the *lógos*, as John 1:1–3 points out, and John's *lógos* consists in the Persons by whom the world was made. Life in the world depends upon relationships. Infants need mothers. Children need parents. Single men and single women long to be in a lifelong relationship as part of a married couple. Civilizations depend on communities of people living and working together. Animal groups, schools of fish, and insect swarms are also relational and work together within their species to survive and

---

62 Vern Sheridan Poythress, *Logic: A God-Centered Approach to the Foundation of Western Thought* (Wheaton: Crossway, 2013), 112–16.

reproduce. The world is definitely relational. It is logical to assume that the world was created by a relational being, namely the trinitarian God. But, how can a being who has been alone for all eternity create a relational universe? He could and would have created a relational universe if and only if He was and is inherently relational. By being One God and Three Persons, the trinitarian God is inherently relational. Each Person has always related to the other two, as noted. God created a universe that logically reflected Himself and we, His creatures, are reaping the benefits of living in that universe.

Believers are baptized in the name of the Father, the Son, and the Holy Spirit. The Trinity is mentioned and often thoroughly discussed in every major creed and confession within Christianity. The Triune Godhead is embedded within the doctrine and life of the orthodox Church of Jesus Christ, because it is absolutely Scriptural and most certainly logical.

Doctrine of God:
The Noncommunicable Attributes of God

God, as the greatest and highest of all Beings, exists on a level far beyond human ability and human comprehension. In this way, He is transcendent, as is evident when the psalmist praised the LORD for being above the nations of the Earth and the Heavens, with no one being like Him (Ps. 113:4–6). Transcendence, in relation to the nature of God, is evidently a non-communicable attribute of God; those attributes are noncommunicable that humans cannot share with God. Among these are eternality, omnipotence, omniscience, omnipresence, omnibenevolence, and holiness.

Possibly the most difficult attribute to understand is God's *eternality*. In short, God has always existed and will always exist. From eternity past to eternity future, God is and always will be. This fact is hard to comprehend for human minds because every person has a point of origin and a life limited by time. Due to this difficulty, many religions, including pagan mythologies, have developed origin stories for their deities. Zeus, Odin, and Vishnu all have myths that describe how they came into existence. Joseph Smith believed that the God of the Bible came into existence as a man and eventually became God.[63] In current theological discussions, there has been

---

63   Robert C. Webb, *The Real Mormonism*, (New York: Sturgis and Walton, 1916), 183.

a move away from the classical theistic view of God as timelessly eternal; some writers now believe God to be one who experiences duration and sequence but is everlasting, since the future does not yet exist. This is called the Openness view of God's eternality,[64] because the future for God, as for us, is open to unknown possible outcomes.

The Bible clearly presents God as eternal. Moses declared that God is eternal (Deut. 33:27), and David described God as "from everlasting to everlasting" (Ps. 90:2). David also declared the same in Ps. 41:13. Another psalmist wrote that God's throne was established forever and He Himself was eternal (Ps. 93:2). Isaiah described the LORD as the "everlasting God" (Isa. 40:28). Peter put it more eloquently by comparing a thousand years with a day from God's perspective (2 Pet. 3:8). Despite the testimony of Scripture, today's Christians face the task of explaining the belief to those who deny God's existence, who often derisively ask the question, "If God made the universe, then who made God?" Those who ask this question fail to realize that God, by the very definition of who He is, has always existed and has no point of origin. So applied to the being of God, the question is nonsensical. It would be similar to asking for a cup of dry water. Dryness has nothing to do with water and origin has nothing to do with God's existence. Eternity, when applied to God, corresponds to a theistic worldview. God created the world and God sustains the world. Should it be possible for God to cease to exist, in that moment the universe would cease to exist. An underlying theme in theism is trust in the deity who is our Maker and Sustainer and is also timeless. We know this to be true because He has declared it of Himself, and the Bible says that He exists in the past, present, and future, that He was and is and is to come (Rev. 1:5, 8, 11; 21:6; 22:13). God by his servants the prophets has also made many predictions of future events; such prophecies are not "self-fulfilling" but indicate that He knows the future with certainty. Such a God must therefore exist, have always existed, and exist into the future he foresees (Hos. 1:4–7; Amos 2:1–3; Mic. 3:12; Zech. 1:12–21). One cannot completely place one's eternal soul's trust in a deity that one day may no longer exist. Nor would one desire to worship a mortal deity. Furthermore, things that have existed since the beginning of time will, by all appearances, exist indefinitely, such as the laws of logic and the principles of mathematics.

---

64 John Sanders, *The God Who Risks: A Theology of Divine Providence*, 2d. ed., (Downers Grove: InterVarsity, 2007), 200–3.

If these have existed prior to the human record of history and will exist indefinitely, is it so unreasonable to conceive of an eternal God who is their possible source of origin?

One attribute of God men have made more controversial in the last century is God's *immutability*. Immutability refers to the changelessness of God. God has been and always is the same, as Scripture testifies. Job in conversation with his friends states that God does not change (Job 23:13). The LORD's words through the prophet Malachi declare the same in Mal 3:6, which is often remembered when discussing immutability. The writer of Hebrews wrote that Jesus Christ has always been the same (Heb. 13:8). Process Theology has been the foremost antagonist of divine immutability, proposing that God is actually affected by what goes on in the world and reacts to it; alteration means a change in direction on His part.[65] Openness Theology maintains a similar position in that God does change in His plans, thoughts, and emotions, i.e., in His character, but His nature stays the same, earning the term "weak immutability."[66]

It would seem that a personal God who expresses emotion would be one who alters and changes. Yet, God always expresses emotions that are consistent with His character. By His consistency, He demonstrates immutability. Even the Son of God's incarnation and death on the cross was consistent with God's character in both His hatred for sin and His love for humanity (Lev. 20:23; Prov. 6:16-19; Isa. 53:4-6; Rom. 5:8). The incarnation did not change God's nature, because Jesus remained fully divine (Phil. 2:5-11). A God who changes is a God who is unreliable. Throughout Scripture, God has displayed His consistency. That is why believers pray to God for His intervention in dire situations and trust in the hope of eternal life. A consistent God is the only Being who could have created the universe, because the universe is consistent. The natural laws and the principles of logic and mathematics consistently stay the same. This would only be possible with an immutable God. Furthermore, people value consistency in relationships. A neighbor who assures another neighbor that he can borrow his ladder any time on one day and then curses the same man for borrowing his ladder the next day would not be considered stable mentally or valued as a friend. The inconsistency of the neighbor would be described as an abnormality, and not a pleasant one at that. People, by and large, anticipate

---

65 Hartshorne, *Creativity in American Philosophy*, 112.

66 Sanders, *The God Who Risks*, 197.

and rely on consistency to manage each day at work, in the community, and at home in order to survive. Too many inconsistencies cause an unstable environment and lead to much anguish on the part of human beings. An unstable environment would be labeled deficient. Stability is valued, since we regard it as a normal and optimal human experience and part of the natural order. A stable and consistent universe must be the product of a consistent and unchanging God.

Omnipotence generally comes to the forefront when one mentally conjures up images of God, referring to God's unlimited power. No action or feat is beyond His grasp of performing. No one and nothing may limit His power. Generally, omnipotence is rarely contested, because the name, "God" in itself is often equated with infinite power. There are, however, some worldviews that contest divine omnipotence. Every polytheistic religion denies divine omnipotence because multiple deities must share divinity and its powers. Dualism subscribes to the belief that two beings, one righteous and the other evil, exist as equal counterparts; like polytheism, it implies that one being does not possess unlimited power.[67] Atheism, agnosticism, and skepticism hold that the Christian conception of God as both omnipotent and omnibenevolent is false since evil exists in the world.[68] Some have attempted to circumvent this problem by stating that God is good, but is limited or "finite" and therefore cannot overcome evil.[69]

The Bible is replete with statements that assert God's omnipotence. From the beginning, God demonstrates a power beyond the understanding of the human mind by creating the Universe via a simple word (Gen. 1:1–21). In fact, each miracle performed by God throughout Scripture is an indication that God possesses unimaginable power over the nature that He created, particularly the ten plagues of Egypt (Ex. 7:14–21; 8:1–6, 16–19, 20–24; 9:1–6, 8–11, 22–25; 10:12–15, 21–23; 12:29–30), the conquest of Canaan (Josh. 6:1–20; 10:1–14; 11:1–11, 16–23), and the resurrection of Jesus (Matt. 28:1–10; Mark. 16:1–8; Luke 24:1–43; John 20:1–29; 21:1–24). Beyond

---

67   Edward John Carnell, *An Introduction to Christian Apologetics* (Grand Rapids: Eerdmans, 1948), 286–7.

68   William L. Rowe, "The Problem of Evil & Some Varieties of Atheism," in *The Evidential Argument from Evil*, ed. Daniel Howard-Snyder (Bloomington: Indiana University, 1996), 5.

69   Carnell, *Christian Apologetics*, 286–7. Good and Evil dualism is in the Babylonian creation myth, below.

these accounts, several others specifically state that God has unlimited power. Jehoshaphat prayed to the LORD when facing an invasion from Moab and Ammon, asking the God who cannot be defeated by any enemy to intervene (2 Chron. 20:5-7). David praised God for the awesomeness of His work and the greatness of His power (Ps. 66:3). Describing the "Most High," Nebuchadnezzar informed his people that God does what He pleases and is answerable to no one (Dan. 4:35). Assuring His disciples that while it was difficult for the wealthy to enter the Kingdom of Heaven, Jesus told them that nothing is impossible with God (Matt. 19:25-26). The angel stated the same to Mary when announcing the birth of Christ (Luke 1:37). Throughout the pages of the Old and New Testament, the messages of God's immeasurable power are consistent and universal. On a popular level, atheists and agnostics have asked the infamous question, "Can God create a stone that He cannot lift?" A question meant to be a dig against God's omnipotence and His very existence is, as several philosophers have pointed out, a logical fallacy because God's omnipotence is part of His essence. To imagine a God that has limitations would be similar to imagining a square circle or a married bachelor. From another angle of attack, skeptics often attempt to pit God's attributes against one another. This is especially the case with omnipotence. "If God has unlimited power and can do anything He desires," they ask, "why can He not sin? Isn't that a limitation?" However, sin is a violation of God's character and thus is a privation, outside of God's character and contradictory to God's nature. God will only do what is true to His nature; therefore, it is not a limitation. Sin, properly understood, corrupts what is and signifies weakness. An all-powerful being would not commit an action that weakened Him, and if He did, He would no longer be God. Omnipotence is closely connected to generic theism, which cannot work as a theological and philosophical system unless God is omnipotent. In theism, God is Creator and Sustainer of the Universe, the orchestra conductor of major events in human history, and architect of the world's final destiny. Theism's God cannot be any of these things unless He is omnipotent. Consider creation: a universe as vast as three trillion galaxies could conceivably come into existence only by a power that humans can never experience nor witness. One can hardly claim that the power that created such a universe could be measured, yet an immeasurable power falls into striking range of omnipotence.

Omniscience involves God's unlimited knowledge: God is all-knowing. This entails every piece of knowledge of the past, present, and future. More than any other book in the Bible, the Psalms indicate God's omniscience. According to Psalm 44, God has knowledge of even the secrets within the human heart (Ps. 44:21). In Psalm 139, David begins by discussing the fact that God knows the very thoughts of His creation and that God knows everything (Ps. 139:1–4). Another Psalm (147:5) describes God as possessing an understanding without end. Outside the Psalms, the New Testament affirms God's all-knowingness. In Matthew 10:30, Jesus discloses that God knows even the number of hairs on each person's head. John, another apostle, writes like the psalmists that God knows everything (1 John 3:20). With these verses as a foundation, omniscience may be taken as a substantiated biblical doctrine.

For centuries, God's omniscience was understood as a logical and essential attribute of His Deity, but later in the Modern era, we see an erosion of that belief. Process Theology denies omniscience, claiming that God has complete knowledge of the past and present but not of the future.[70] Openness Theology draws a similar conclusion, arguing that since the future does not yet exist, God has "dynamic omniscience --" perfect knowledge of the past, present, and a future not yet determined. He does not possess perfect knowledge of the indefinite future; God has awareness only of future possibilities and probabilities.[71] It is hard for many to conceive of absolute knowledge because no one outside of God has absolute knowledge. Yet, if God is the source of all existence, then it is logical to assume that God's knowledge has no finite limit since He possesses the know-how to create the universe and all that is within it. It is humanly impossible to acquire all knowledge that pertains to the universe. At this point, scientists are only estimating the number of galaxies that are contained in the universe. To create the universe, the One responsible would have to possess a level of brilliance and knowledge far beyond anything that anyone can conceive. He would require that same unlimited capacity of knowledge to sustain the universe as well. The fact that the universe is not falling apart at the seams is another indication that God possesses infinite knowledge. Pertaining to the matter of future knowledge, God knows the future because He transcends His creation and exists above it. God is not bound to the existence He created, but his

---

70 Charles Hartshorne, *Creativity in American Philosophy* (Albany: State Univ. of New York, 1984), 112.

71 Sanders, *The God Who Risks*, 213–216.

superiority to it is literal. Existing outside of creation as an Eternal Being, God knows all the events occurring among those whom He made: past, present, and future.

God's *omnipresence* refers to His ubiquitous nature: God is everywhere. Psalm 139:7-10 gives us a perfect description of the divine being present wherever David goes; there is nowhere where he can hide from God. David's son Solomon admits in his prayer of dedication to the temple that the universe itself could not contain the LORD (1 Kgs. 8:27). Further evidence is found in Proverbs, where it is stated that God's eyes are in all places (Prov. 15:3). At times, God proclaims His omnipresence from His own mouth, such as Isaiah's description of heaven as God's throne and earth His footstool so that no house could contain Him (Isa. 66:1). God told Jeremiah that no one can hide from Him because He fills the earth (Jer. 23:23-24). In his sermon to the Athenians, Paul explained that God was near each of them, implying God's omnipresence (Acts 17:26-28). Omnipresence is thus quite clear from Scripture.

The human psyche points to the probability of divine omnipresence by the fact that people, often in desperate circumstances, cry out to God for help. This occurs not only for self-identified Christians, but also for non-Christians, including atheists and those who do not have any religious affiliation. People all over the world cry out to God for physical healing, for intervention in difficult circumstances, for financial assistance, for comfort during the midst of grief, and for spiritual salvation. They pray to God hoping for answers, but before they hope for God to answer their prayers, they hope that God will hear their prayers. How could God hear unless He was near? Why would individuals of many different worldviews and religious beliefs automatically think that God could possibly be near enough to hear their prayers? Created in God's image, humans, when reflecting on the nature of God, accept the nearness of God everywhere. Ancient mythologies depict the gods as being confined to one space at one time. When Zeus or Thor made an incursion on Earth, they had to physically leave Mt. Olympus or Asgard to venture to another location. Pagan mythology found it difficult to conceive of divine omnipresence. Others have found this concept difficult even in the modern era and stress that God has a physical body. The Church of Jesus Christ of Latter-Day Saints' official doctrine states that God the Father has a physical body of flesh and bone.[72] Popular depictions of God

---

72   Martin, *The Kingdom of the Cults*, 273.

in paintings and in media present Him in a way that the observer might conclude that God the Father indeed has a physical body. Perceptions such as these must be avoided within the minds of believers and in communications concerning God's nature.

Yet, belief in God's omnipresence is actually rational. Skeptics cannot discount this as superstition, because superstitions are passed down from one generation to the next. There are many instances where a person first prays and has little biblical knowledge about God. They may pray because it is sensible to think of God with His unlimited ability to be present everywhere at the same time. Humanity would have God no other way, for an inaccessible God is not a God worthy of our worship or service. From the perspective of a theistic worldview, a God who sustains the universe would require a constant presence, and a constant presence in as vast a universe as this one requires an omnipresent God.

Omnibenevolence is not as common a word used in the language discussing the nature of God, but it necessarily belongs to His nature. The term describes God as having perfect goodness. Believers have long enjoyed declaring that "God is good." In the Psalms, God is declared outright as "good," and for this reason He deserves praise (Ps. 118:1; 136:1; 143:10). Jesus stated the same when He spoke to the rich young ruler (Matt. 19:17; Mark 10:18). In many more places, the Bible speaks of God's everlasting and abundant mercy (Deut. 7:9; 2 Sam. 22:51; 1 Chron. 16:34, 41; 2 Chron. 5:13; 7:3, 6; 20:21; Ezra 3:11; Ps. 100:5; 106:1; 118:1–4; 136:1–26; Jer. 33:11; Eph. 2:4; 1 Pet. 1:3). As much as such writers testify to the power and majesty of God, they equally assure readers of God's goodness and mercy.

The most vocal opponents of God's omnibenevolence are, again, atheists, agnostics, and skeptics who give voice to the philosophical argument known as "the Problem of Evil." The evidence they use is from the pages of the Bible itself. Pointing to events such as the Israelite conquest of Canaan, they claim that the God of the Bible is evil or, at least, is portrayed as such.[73] Furthermore, those who deny God's goodness point to all of the evil in the world, asking the question, "If God is good and God is also Almighty, then why does He not put a stop to the evil of this world?"[74] Many volumes have been written on this subject by

---

73 Richard Dawkins, *The God Delusion* (Boston: Houghton Mifflin, 2006), 237–47.

74 Rowe, "The Problem of Evil," 5.

Christian philosophers and apologists. Though this argument is one of the most used in the atheist's arsenal, Christians need not fear the problem of evil; they can be assured that God is indeed good. Scripture consistently testifies of God's goodness. In addition to the testimony of Scripture, God's omnibenevolence can be argued from the concept of goodness. How does humanity know goodness in any of its forms to distinguish it from evil? Human beings throughout the world understand right and wrong and that certain actions, such as stealing, assault, rape, and murder are perverse and wrong and others such as gift-giving, grief consoling, and life-saving are right and good. Generally, humans instantly recognize goodness without relying on complicated reasoning, which leads to the conclusion that goodness is instinctive or innate within humans. Its virtual universality demonstrates that goodness exists as an idea outside of mere human experience. Where did goodness originate if not from humanity? Goodness must have a source and a source that must be intelligent, because goodness is an attribute that is recognized through the intellect. The source must be greater than humanity, because humans can only recognize and do good acts rather than inventing goodness. Humans did not create goodness, and so the source, its origin, must transcend humanity. The sensible suggestion is that God is its intelligent and transcendent Source, and if God is indeed its source, then it is reasonable to suggest that God is good.

The goodness of God is found in the nature of reality. Reality, though it admits of evil acts, also has many good and beautiful things. Creation, with its majestic mountains, impressive oceans, fields full of flowers, and amazing starlit skies, displays the desires of One who would have those whom He made enjoy the world and the universe where He placed them. A good God would create a world and a universe of beauty and wonder; which describes the universe itself then and now.

Holiness, in relation to the description of God, refers to the fact that God is set apart and unlike any other. It also signifies His purity and sinlessness. This is an attribute that one finds consistently throughout the Bible, from the LORD's declarations concerning His own holiness (Lev. 11:44–45; 19:2; 20:7, 26; 21:8; Ps. 86:2; Isa. 29:19; 43:3, 15; 1 Pet. 1:6) to designations of His Name as holy (Lev. 22:2; Ps. 106:47; Ezek. 36:21–22; 39:7). In addition, places and items used in worship that the Bible associates with the LORD are designated as "holy" (Ex. 28:38, 43; 29:30, 37; 30:36; 40:9–10; Lev. 6:16, 26, 30; 16:16–20; Num. 4:4, 15; 1 Kgs. 6:16; 7:50;

8:6; 2 Chron 4:22; 5:7; Ps. 5:7; 11:4; 138:2; Isa. 64:11; Ezek. 48:21; Jon. 2:4, 7; Joel 3:17; 1 Cor. 9:13). Even certain days are called "holy" due to the fact that they are set aside for worship, particularly the Sabbath and the Feast and Festival days (Ex. 20:8; 31:15; 35:2; Lev. 23:3, 8, 21, 24, 27, 35–37; 27:23; Num. 28:18, 25–26; 29:1, 7, 12; Deut. 5:12; Neh. 8:9–11; Isa. 58:13). With the adjective "holy" attached to God and to what is associated with Him throughout the Bible, it can be safe to assume that the writers of Scripture understood the LORD to be holy.

Concerning the holiness of God, no belief system outside of Christianity truly matches the biblical concept. The polytheism of pagan mythology lowered the divine to something very similar to humanity, whose gods possess all the flaws and faults of mankind besides immortality and certain special abilities. The pantheism of Hinduism and the New Age movement regards God as separate, but without the distinctions of personhood and therefore without the ability to establish any relationship with humans.[75] Islam acknowledges that Allah is set apart, but he is not pure, since, as the ruler over a deterministic reality, he presides over all things deemed acceptable to his will, moral or not.[76] Christians believe in a God set apart and like no other. If God is like humans, then there is no reason to worship Him; but many do, in fact, worship Him. Hymns in languages representing nationalities and ethnicities all over the world praise God because His people have had glimpses of His holiness. Skeptics might protest by objecting that there is no tangible evidence of holiness, in contrast with God's omnipotence. Yet, tangible evidence exists in the changed lives of the millions of individuals who call Him "Lord." They have become moral, compassionate, humble, patient, and generous, whereas prior to their conversion they failed to display these qualities. Their transformation exhibits, albeit imperfectly, God's holiness.

God's non-communicable attributes display His transcendence. No one created can be like God. For that very reason, it is reasonable to believe in the non-communicable attributes shown in this section. By definition, God has abilities and characteristics unlike anyone or anything else and so, when applied to God, these particular attributes describe God perfectly. Non-communicable attributes are often dismissed as nonsense,

---

75 Newport, *The New Age Movement*, 5.

76 Norman L. Geisler and Abdul Saleeb, *Answering Islam: The Crescent in Light of the Cross*, 2d. ed. (Grand Rapids: Baker, 2002), 30.

but they are certainly sensible both from a definitional standpoint and by coherence with the Christian system of belief. God simply is beyond our full understanding, because He is God and we are His creation.

Doctrine of God: The Communicable Attributes of God

Communicable attributes are attributes that humans may have and share, at least in part, with God, their Creator. But because of man's sinful nature, humans share them imperfectly. Just as believers cherish God's non-communicable attributes, they revere God for those attributes He does communicate to us, such as His wisdom, His mercy, His patience, His faithfulness, His righteousness, and His holiness.

Much would be missing from the Bible if one removed all the verses pertaining to the Lord's communicable attributes, because Scripture contains many descriptions of them and encourages God-followers to imitate Him in character. A number of passages describe the wisdom of the Lord (Job 9:4; Rom. 16:27; 1 Cor. 1:25; 1 Tim. 1:17; Jude 1:25). Other passages encourage God's people to embrace wisdom (Prov. 1:2-3; 3:13; 4:5; 16:16; 28:26; Eccl. 2:26; Jas. 1:5). As God's mercy is everlasting, Scripture instructed those who follow Him to show mercy (Ps. 37:21; Zech. 7:9; Jas. 2:13). Despite human sinfulness, God demonstrates tremendous patience (Ex. 34:6; Num. 14:18; Ps. 86:15; Rom. 2:4; 2 Pet. 3:9, 15), and those who believe in Him are told to be patient with others (2 Cor. 6:6; Gal. 5:22; Eph. 4:2; Col. 1:11; 3:12; 2 Tim. 3:10; 4:2). Whereas mankind has largely been unfaithful to God, He has continued to be faithful or loyal (Deut. 7:9; Ps. 71:22; 89:5, 9; 98:3; Hos. 11:12; 1 Cor. 1:9; 10:13; 2 Cor. 1:18), and true believers are also to demonstrate their faithfulness (Prov. 28:20; Matt. 25:21-23; Luke 16:10-12; 1 Cor. 4:1-2; 1 Tim. 3:11; Rev. 2:10). Because of God's perfection, He has proven time and again that He is righteous or always upholds the law (Ps. 7:17; 11:7; 22:31; 50:6; 97:2, 6; 111:3; 112:3, 9; Jer. 23:6; 2 Cor. 9:9). Those who trust in Him inherit His righteousness and practice it (2 Chron. 9:8; Ps. 15:2; 23:3; Prov. 11:19; Isa. 11:4-5; Zeph. 2:3; Matt. 6:33; Rom. 3:25-26; 4:5; Heb. 11:7; 1 Pet. 2:24; 1 John 3:10). As discussed previously, God is Holy and God told the Israelites to be holy as He was (Lev. 11:44-45; 19:2; 20:7, 26; 21:8). Quoting Leviticus, Peter urged Christians to do the same (1 Pet. 1:16). Therefore, the Bible not only informs its readers of God's characteristics, but exhorts them to emulate certain of His attributes that the writers say may also be ours.

Thinking Rationally About Christian Theology
A Handbook on Polemics

On its surface, the Bible's treatment of God's communicable attributes seems uncontroversial and, in its profound simplicity, nearly impossible to distort or deny. However, certain belief systems cannot accept the attributes in their biblical form. This includes agnosticism, which not only claims that there is not enough evidence to prove that God exists, but that even if He does exist, He would be unknowable.[77] Deism depicts God as a mere observer of the world who does not communicate with it. The deistic God is not really known by the earth's inhabitants nor His attributes, let alone shared attributes. Some popular portrayals of God conceive of Him as a list of abstract ideals, rather than having concrete attributes that humans can share with Him to a lesser extent. The danger of such a conception is that it denies the ability to have any serious relationship with God or the possibility of man to aspire to be like God in any way.

An argument for attributes "shared" between God and man can be found in morality. During mankind's history, almost every culture has valued the noble characteristics of wisdom, mercy, patience, and faithfulness. Why are such behaviors praised in the world's societies? A reasonable explanation is that having been created in God's image, mankind recognizes goodness and appreciates it. These qualities cannot be said to have originated with humans, because no human, apart from the fully human and fully divine Christ, has exhibited these qualities to perfection. However, we may safely acknowledge the existence of the perfect forms of these attributes, because people have aspired to improve their personal fidelity to moral qualities. With the additional understanding that these noble characteristics are appreciated with near universality around the world, we would argue that a noble and upright Source exists who demonstrates such qualities with perfect completeness and vigor.

Another support for God's communicable attributes centers in the life of Jesus. No other life in the entirety of the world's history has inspired so many. Christ's miracles, sermons, and parables continue to excite the desire to emulate Him in many who read about them, but what attracts so many to Him is the written record of His compassion for the sick, poor, and ostracized, His willingness to forgive even those who persecuted and betrayed Him, and His love for those who hated Him. When one examines

---

77   Julian Huxley, *Religion Without Revelation*, 5-7.

the life of Jesus, there is nothing that is not admirable. Paul declared that the world saw God in all of His holiness, righteousness, mercy, compassion, patience, and wisdom when they observed Jesus in all that He said and did. In Jesus, God's communicable attributes exist in their perfection. Since strong evidence points to the Gospels as historically reliable accounts of the life of Jesus, it is hard to dismiss the virtuous character of Jesus. When considering the life of Jesus, one is attracted to the communicable attributes of God.

Believers stand in awe at the non-communicable attributes of God, but they find comfort in His communicable attributes. Because God has shared attributes with His people, believers live not only as worshippers but as partakers on a journey to spiritual maturity. Also, because of these shared attributes, Christians look to Jesus as the ultimate model for living out their faith.

Doctrine of God:
The Sovereignty of God

Nothing in the entire realm of existence is beyond the reign and rule of God. Every event that happens occurs because directly willed it to be so or because He allowed it. Many Christians utter their support of this doctrine by quoting the oft repeated and cherished phrase, "God is in control."

The doctrine of God's sovereignty finds itself in a struggle between two perspectives: determinism and libertarianism. For determinism and libertarianism, each has a hard and a soft version. Hard determinism suggests that free will does not exist, and has two further variants. One is Islamic determinism. According to Islamic theology, everything that happens occurs because Allah directly willed it.[78] This presents a problem for Christians who rarely entertain the thought of a god responsible for both good and evil circumstances. Naturalism also has its form of hard determinism, developed by B.F. Skinner (1904 - 1990), which argues that man ultimately is a slave to natural processes and to the stimuli of his own environment and has no free will at all.[79] So, rather than a supreme being controlling events, the laws and processes of nature and mankind's

---

78 Geisler and Saleeb, *Answering Islam*, 30.

79 B. F. Skinner, *Beyond Freedom and Dignity* (New York: Alfred A. Knopf, 1972), 208–11.

environment direct all circumstances and all human decisions. Soft determinism, or compatibilism, recognizes that though much in the universe is determined and beyond human control, individuals do have a degree of freedom to choose according to the dictates of their desires according to their nature. Libertarianism, in its hard form, states that humans have the ability to make all decisions completely free from any external influence. The softer view of libertarianism posits that God has granted individuals the ability to choose from a variety of choices, but that the consequences of choices can restrict our freedom.[80]

Unfortunately, secular humanism has adapted the concept of free will to make humans gods unto themselves, having free control and mastery of their universe. No social mores, ethical codes, or religious creed can dictate their personal choices. Such is the impact of secular free will that many Christians or nominal Christians place free will over divine sovereignty; in that case, God has little to do with the daily lives of His creatures or specifically His people. In recent years, Moralistic Therapeutic Deism, terminology coined by Christian Smith and Melina Lundquist Denton, is a common belief among secular persons and even among Christians in Generation Z. According to this view, God accepts humans in their sinful state and without any desire for them to change. As with any Deism, God interacts little with humanity and cares little about their ethical decisions so long as they are for the happiness of everyone, but He is present to help any person in crisis who desires to help himself.[81]

Scripture's testimony doubtless affirms God's sovereignty. In Psalm 33, God is described as One who overcomes the plans of man and whose own plans cannot be undone (Ps. 33:8–11). According to Psalm 97:1–12, Yahweh reigns supreme as Lord over all creation, and nothing is greater than Him. Echoing Psalm 97, Psalm 104 attributes to the Lord the sovereignty to command creation to do His bidding (Ps. 104:2–26). Paul recognized that this same absolute authority was used to bring about the

---

80 Kenneth Keathley, *Salvation and Sovereignty* (Nashville: Broadman and Holman, 2010), 65–77.

81 Rachel Bratton, "The American Church has Fallen: Shocking Poll Shows 'Fake Christianity' Has Supplanted Biblical Worldview," *The Western Journal*, (July 4, 2021) https://www.westernjournal.com/american-church-fall-en-shocking-poll-shows-fake-christianity-supplanted-biblical-worldview/ (accessed January 31, 2023).

salvation of mankind through the Son of God (Gal. 4:4–5). Additional Bible passages state that God's will cannot be thwarted and that He does as He pleases (Ps. 115:3; Prov. 19:21; Jas. 4:14–15).

With the Bible's affirmation of God's sovereignty, it leads people to question whether humanity can have any ability to act in freedom. In the sovereignty versus free will debate, neither extreme represents reality. A fully deterministic worldview, in which man has either absolutely no freedom or has but a small degree of freedom, does not represent a realistic understanding of the world. Man has some freedom due to the fact that each person, in whatever culture around the world, is held responsible for his or her own actions, decisions, and language choices. The Bible strongly testifies that people of the Earth will answer for their sins (Rom. 3:5–6; 1 Pet. 4:4–6; Rev. 20:12–15). At the same time, human beings must acknowledge how little control they do have over the universe. They did not consent to the time they were born. They cannot change the scientific laws that govern the universe. They do not control nature or sustain the orbit of the planets in the solar system. A quick inventory of reality will suffice to demonstrate how little authority man does have, especially to remove himself and his actions and decisions from a world predisposed to self-motivated activity. God is obviously sovereign, and man has some ethical and spiritual freedom during his lifespan. The logical conclusion based on Scripture and observation is that God chooses to give a degree of freedom to each person without handing mankind complete control of the universe and determination of the eternal fate of human existence. God, then, is Sovereign and in control, but every human being has the responsibility to commit to Him, obey Him, and live according to His standards and to emulate Christ's life of obedience on earth.

Defending the rationality of God's Sovereignty is relatively easy, as it is so closely related to God's nature. If God created the universe, then He is certainly omnipotent, and if He is omnipotent, then He has the power to control it. By its nature, the universe is orderly and organized. Its laws are constant, and its processes and systems are regular and predictable. The earth continues to orbit around the sun without interruption. The principles of mathematics remain the same. The elements do not change their properties from day to day. Mathematical constants, as to their fine tuning, betray a supreme hand that guides the universe on a consistent basis.

History also demonstrates divine sovereign control. Humanity has yet to completely destroy itself, though it has certainly tried through two world wars and dictatorial genocides that seem to have begun with the pogroms of Stalin, or earlier with barbarians before the gates of Rome. Neither has one civilization entirely subjugated the earth to enslave and exploit the populations it has conquered, although various "civilizations" and Empires have attempted to subdue whole populations; if this were successful, it would leave the entire human race at the mercy of their subjugators. Despite the existence of thousands of diseases on the planet, some spread by human ills and some man-made, illness has not eradicated life on earth. The fact that humanity has not only survived but thrived should make one wonder if a Being is directing events around the world for the purpose of preserving the human race and life on earth.

Evidence within Scripture, nature, and history demonstrates the sovereignty of God. Not one moment and not one section of the universe exists when and where God is not in control. For that reason among others, believers trust God for their eternal salvation and look to the future with hopeful assurance.

Doctrine of God:
Creation

All that exists originates from God and God alone. God created the Universe *ex nihilo* or "out of nothing." Of all the acts of God, there is none more foundational to Christian faith than the creation of the universe by God. For in creation all the non-communicable attributes of God (His omnipotence, omniscience, omnibenevolence, and holiness) are made known. Creation also explains the world and humanity's point of origin. Without creation, the history of the world cannot and will not make sense.

When seeking to learn about the origins of the universe, the first passage of Scripture to study is obviously Genesis 1:1-28. However, references to creation exist throughout the Bible. Genesis 2:1-7 offers a summary of creation, instead of a contradictory account as postulated by some Old Testament scholars and theologians. Furthermore, numerous passages refer to creation as being the handiwork of God (Ps. 104:5; Isa. 42:5; 45:5-12, 18; Mark 13:19; Eph. 3:9; Col. 1:16; Rev. 4:11; 10:6). Others mention that God is Creator of man (Gen. 5:1-2; 6:7; Deut. 4:32; Ps. 89:12, 47; 102:18; 148:5; Mal. 2:10; 1 Cor. 11:8-9; Eph. 2:10; 4:24). Creation, then, is not a doctrine built upon an obscure biblical reference, but a belief based on numerous passages of in-depth and coherent content explaining the origins of the universe and of humanity.

If one approaches the creation narrative of Genesis 1:1–28 from a simple, literal reading, the obvious conclusion to make is a six-day young-earth perspective of God's creation of the world. For much of the Church's history, the literal interpretation held sway. A notable exception to that would be the dualism espoused by the Bogomils in the thirteenth-century Balkans and a portion of the Cathari of southern France during the twelfth through fourteenth centuries, who claimed that it was Satan who created the original elements of the world.[82] However, the advent of theoretical Evolution as taught beginning in the middle of the nineteenth century has resulted in a much more widespread abandonment of the biblical understanding of creation. Evolution has led many to dismiss the literal interpretation of the Creation account and search for alternatives that align closer to prevailing scientific theory. Since Charles Darwin's (1809 – 1882) publication of *On the Origin of Species*, several additional interpretations of the Genesis creation account, aside from the literal interpretation, have emerged. The Gap Theory became popular through the promotion of Thomas Chalmers (1780 – 1847) and the first edition of the Scofield Reference Bible (1917). It proposes that a gap exists between Genesis 1:1 and 1:2, and that between that gap were millions of years. During that gap of millions of years, Satan's rebellion against God and the subsequent war destroyed the first world that God created and all life that was contained in it. Therefore, Gen. 1:2 and the rest of the passage describe God's recreation of the world, which only took six literal days. Progressive creationism or Old Earth creationism proposes that the universe and the earth began billions of years ago, but evolution was not the primary agent of bringing about new ages and new species. Initiated by Bernard Ramm (1916 – 1992), the theory claims that God intervened in each step of the process to usher in a new age and create new species over billions of years. Theistic evolution was popularly embraced by many Christian biologists, theologians and pastors when the theory of evolution became accepted in the scientific community during the second half of the nineteenth century. Simply put, the theistic account holds that God used evolution to

---

82   Jaroslav Pelikan, *The Christian Tradition: A History of the Development of Doctrine*, vol. 3 (Chicago: University of Chicago, 1978), 3:239.

create the universe, earth, and life on earth over the process of billions of years. Finally, some, believing (some would say in a "religious" way) that evolution has disproved God's creation of the world, completely dismiss Genesis. Some, persuaded by philosophical naturalism, hold that human existence and life emerged out of unguided evolution.[83]

With regard to creation, Christians have many different views. One should never suggest that if a believer does not have a specific view on the origins of the world, then he or she is not a follower of Christ. Yet, it is also important for the believer to ensure that Scripture guides his beliefs. Any view that radically departs from the Genesis account must be abandoned since Jesus himself affirmed Genesis (Mark 13:19). Christians, then, should consider a biblical understanding of creation as one that includes God's direct involvement with creation, demonstrating His omnipotence and omniscience with no process bearing responsibility in full or in part with bringing about existence. Theistic evolution cannot be easily reconciled with the Genesis account, because God directly created species (Gen. 1:12, 24–25) and had a constant and active hand in the making of the universe. Furthermore, Theistic evolution stresses the work of evolution rather than the effort of God, suggesting that evolution is a force almost unto itself and God had little to do with creation. Gap theorists have sincerely attempted to bring harmony to the Bible and the supposed evidence that the earth and the universe are billions of years old. Yet, little evidence exists for such a gap within the whole text of Scripture; where does it specifically state that an age-long gap exists between the first two verses of Genesis 1? The same could be said for the Day-Age Theory, due to the fact that the language and context of Genesis 1 indicate that God created in days and not ages and little-to-nothing within Scripture suggests otherwise. Among progressive creationists are brilliant scientists and philosophers who are equally devout Christians supporting their position. They attempt to harmonize the biblical account with scientific evidence. William Lane Craig (1949-) has offered an interesting harmonization by suggesting that the first human couple came from a population of hominids or creatures that are similar to humans, but who did not have rational thought capabilities. Craig asserts that God gave the first couple

---

83 Weston W. Fields, *Unformed and Unfilled* (Phillipsburg: Presbyterian and Reformed Publishing, 1976), 165-7. Such a view may be taken as a kind of pre-philosophical or pre-scientific (i.e., not from science) naturalism.

(i.e., Adam and Eve) souls and thus created the human race.[84]

When approaching the doctrine of creation, a word of caution should be issued. Typically, when harmonizing Scripture with scientific theory, science is given precedence over Scripture, and scientific theory becomes authoritative over it and over the historic creeds. For biblical Christians, the Bible should always be our supreme authority for faith and practice. When approaching the origins of the universe, Christians should, as with any other doctrine, make sure that their beliefs are biblically grounded. Moving further away from the biblical description by definition makes a doctrine less biblical and more unbiblical. This diagram illustrates that principle:

Biblical	Quasi-Biblical	Allegorical-Biblical	Unbiblical
Scripture is accepted as trustworthy	Scripture must be adapted to be factual	Scripture communicates spiritual truth but not facts	Scripture is disregarded

A long list of books and journal articles have covered the plethora of scientific indicators that the universe and the earth did come to being through natural processes but through the efforts of a Designer. Though the two major movements would not necessarily consider themselves allies, biblical creationists and proponents of intelligent design have submitted substantial, difficult-to-ignore evidence that the universe is the product of a Creator. Yet, many object to such tactics; those that buttress the creation accounts in the first place are dismissed out-of-hand. Claiming that the Genesis account reflects the mythology of an earlier era, those who deny the possible historicity of Creation argue that the narratives were not written to describe an actual event but are figurative, and, as figurative, they portray an unscientific beginning for an uncultured and ignorant community. What those who regard the Genesis account as figurative fail to realize is that the biblical narratives contrast sharply with ancient mythology. The Babylonian creation

---

84   William Lane Craig, "The Historical Adam" in *First Things*, (October 2021) at URL https://www.firstthings.com/article/2021/10/the-historical-adam (accessed January 27, 2023).

account, for example, describes the world as beginning as the result of a conflict between the sea monster, Tiâmat and the king of the gods, Marduk. Hindu mythology, on the other hand, claims that the world came from the body of the giant creature known as Purusha after he had been sacrificed by the gods. In no mythological account did deities create the universe out of nothing.

In the secular-dominated societies of the twenty-first century, submitting a defense of the doctrine of Creation often meets stiff resistance. Any believer who regards the Genesis account as accurate, whether fully or partially, is labeled as an enemy of science. Knowing this, many Christians opt to refrain from any debate concerning the origins of the Universe. Tragically, followers of Christ have failed to realize that the doctrine of Creation possesses a solid foundation of rationality. For instance, the universe contains a vast amount of information. The amount of information is so vast that no technology, whether book, computer, or data storage device has the capacity of storing every piece of human knowledge in one place. Even more intimidating is the fact that the knowledge available to mankind is a mere fraction of the totality of information that exists in the universe. Could this universe, owing its existence to the randomness of the process of an unthinking and undirected evolution, have so much knowledge contained within it? As epistemologists (theorists of knowledge) have determined through the centuries, knowledge must come from a source. There are many sources of knowledge, but they, in turn, received their knowledge from another source. Therefore, there must be an ultimate Source of knowledge. A universe that came into existence accidentally or with little direction could not have such an ultimate Source of knowledge. Because this universe, with the totality of its knowledge requiring a Source, is the way it is, it must have been created by a Creator.

Not only is the universe an informational collection, but it is also orderly. As has been discussed previously concerning God's Sovereignty, the Universe operates under laws, laws that cannot be changed if it is to stay the same (not necessarily statically but dynamically) and, e.g., continue to support human life. The universe's consistent regularity points to a Designer who created it according to His plan. He constructed it to run a certain way from the beginning, and it continues as such. A universe that simply happened without the guidance of a Creator would not have consistency and regularity.

Doctrine of God

The first words of the Bible describe the creation of the universe by the spoken word of God. One of the earliest biblical events that children growing up in churches learn is the six days of the creation. Those reading the account of earth's origins are often struck by the simplicity as well as the awesomeness of what God achieved. During the last two centuries, many Christians have opted to speak less about this fundamental belief due to the opposition of prevailing scientific theory. They should not continue to hold their silence, because the rational arguments outlined here support Creation, and the very fact that we live in a rational universe suggests that it originated from a Divine Being.

Chapter 4

Christology

Historical Background:

Renaissance artist, Raffaello Sanzio da Urbino (1483-1520), more commonly known as Raphael, finished his last and most famous work shortly before His death. Entitled, The Transfiguration, it depicts the transfiguration of Christ as depicted in the Gospels (Matt. 17:1-21; Mark 9:2-29). In his painting, Raphael portrays Christ transfigured with a white robe, floating above and conversing with Moses and Elijah. Beneath Christ's transfiguration, Raphael illustrated the scene of Jesus' disciples vainly attempting to exorcise the demon from the epileptic boy. Raphael's painting is unique in that it represents Christ's divinity. Many of the paintings of Christ depict His ministry, particularly His crucifixion, but few illustrate the divine identity of Jesus as God, the Son.[85]

From the beginning of His ministry, Jesus has been the center of controversy and the subject of many unbiblical beliefs. A popular figure in many different cultures, Jesus has been reinterpreted to be a prophet of Islam, a radical Feminist, a social revolutionary, and a New Age guru. Although biblical Christians might find encouragement in the fact that Jesus is so attractive a historical figure, they should be warned that the subject of the identity and ministry of Jesus has been considered fair game for any theory about Him. The doctrines pertaining to Christ represent the cornerstone of Christianity. If Jesus is misrepresented or if the beliefs about Him are distorted,

---

85 Bette Talvacchia, *Raphael* (New York: Phaidon, 2007), 218–22.

> *then the entire belief system collapses. Due to the widespread devia-*
> *tions concerning Jesus in the twenty-first century, believers must pre-*
> *pare themselves to defend the biblical beliefs about Him.*

Christology :
The Incarnation

The most amazing event after the creation of the universe came when God the Son became a man. As fully human, He lived with His creation, the bearers of His image. As fully God, the Son displayed divine power through various miracles during His ministry. As a fully human and obedient sacrifice, yet as God's anointed, Christ died as a substitute for humanity in payment for their sins.

What presents the largest problem for skeptics of the incarnation is the dual nature of Christ. Several heresies arose to attempt to explain or correct supposed problems with the doctrine. Though Nestorius (ca. 386 – ca. 450) probably did not hold to the extreme versions of his teaching to which others subscribed, the heresy known as Nestorianism assaulted the biblical understanding of the union between the two full natures of Christ. To preserve the fully human and the fully divine natures of Christ, Nestorianism resists the idea of a union between the two natures, making Christ's natures separate. This leads to the unbiblical conclusion that Christ is actually two persons in one body.[86] Arguing the opposite point, Monophysitism confused the language between "person" and "nature" and proposed that Christ has only one nature.[87] Originating in the seventh century, Monothelitism (a later attempt) declares that Christ has only a divine will. Similar to the denial of Christ's human nature by Monophysites, Monothelitism denies His human will and therefore, His full humanity.[88] Another unbiblical belief, this time arising in the late twentieth century with the New Age Movement, is the idea of a Cosmic Christ or a Christ

---

86 Aloys Grillmeier, *Christ in Christian Tradition*, vol. 1, 2d ed. (Atlanta: John Knox, 1975), 503.

87 Philip Hughes, *The Church in Crisis: A History of the General Councils 325 – 1870* (London: Burns and Oates, 1961), 55–6.

88 Hughes, *The Church in Crisis*. 101.

who exists in the spiritual awareness of the human consciousness. Jesus, then serves as the model to enable one to attain personal enlightenment.[89]

Biblically, the incarnation is attested most famously by the statement found in John 1:14 that the Son of God took on human flesh "... and dwelt among us, and we have seen his glory, glory as of the only Son from the Father, full of grace and truth." (ESV). Explaining the doctrine of the resurrection to the church at Corinth, Paul designated Christ as the "Second Adam," indicating that Jesus had a fully human body (1 Cor. 15:42–49). The apostle gave a more explicit description of the incarnation to the church at Philippi when he inserted a hymn explaining Christ's life on earth. The hymn describes Jesus as lowering Himself by leaving Heaven and taking on a human body (Phil. 2:5–8). Writing to Timothy, Paul refers to Christ specifically as a man (1 Tim. 2:5). The book of Hebrews deals extensively with the incarnation, informing its readers that Christ lived on earth in human flesh (Heb. 5:7–9) and that His body became a sacrifice to atone for sin (Heb. 10:10). In two of his letters, John warned that only true believers acknowledge that Christ took on human flesh (1 John 4:1–3; 2 John 1:7). Beyond John's familiar declaration in his Gospel's first chapter, Christian teaching of the incarnation is firmly rooted in the New Testament through several sentences that offer detailed descriptions of the Son of God becoming fully man.

A major objection to the incarnation is the seemingly impossible combination of two full natures in one Person. This leads many to the false conclusion that Christians claim that the Incarnate Son of God is actually two persons who share one body, as Nestorians believe. Part of the difficulty comes from the attempt to conceive how the two natures share Christ's body at the same time. The incarnation, as a miracle, cannot be fully fathomed or completely explained. Believers accept that God created the Universe by speaking it into existence even though they do not fully understand how God performed this awesome feat. Attempting to explain God's incarnation in Christ often leads to misconceptions and unbiblical conclusions.

Another objection to this doctrine is the seeming inconsistency of God, an uncreated being, becoming incarnate "in" a created human. The two natures are not only completely different, but, according

---

89 Deepak Chopra, *The Third Jesus: The Christ We Cannot Ignore* (New York: Harmony Books, 2008), 138-9.

to the argument, seem incompatible. For students of Scripture, the incompatibility is overcome in that Scripture states that God created human beings in His image (Gen. 1:26–27; 9:6). By his very origins and nature, man, designed by God Himself to be part of His family, has a special connection to God. To say that Jesus' divine nature is incompatible with His human nature would be to deny that any person created by God has any link to God. Yet, humans have religious inclinations, such as curiosity about God's existence and the urge to pray in times of need. Such inclinations reveal a connection to their supernatural Creator. Also, when the first humans were created by God, they were sinless (Gen. 2:25; 3:6–7). Jesus, being conceived by the Holy Spirit, did not inherit mankind's sin nature ("yet without sin" Heb. 4:15) and thus has a human nature compatible with His divine nature (Luke 1:4–35; 2 Cor. 5:21).

Fundamentally, God's personal nature corresponds with the incarnation and with the Son of God's ministry on Earth. Though different in substance due to His divinity, God is also a Being who thinks, makes judgments, and expresses emotions. He has the ability to relate to humans. God, then, could easily live amongst the people He created and live fully as a human. So, in the biblical-theistic worldview, the incarnation does not defy logic, but logically fits and coheres with other Bible teaching.

The incarnation agrees perfectly with the biblical concept of God. As an omnibenevolent Being, the God of Scripture would have sincere and earnest compassion for His creation, so earnest that He could become human to save His creation and its people. As fully divine, the Son of God was sinless, making Him the perfect and only sacrifice for the sins of the world.

Christology:
The Virginal Conception of Christ

It was the conception of Jesus that began the incarnation of the Son of God. According to Scripture, the birth itself—Mary having all the normal, physical experiences of bearing and giving birth to Jesus (Luke 2:6–7)—was not the miracle. Rather, it was the conception of Jesus that was the miracle (Matt. 1:20; Luke 1:35). The Holy Spirit visited Mary and miraculously conceived the child who was both fully God and fully man. While the conception was the miracle, the birth, of course, was significant in the fact that it represented the arrival of Christ into the world to eventually save the world through His death and resurrection.

Christology

In the attempt to explain the miraculous conception of Christ, a false version of the virginal conception has been proposed. According to the doctrine of the Church of Jesus Christ of Latter-Day Saints, God the Father instigated sexual intercourse with Mary in order to conceive Christ.[90] Luke's account definitely describes a miracle. Divine physical intercourse with humans is not miraculous but a devaluing of the nature of God. False versions of virginal conception limit the deity's ability in claiming it cannot bring about conception without the act of intercourse, and has them commit intimacy outside of marriage, which is sin.

Early on, the virginal conception faced denials. Celsus (late second century) charged that Jesus was conceived humanly but outside of marriage.[91] Interestingly enough, radical feminists such as Mary Daly (1928 –2010) later echoed Celsus's conclusion.[92] Twentieth-century deniers sought to draw parallels between the Gospel accounts and myths from Zoroastrian, Buddhist, Mithraic, Egyptian, and Krishna sources. Emil Brunner (1889 –1966) saw the virginal conception as a product of docetic influence from the Gnostics.[93]

Though numerous explanations abound to reject the virginal conception, the primary reason behind its denial is on scientific grounds. Biologically, females cannot conceive on their own. Therefore, the conception of Jesus by the Holy Spirit could not have happened. Of course, this denial is an outright refusal to accept any occurrence that cannot be explained within the limits of the experiences and data science studies, which shows prejudice against a biblical worldview and reveals a predisposition against the miraculous. To deny a claim before examining the evidence would be to commit a logical fallacy. For theists, belief in the miraculous conception of Christ is not difficult, because God, with His unlimited power, can do anything He wills that does not contradict His nature.

An additional argument has been made by Marcus Borg (1942 – 2015), Bart Ehrman (1955 –), *et al* that Scriptural evidence for Christ's

---

90   R. Philip Roberts, *Mormonism Unmasked*, (Nashville: Broadman and Holman, 1998), 69–71 .

91   James Leo Garrett, *Systematic Theology*, vol. 1, (Grand Rapids: Eerdmans, 1990), 591–4.

92   Mary Daly, *Beyond God the Father: Toward a Philosophy of Women's Liberation* (Boston: Beacon Press, 1973), 84–5.

93   Garrett, *Systematic Theology*, 593–4.

virginal conception is weakly attested from the New Testament, since the circumstances surrounding Jesus' birth are only mentioned in two of the four Gospels: Matthew 1:18-2:23 and Luke 2:1-20.[94] What should be observed in the Gospel accounts, however, is that the narratives are not mere mentions or slight references to Jesus' conception and birth, but descriptions with many details that mention historical figures, namely Herod the Great (Matt. 2:1, 3, 16-22), Archelaus (Matt. 2:22), Augustus (Luke 2:1), and Quirinius (Luke 2:2), as well as the historical event of the census conducted by the Roman Empire (Luke 2:1-2) and the actual locations of Nazareth (Luke 1:26), Jerusalem (Matt 2:3), and Bethlehem (Matt. 2:1, 5, 8; Luke 2:4, 15). Even with the seeming discrepancies of the timing of the census at Jesus' birth and the dates of Quirinius' time as governor in Syria in Luke's account (Luke 2:2), for which reasonable explanations can be given, Matthew and Luke's accounts demonstrate a consistent reliability.[95]

Historical details included in the birth narratives certainly give Matthew's and Luke's accounts significant credibility. Besides the accurate, historical information included in those Gospels, historians have examined the overall credibility of the two Gospels and found them dependably reliable. Other explanations, such as an illegitimate birth or dependency on pagan influence make little sense in light of the superb and proven historical accuracy of the Gospels. The only reason left to reject the birth narratives as history would be the predisposed prejudice towards miracles and supernatural events.

When discussing the actuality of the virginal conception, the objection often arises that it is an unnecessary doctrine. The argument states that Christians should focus on Jesus' death and resurrection,

---

94   Marcus J. Borg, *Meeting Jesus Again for the First Time* (San Francisco: Harper, 1994), 23-4. Bart D. Ehrman, *Jesus: Apocalyptic Prophet of the New Millennium* (New York: Oxford University Press, 1999), 36-9.

95   Walter Liefield, *Luke* in The Expositor's Bible Commentary Series, ed. Frank E. Gaebelein (Grand Rapids: Zondervan, 1984), 843. The issue concerns the timing of Quirinius' stint as governor of Syria and the census, which occurred in 6 A.D. Jesus was born before that time, between 6 and 4 B.C. Though some have argued that Luke was in error, the problem can be easily solved. A partial manuscript suggests the possibility of Quirinius serving as governor on two different occasions. Also, the preposition, *prote*, can be translated as "before" the census during Quirinius' administration.

which have important bearing on the foundation of their beliefs. Whether the virginal conception happened or not is unimportant to these critics. However, Christians do think of the cross and Christ's atonement when they consider the conception of Jesus. If Jesus were not miraculously conceived and, instead, had two biological parents, then He would have inherited man's sin nature (Ps. 51:5). Jesus would have then been born a sinner, and a sinner who died on a cross could not save the world from their sins, since the sacrifice requires the perfect obedience of an unstained Lamb (Heb. 4:15–16; cf. Lev. 3:1, 6, 7, 4:32, 9:3; John 1:29; Rev. 5:6–13). The virginal conception is not dispensable; it is indispensable.

Christians celebrate Christmas every year, primarily in December except for the eastern church. They have reason to celebrate it. The event inaugurates the coming of the Son of God to the Earth to rescue humanity from sin and eternal destruction. Believers celebrate the birth of Christ not simply as a cherished story, but as an actual historical event, and they have solid reasons to believe it.

Christology:
The Deity of Christ

Jesus of Nazareth was and is not only a first-century Jewish rabbi ministering in Galilee and Judea, but God the Son, Second Person of the Triune Godhead, Creator and Sustainer of the Universe. He is eternal, along with God the Father and God the Spirit, and equal in power, majesty, holiness, and all the divine attributes of the other Persons of the Trinity. In short, Jesus is fully God.

The first onslaught against Christ's divinity occurred with Ebionism, a sect that flourished in the second century. Ebionites proclaimed that Jesus was simply a human prophet and did not exist prior to His birth.[96] A fourth-century heresy developed by Arius of Alexandria (250 – 336), Arianism understood the Son of God to have possessed some divinity, but denied His full deity by rejecting His eternity, since it argued that God the Father created the Son of God.[97] A variety of Arianism continues with the Jehovah's Witness Watchtower

---

96   Justo L. Gonzalez, *A History of Christian Thought in One Volume*, rev. ed. (Nashville: Abingdon, 1987), 125.

97   Arius, *Confession of the Arians*, 332-4.

Society, whose members claim that the Son of God was the first among God's creation in angelic form.[98] During the late eighth century, Felix of Urgell (d. 818) advocated adoptionism, proposing that the human Jesus of Nazareth was, after birth, adopted by God the Father to be the Son of God. This means that Jesus was a son in the same sense as all believers are sons and daughters of God, and also that His human nature and divine nature were separate.[99] Modern doubt over the deity of Christ began with the rise of skepticism in the eighteenth century. Skepticism triggered the quests for the Historical Jesus. Beginning in the eighteenth century, the first such quest for the Historical Jesus determined that the Jesus of history and the Christ of faith were completely separate; the Christ of faith is on this view so embedded within the Gospels that people faced great difficulty extracting the historical Jesus from them. A "no quest" era was dominated with the notion that little could be found with regard to the Jesus of history. Rejecting this argument, the second quest in the middle of the twentieth century accepted many of the teachings of Jesus, but did not believe that Jesus believed Himself the Messiah.[100] Continuing in this tradition, members of the Jesus Seminar claim that the Jesus of history was only a human and never arose after His crucifixion, but later became the Messianic figure important for the community of faith within Christianity.[101] Moving the search for Jesus back to its historical roots, a third Quest has centered the study on Jesus' first-century Jewish background and has found much value in the Gospel accounts. However, many of the scholars in this quest still do not believe that Jesus understood Himself as Messiah.[102] Radicals such as G.A. Wells (1926 - 2017) question the very existence of Jesus.[103] Surveying the spectrum of unbiblical beliefs in relation to Christology, any heresy

---

98 George D. McKinney, *The Theology of the Jehovah's Witnesses* (Grand Rapids: Zondervan, 1962), 65-6.

99 Louis Berkhof, *The History of Christian Doctrines* (Carlisle: Banner of Truth Trust, 1937), 111–12.

100 Darrell L. Bock, *Studying the Historical Jesus,* (Grand Rapids: Baker Academic, 2002), 143–6.

101 John Dominic Crossan, *The Historical Jesus* (San Francisco: Harper, 1991), 421–2.

102 Bock, *Studying the Historical Jesus,* 147–8.

103 G.A. Wells, *Cutting Jesus Down to Size* (Chicago: Open Court, 2009), 6–21.

Christology

concerning the deity of Christ is a lessening of His fully divine nature. This illustration provides a synopsis of "progressive" thought:

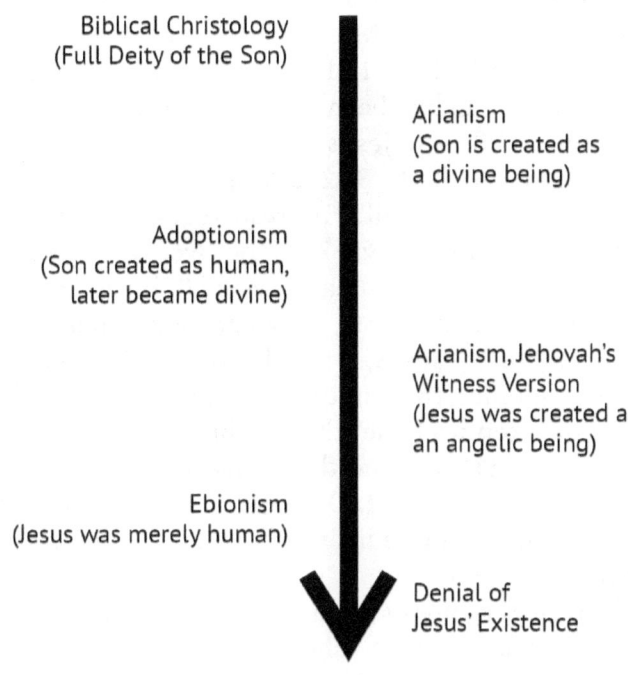

Biblical Christology
(Full Deity of the Son)

Arianism
(Son is created as
a divine being)

Adoptionism
(Son created as human,
later became divine)

Arianism, Jehovah's
Witness Version
(Jesus was created as
an angelic being)

Ebionism
(Jesus was merely human)

Denial of
Jesus' Existence

At the onset of Christianity, believers proclaimed the identity of Jesus of Nazareth as the Son of God. The fact of Christ's deity is evident through His life and ministry. Out of His own mouth, Jesus confirmed that He was the Son of God and Second Member of the Trinity. He declared that "before Abraham was, I AM," pointing to His eternality and identification with the divine name Yahweh (John 8:58). By His statement, Jesus has the authority to forgive sins, an attribute of God alone, which is why this claim was regarded as blasphemy (Mark 2:5-12). Regarding His return, the remarks Jesus made are also confessions that He is fully divine. Jesus told His disciples that He would return, coming in the clouds in power and majesty (Matt. 24:30; Mark 13:26). When asked by Caiaphas, then the High Priest, if He was the Son of the Blessed, Jesus responded in the affirmative and informed Caiaphas that he would see Him sitting at the right hand of God the Father and one day returning in the clouds (Mark 14:60–62).

Thinking Rationally About Christian Theology
A Handbook on Polemics

In addition to His own words, Jesus performed a large volume of miracles given His relatively short period of earthly service. He healed the blind (Matt. 9:27–31; 20:29–34; Mark 8:22–25; 10:46–52; Luke 18:35–43; John 9:1–7) and the lame (Matt. 21:14; Mark 2:1–12; John 5:2–9), fulfilling the prophecies of Isa. 29:18, 35:5, 42:7, 18, etc. Jesus cured several lepers (Matt. 8:1–3; Mark 1:40–42; Luke 5:12–13; 17:11–14). He resuscitated one girl and two men to life, one of whom had been deceased for four days (Mark 5:35–43; Luke 7:11–15; John 11:38–44). Jesus even displayed power over nature (Matt. 8:23–27; Mark 4:35–41; Luke 8:22–25). Beyond the miracles of Jesus' ministry stands the greatest of all, His resurrection, signifying to His disciples that He is Lord (Matt. 28:5–7; Mark 16:6; Luke 24:5–31, 36–43; John 20:11–18; 1 Cor. 15:3–8), as Thomas attested (John 20:26–28).

Aside from biblical statements, how can one defend the deity of Christ? The resurrection of Jesus, with the preponderance of support from eyewitness testimonies, the empty tomb (Luke 24:5–12; John 20:1–8), the conversions of the skeptics James the half-brother of Jesus (1 Cor. 15:7) and Paul of Tarsus (Acts 9:1–18), and the changing of the day of worship to the first day of the week (Rev. 1:10) all point to the likelihood of the event. More so, the resurrection indicates that Jesus is divine, for no mere human can rise from the dead.

By itself, the resurrection is strong support for the divinity of Christ. However, far more evidence exists. The fact that Jesus in precise detail fulfilled close to one hundred prophecies, including some beyond His human control, signifies that He, as deity, had the ability to orchestrate events and worked closely with God the Father, who orchestrated events far beyond human ability. Additionally, since Jesus' crucifixion, those who have identified themselves as His disciples have worshipped Him as God. Early hymns recorded in the New Testament acknowledge Jesus as divine (Phil. 2:5–7). Pliny the Younger's description of Christian worship services in the second century indicates that followers of Christ venerated Him as God.

Of all the persons who have lived on Earth, Jesus of Nazareth fascinates more people than any other individual. One reason alone can explain this fascination: His life is unique among the rest of humanity. What makes Jesus so unique? Simply put, Jesus is God. His power, His wisdom, and His character all indicate that Christ fully partakes of divine nature. Christians all over the world call upon His name, and unbelievers pray to Him for the first time to join the Church, the Body of Christ, not because Jesus was merely an exemplary human being, but because He arose and is God the Son.

Christology:
The Humanity of Christ

Jesus, the Son of God, is fully divine and has been for all eternity. When He came to earth through the incarnation, Jesus also became fully human, without losing any of His divinity. As an inhabitant of the world, Jesus possessed all of the qualities of a human being and all the experiences involved in human life.

While it would appear that the humanity of Jesus Christ has few detractors today, it would be wise to remember the Docetic and Apollinarian heresies of the second century. A main component of the Gnostic belief system, Docetism claims that the Son of God possessed full divinity but no human nature. Considering all flesh and everything material corrupt, the Gnostics stated that the Son of God was spirit alone and not flesh at all. Therefore, Christ came to earth as a transfigured man or possessed Jesus of Nazareth at His baptism.[104] Apollinarianism did not go as far as Gnosticism, but describes Jesus' human nature as incomplete. By incomplete, Apollinarius (or Apollinaris, c. 310 – c. 390) intended that the Son took a human form, but did not possess the fully human nature in that the Son did not have a human soul.[105] Unfortunately, such unbiblical beliefs related to the humanity of Christ were not alone. As described earlier, Monophysitism argues that Christ has one nature, thus detracting from His human nature.[106] Monothelitism believes that Christ has only one will, thus detracting from His human will.[107]

Addressing the attacks on the deity of Christ, pastors and church leaders have ignored the equal necessity of His humanity. Because of this and due to misleading media depictions, many Christians feel uncomfortable contemplating Jesus as fully human and doing the

---

104 Irenaeus, *Against Heresies* (Selections) 3, 11, in *Early Christian Fathers* ed. Cyril Richardson, Library of Christian Classics (Philadelphia: Westminster, 1953), 379.

105 Grillmeier, *Christ in Christian Tradition*, 331–2.

106 Hughes, *Church in Crisis*, 55–6.

107 Ibid., 101.

regular, mundane, and even uncomfortable things that humans must do. They would rather think of Jesus as not quite human, even odd and unapproachable; as some motion pictures about Christ portray.

What many Christians do not understand is that the humanity of Christ is just as essential for Christology as the deity of Christ. By identifying with His creation and taking on the fullness of humanity, the Son of God serves as an exemplar of the righteous life for every one of His followers. Without Christ's humanity, there would not have been an atonement. Only One who was fully human could take on the role of substitute for humanity in full payment of their sins. That One is Jesus.

Perhaps the easiest Christian doctrine to defend is the humanity of Jesus Christ. Scripture is replete with references of Jesus living a human life and doing very human things. The Gospels record Jesus walking (Matt. 4:18; Mark 11:27; John 1:36; 7:1), eating (Matt. 26:26; Mark 14:18, 22), drinking (Matt. 11:19; Luke 22:20), sleeping (Mark 4:38, Luke 8:23), weeping (Luke 19:41; John 11:35), coming into physical contact with other human beings (Matt. 26:50, 67; Mark 5:27; 15:19; Luke 8:44–46; 13:13; 22:41), and even spitting (Mark 7:33; John 9:6). More importantly, all four Gospels record Jesus' death. Each of the Gospel writer's descriptions indicate that Jesus suffered a very torturous and human demise by means of crucifixion. He was beaten (Matt. 26:67; 27:30; Mark 15:19), mocked (Mark 14:65; 15:19; Luke 22:63; John 19:2-3), scourged (Matt. 27:26; Mark 15:15; John 19:1), forced to carry the instrument of His execution (Matt. 27:32; John 19:17), stripped (Matt. 27:35; Mark 15:24; John 19:23), and nailed to a cross (Mark 15:24; Luke 23:33; John 19:18; 20:25). On the cross, Jesus was in extreme agony and declared that He was thirsty (John 19:28). Finally, He gave His last breath and died on the cross (Mark 15:37; Luke 23:46; John 19:30). Years after Jesus' ministry, His disciple John declared that he himself witnessed the ministry, death, and resurrection of Jesus, acknowledging that he saw, heard, and even touched Jesus (1 John 1:1-3). All of these are indicators of Jesus' complete human nature, about which the New Testament leaves no doubt at all.

Besides the Gospel accounts, ancient historians without seeming to have any interest in the Gospel, such as Josephus (c. 37 – c. 100)[108] and Tacitus (c. 56 – c. 120),[109] refer to Christ's life and the ministry of Jesus as

---

108 Josephus, *The Antiquities of the Jews*, 18. 3. iii. in *The Works of Josephus*, 2d ed. trans. William Whiston (Peabody: Hendrickson, 1987), 480.

109 Tacitus, *Annales*, 15, 44, trans. Alfred John Church and William

historical events that influenced the ancient Jewish and Roman worlds, respectively. None of the accounts by ancient historians go into the lengthy detail provided by the four Gospels, but they mention His ministry, His execution, and the devotion of His followers toward Christ. No historical record of such a life would have been mentioned had Jesus never lived and if Jesus had never been human, given the relatively commonplace occurrence of insurrectionists and criminals executed under the auspices of Roman law and the *pax Romana* (the order of Roman legal codes to keep the peace).

By all accounts, Jesus lived a fully human life. He was born; He grew to manhood; He worked, He ate, He slept, He hungered, He bled, and He died. Only by ignoring the evidence can one assert that Jesus lacked human nature. The Son of God really did walk among the people He created and died a very human death for their salvation.

Christology:
The Sinlessness of Christ

Throughout His life and ministry and throughout all eternity, Jesus never sinned, neither intentionally nor unintentionally, and neither by omission nor by commission. Christ never committed a sin of commission or actively performed an act of wrongdoing. Neither did He commit a sin of omission by failing to do what He should have done. The life of Jesus Christ signifies absolute ethical and moral perfection. For two thousand years, Christ's sinlessness has served as an example to His followers, who strive to emulate their Master as they are directed by the Holy Spirit living within them.

While Christians find inspiration in the sinlessness of Jesus, others find it a source of ridicule. Secular humanism, due to its dominance in Western culture, has especially impacted the perception of the doctrine negatively. The argument against this doctrine is rather straightforward. Throughout the history of humanity, no person has attained perfection. Even Jesus, who even many skeptics believe lived an extraordinary life, could not, such skeptics believe, have lived a life absent of flaws. Theological developments during the twentieth century, by deemphasizing Jesus' divinity and emphasizing Jesus' humanity, have relegated Jesus to functioning only as a

---

Jackson Brodribb (The Internet Classics Archive, 1994 – 2009) http://classics.mit.edu/Tacitus/annals.htm accessed February 1, 2023).

spiritually-conscious exemplar of morality.[110] According to recent statistics, many who consider themselves Christians believe in the possibility that Jesus sinned during His time on Earth.[111]

As with His humanity, Christ's sinlessness is essential for the atonement. A sinner cannot atone for another sinner or a world of sinners, but a sinless man can offer redemption through a sacrificial death. Some make the claim that the sinlessness of Christ is not biblical, but Scripture clearly testifies to Christ's moral perfection. Paul declared clearly that Jesus "knew no sin" (2 Cor. 5:21). Peter testified that Jesus never committed a sin, nor deceived He anyone (1 Pet. 2:22). Unbelievers also attested to Jesus' innocence. The Roman Procurator of Judea, Pontius Pilate, found Jesus not guilty of any crime (John 18:38). At Jesus' crucifixion, the Roman centurion confessed that Jesus was "innocent" (Luke 23:47). Added to these professions, a demon called Jesus "the Holy One of God" (Luke 4:34), language first used of Yahweh in the Old Testament. Jesus' sinlessness is certainly supported by multiple passages in the New Testament from multiple writers that make the doctrine a strongly asserted and biblical belief.

Defending Christ's sinlessness hinges upon Christ's deity. If one can make a strong case for the divinity of Jesus, then His sinlessness is a foregone conclusion. In addition to arguing from Christ's deity, from historical accounts of His life, one may assert that there is no record of any immoral act committed by Jesus. To say that all of the accounts of Jesus are biased and therefore glossed over any flaws Jesus may have had is a very weak argument. Of the historical accounts of religious founders, including Buddha and Muhammed, they present glowing reports of their lives but still reveal character flaws. Buddha left his wife and son to pursue enlightenment. Muhammed married a six-year-old girl and spread his new established religion through violent conquest. Not one instance of a flaw, crime, or act of indiscretion is mentioned concerning the life of Jesus of Nazareth. This lack of historical evidence for any flaw of Jesus cannot be labeled as positive and conclusive evidence for Christ's sinlessness, but it does beg the question why such evidence did not surface in any account of or reference

---

110 Berkhof, *The History of Christian Doctrines*, 123.

111 Ian M. Giatti, "Nearly 40% of Gen Z adults believe Jesus wasn't sinless: Survey" in Christian Post (May 18, 2022) https://www.christianpost.com/news/nearly-40-percent-generation-z-adults-believe-jesus-sinned-survey.html (accessed February 1, 2023).

to His life in an age when societal leadership sought to bring accusation against him or against his disciples (e.g., Matt. 27:64). For the curious, one can make a strong claim that the life of Jesus was extraordinarily unique and bears a closer examination. A closer study of the life of Christ leads the student to examine what type of person Jesus was and is and, therefore, such a study may take him or her, even those initially unbelievers, down the path to understanding Jesus to be God the Son.

Christology:
The Atonement

Before Jesus, to common people, crucifixion represented only a cruel method of execution utilized by the Romans. After the ministry, death, and resurrection of Jesus, the cross became the symbol of triumph, forgiveness of sin, hope, and the ultimate expression of love from God to His rebellious and fallen creation.

Historically, it would be extremely difficult to deny Jesus' atoning death by crucifixion as fact, but some have tried. The Gnostic *Apocalypse of Peter* claims that the spiritual Jesus, who was the actual Jesus, did not die on the cross, but left the human Jesus to suffer and die.[112] Praxeas (second century) stated that the Father suffered on the cross instead of Jesus.[113] Muslims reject the fact that Jesus died at all, believing that God would never allow His prophet to die in such a humiliating way. They offer two counter-narratives to circumvent the passion story of the Gospels. Some Muslim apologists hold that God deceived the Jewish religious leaders and the Romans, and they arrested and executed the wrong person, namely Judas Iscariot or the watchman assigned to guard over Jesus.[114] The Unitarian Faustus Socinus denied that justice required an atonement, so then Jesus' death did not function as a payment for human sin but merely served as the ultimate example for forgiveness.[115] The New Age movement does not deny Jesus' crucifixion outright, but dismisses it as a mere historical event, portraying Him no longer as a

---

112 N.T. Wright, *The Resurrection of the Son of God* (Minneapolis: Fortress, 2003), 544.

113 Tertullian, *Praxeas*, 1.

114 Shorrosh, *Islam Revealed*, 109–10.

115 Allison, *Historical Theology*, 402.

Savior but a guru who imparts mystical truth.[116] Due to the strong record of Jesus' execution from non-Christian chroniclers such as Josephus[117] and Tacitus,[118] a majority of contemporary historians readily accept that Jesus lived and that He endured execution at the hands of Roman soldiers by means of a wooden cross. However, overall, the debate does not center on the fact of Jesus' crucifixion, but on its significance.

Naturally, atheists, agnostics, and skeptics again reject the notion of any further significance to the cross. Jesus' disciples or subsequent generations of followers, they charge, promoted a myth about Jesus' resurrection and thereby added a spiritual significance of atonement. On closer examination, this argument falls apart. The Gospels record only negative reactions on the part of Jesus' disciples at His arrest and His crucifixion. They were dismayed at Jesus' death (Luke 24:17–21; John 20:11–13). They feared for their own lives (John 20:19). During the first reports of the empty tomb, the angels' declaration of Jesus' resurrection, and the appearances of Jesus, the disciples reacted with disbelief (Luke 24:11; John 20:24–25). The collective mood of the disciples was hardly the source for the beginning of a well-constructed resurrection myth. According to the Gospel accounts, prior to the resurrection, the disciples understood only one fact about Jesus' crucifixion: His death.

When the resurrection occurred, everything changed. Jesus, when He appeared to His overjoyed disciples, explained the reason behind His death (Luke 24:25–27, 44–49). At that point, the crucifixion of Jesus took on significance that the event could have had only if Jesus rose again on the third day. His execution now had a purpose, a profound, spiritual purpose.

Every Christian accepts some form of spiritual significance of the cross of Jesus, but even among believers, we debate its formal significance. Typically, however, the discussion as to the meaning of Jesus' death has focused on the purpose and outcome of the crucifixion. Over the centuries, several different models of the crucifixion have been put forth. (1) the "Christus Victor" approach portrays the crucifixion as Christ's victory over evil. (2) The Moral Influence theory establishes the death of Christ as having the purpose of bringing about a positive transformation in the

---

116 John P. Newport, *The New Age Movement and the Biblical Worldview* (Grand Rapids: Eerdmans, 1998), 201.

117 Josephus, *Antiquities of the Jews*, 18, 3, iii, 480.

118 Tacitus, *Annales*, 15, 44.

world. (3) The Satisfaction theory argues that the death of Christ was to satisfy God's justice. (4) The Ransom theory views Jesus' death as a payment to Satan for the souls of man. (5) The Penal Substitutionary model holds to Jesus' death being a sacrifice for the sins of the world as a propitiation of God's wrath.[119] (6) Hugo Grotius' (1583 - 1645) Governmental theory postulates that the crucifixion demonstrated God's displeasure for sin, but not for the actual remission of sins, rather to appease God's wrath at sin generally in all its influence.[120]

The single view which has endured the most attacks in the last century is the Penal Substitutionary model. Both the Emergent church movement and progressive Christians have been some of the most vocal against this model, calling it "cosmic child abuse," after Steve Chalke's (1955 -) now famous description in *The Lost Message of Jesus*. Viewing the atonement as child abuse, opponents of penal substitution observe that the doctrine depicts God the Father as the vengeful punisher of His Son who committed no crime.[121] Clearly, however, the New Testament indicates that Jesus was not forced to die by crucifixion, but gave His life willingly (John 15:13; 18:11; Phil. 2:8). Furthermore, Scripture identifies Jesus as the Son who is equal to the Father in His deity and not a helpless victim (Mark 14:62; John 1:1; 20:28; Phil. 2:6).

In contrast to the denials of the atoning nature of Jesus' death, the New Testament strongly affirms that Jesus died for the sins of the world. The writings of Matthew (Matt. 20:28), Paul (Rom. 3:21-26; 5:6-11; 2 Cor. 5:21), John (1 John 2:2), and Peter (1 Pet. 2:24) all declare that Jesus died by Roman crucifixion for the express purpose to atone for the sins of humanity. That is not to say that no other theme can be found in Jesus' crucifixion, such as His victory over death in 1 Corinthians 15. Yet the New Testament clearly states that sin is the reason for the Son of God's incarnation and atoning death (Rom. 5:12-21; 1 Cor. 15:3; Heb. 9:28; 1 Pet. 3:18). Therefore, this should be the main theme when considering Christ's crucifixion.

If Penal Substitution represents the strongest biblical interpretation, then the other models have deficiencies. Within the Christus Victor view,

---

119 Joel B. Green and Mark D. Baker, *Recovering the Scandal of the Cross* (Downers Grove: InterVarsity, 2000), 117–150.

120 Allison, *Historical Theology*, 403.

121 Steve Chalke and Alan Mann, *The Lost Message of Jesus* (Grand Rapids: Zondervan, 2003), 182–3.

Christ's death and resurrection signified a victory over evil and spiritual darkness, but the Omnipotent God did not need a death on the cross to defeat evil. Regarding the Ransom Theory, Anselm deftly observed that God owes nothing to anyone, especially not to Satan. The Christus Victor, Moral Influence, and Scapegoat theories diminish the significance of the evil of human sin and focus the attention of Christ's death on abstract ideals. Though the Satisfaction and Governmental theories note the significance of sin, they do not recognize the need for the removal of personal sin for the salvation of each man or woman.

Sin's presence is universal; sin is within every human being. Since the fall of mankind, sin has always been the fundamental problem of humanity, wreaking havoc upon every individual with every generation in every age. With every age, sin does not diminish, but increases. Modern wars have had a larger death toll than ancient ones due to increasingly sophisticated technology, which has also made life easier and sin more accessible, internet pornography being one tragic example. Despite the advances of the human race, no one besides God has devised a means to rid the world of sin. Sin is an enemy that requires an extraordinary act to defeat it. The atoning death of Christ is that extraordinary and very necessary act. Upon recognition of the magnitude of sin's evil and the impossibility of its defeat by human means, Jesus' atoning death on the cross stands as the only answer to the world's ultimate problem.

Christology:
The Resurrection of Jesus

After His execution by crucifixion, Jesus was buried in a tomb that had never before been used (Luke 23:53). On the first day of the week, Jesus arose with an eternal body, appearing before His disciples on several occasions and in different locations. Jesus died but now lives again, and that truth was ecstatically propagated by His disciples.

Much work has already been done on the resurrection by practitioners in the field of apologetics, particularly by William Lane Craig,[122] Gary

---

122 Craig, *Reasonable Faith*, 333-400. See also *The Son Rises: The Historical Evidence for the Resurrection of Jesus*, (Chicago: Moody, 1981).

Habermas,[123] and Michael Licona.[124] To attempt a full reiteration of this subject matter would be redundant and inadequately brief. Unfortunately, Christians are often tempted to defend the resurrection solely against atheists and agnostics, who are its most vocal deniers. What many fail to understand is that the resurrection is not only denied, but reinterpreted under the banners of modern biblical interpretation and post-modern reductionism. A host of different perspectives will acknowledge that the resurrection did occur, but will not accept the literal, biblical interpretation of a bodily resurrection of Jesus. According to belief in Gnostic Docetism, Jesus appeared to His disciples after the crucifixion, but only as a spirit and not in a physical form.[125] Reinterpretation of Jesus' resurrection increased dramatically in the nineteenth century. The subjective-vision theory, popularized by David Fredrich Strauss (1808 – 1874), argues that the faith of the disciples inspired delusionary visions of Jesus after His crucifixion.[126] Twentieth century theology witnessed a move to a metaphorical interpretation of Jesus' resurrection. Rudolf Bultmann (1884 – 1976) understood the resurrection to be symbolic in that it was found in the kerygma (or the preaching of the Gospel) by Jesus' disciples. The resurrection, then, occurred solely through faith in Christ and belief in the preaching about Jesus rather than as an historical event.[127] Willi Marxsen (1919 – 1993) concluded that certainty as to what happened on the First Easter was unattainable, so the resurrection was found in the faith of Peter and the other disciples.[128] Later scholars, including Géza Vermes (1924 – 2013), Michael Goulder (1927 – 2010), Gerd Lüdemann (1946 – 2021), and John Dominic Crossan (1934 –) followed in the tradition of Straus in that

---

123 Gary R. Habermas, *The Risen Jesus and Future Hope* (Lanham: Bowman and Littlefield, 2003).

124 Michael R. Licona, *The Resurrection of Jesus: A New Historiographical Approach* (Downers Grove: InterVarsity, 2010).

125 Ross Clifford and Philip Johnson, *The Cross is Not Enough: Living as Witnesses to the Resurrection* (Grand Rapids: Baker, 2012), 213.

126 Habermas, *The Risen Jesus*, 13–14.

127 Stanley J. Grenz and Roger E. Olson, *20th Century Theology* (Downers Grove: InterVarsity, 1992), 95.

128 Willi Marxsen, *The Resurrection of Jesus of Nazareth*, trans. Margaret Kohl (London: SCM Press, 1970, orig. published as *Die Auferstehung Jesu von Nazareth* [Mohn: Gütersloher, 1968]), 126–7.

they reason that Jesus' disciples had a spiritual or psychological experience that they interpreted as the resurrection of Jesus, but these scholars do not believe in a literal, bodily resurrection.[129] The New Age movement also spiritualizes the resurrection to the point that it is no longer a historical event and describes it as a mythologized occurrence that signifies Jesus' role as a mystical teacher.[130] Progressive Christians downplay historical evidence to view the resurrection as a metaphor for spiritual truth.[131] Tragically, the pastors of many Evangelical churches rarely give expository sermons about resurrection, focusing only on the crucifixion of Christ. Worse still, many churches take little thought to Christianity as a historically grounded system of beliefs, but rather consider it to be a means of being spiritually well-rounded, to produce better people in an ethical sense. The resurrection in many modern churches has become unimportant to their worship or irrelevant to the point that one may question the worship's purpose.

If creation is the foundation of the biblical worldview, then the resurrection is the keystone of Christianity. Each of the four Gospels recorded the resurrection (Matt. 28:1–20; Mark 16:1–8, Luke 24:1–53; John 20:1–21, 24). As Paul pointed out to the church at Corinth, if Christ has not been raised, then he and his fellow believers were still spiritually dead (1 Cor. 15:12–14). Paul certainly did not write this from a merely intellectual viewpoint. The resurrection featured prominently in his preaching, along with the apostles and early Christians (Acts 2:24–36; 3:15; 10:40–41; 13:30–38; 17:31; 26:23). John wrote confidently to the Church that he witnessed Christ's post-resurrection appearances (1 John 1:1–4). Throughout the New Testament, passages consistently affirm that Jesus has risen.

Theologically, the resurrection has been largely ignored in contrast to the benefit of the atonement, particularly from the pulpit. Fortunately, the rise of making an evidential argument for Christ's resurrection in the last half of the twentieth century and into the twenty-first has influenced some evangelical pastors to return to proclaiming the resurrection to their congregations. It is important for all believers to realize how essential the communication of the resurrection is in sharing the Gospel (Rom. 10:9–10). Without the resurrection, the entirety of Jesus' teaching is suspect, since He predicted His death and resurrection on several occasions (Matt.

---

129 Licona, *The Resurrection of Jesus*, 469–532.

130 Newport, *New Age Movement*, 201.

131 McLaren, *A New Kind of Christianity*, 139.

16:21; 17:22–23; 26:31–32; Mark 14:27–28 Luke 9:22; 13:32; 18:33). Without the resurrection, there is no hope of eternal life, because it is the leading evidence of life after death. Therefore, the resurrection should be at the forefront of the content of preaching in the pulpit of every church and in the sharing of the faith with every unbeliever.

No biblical Christian can deny that historical evidence is the best argument for the resurrection of Jesus. As stated previously, the list of the evidences, from the empty tomb, to the eyewitness testimonies, and to the conversion of skeptics of the resurrection, strongly indicates that Jesus is alive. This should be the foundation for any apologetic for the resurrection. However, those who claim to accept the resurrection but reject it as a historical event need a different line of reasoning. Some, such as Marxsen, have proposed that the Church may not have focused on the particular mode of resurrection, whether actual or figurative.[132] This assertion of the lack of focus on a particular mode is negated by the fact of the early Gospel proclamation that Jesus was physically risen (Acts 2:22-32; 10:39-41; 13:29-37). If early Christians did not preach a literal resurrection, it begs the question as to why there has been so widespread an acceptance of a Gospel that depends on a literal resurrection across the world and a multitude of cultures. A figurative resurrection would not bring hope to so many people.

The finality of death is sobering and frightening to most people, who look for hope that some sort of life exists after death. This hope figures into most of the various belief systems in the world. Thus, widespread hope for life after death exists, and hope becomes more certain, when there is tangible proof. Jesus' resurrection, with a host of historical evidences, offers tangible verification of life after death. This historical evidence leads one to consider a literal acceptance of the bodily resurrection of Jesus as the proper understanding of the event, in contrast to more figurative and subjective conceptions. Just as creation's intricate design witnesses to a Divine Creator, the resurrection of Jesus ("the firstborn of the dead" Col. 1:18; Rev. 1:5 ESV) provides evidence for the possibility and the actuality ("for Christ has entered... into heaven itself"; Heb. 9:24-8 ESV) of life after death.

Every year, thousands of visitors come to the Church of the Holy Sepulcher, likely the site of the empty tomb of Jesus. These visitors come

---

132 Marxsen, *Resurrection*, 78.

not to witness the place where Jesus became enlightened or to see the location of the metaphorical resurrection. They come to see the place where Jesus was buried and the tomb from where He arose. The resurrection is a fact; Christ having arisen for us and ascended into heaven is a fact that changed the world. The Church should have confidence in that fact and proclaim it.

Chapter 5

Pneumatology

Historical Background:

During the second century, the Church, already dealing with other dangerous heretical movements, had to confront another false teacher by the name of Montanus (active 157–172). Claiming to receive direct revelation from the Holy Spirit, along with his two female disciples, Maximilla and Prisca, Montanus called for the Church to reform. By his observation, Montanus believed that the Church had fallen into legalism. This reform needed to occur immediately, for Montanus asserted that the Holy Spirit informed him that Christ was returning soon. Therefore, Montanus commanded all Christians to abstain from marriage and married Christians to dissolve their marriages. Even when Christ failed to return at the time Montanus predicted, the movement was tremendously popular. Tertullian himself joined the ranks of the Montanists.[133] What eventually ended Montanism was the Church's official closing of the biblical cannon, effectively affirming that any new revelations were not of divine origin.

Though Montanus is a somewhat obscure figure in Christian history, his movement signified an important turning point for Christianity. From that point on, Christians would identify their beliefs with the complete revelation that is the Bible. Montanus also brought special attention to the Holy Spirit. The fact that his teachings were so popular demonstrates that many Christians of the

133 Eric Osborn, *Tertullian: First Theology of the West* (Cambridge: Cambridge University Press, 1997), 209–13.

> *second century longed for "new" and "fresh" revelations. This was the beginning of a long history of the misinterpretation of the nature and role of the Holy Spirit. Unfortunately, perpetrators of such errors were not solely confined to heretical movements; Christians who largely have a biblical theology have often been confused over the doctrine of Pneumatology or the study of the Holy Spirit and the beliefs pertaining to Him. The doctrine of God the Spirit is often ignored or distorted. To have a sound, biblical theology, the Christian must stand on the themes of Scripture, which affirm the necessity of the Holy Spirit as God over all Creation and the Comforter who bears witness of Christ to the Church and to the world. To defend the belief in the Holy Spirit, the believer must be aware of the Spirit's role in the Trinity and in the life of the Church, and speak and practice the theology of the Holy Spirit both within the walls of the Church and outside it in the life of the mind and in the tasks of daily living.*

Pneumatology:
The Holy Spirit

God is Triune, having Three Persons: Father, Son, and Holy Spirit. The Holy Spirit is equally God in substance, nature, power, and personality along with the Father and the Son. Having all the divine attributes and acting in the roles of inspiring the writing of the Word of God, the Spirit empowers believers to accomplish divinely assigned tasks and indwells them and gives them their unique gifts.

Given the Spirit's necessary role in the birth (Acts 2:1-4) and continued ministry of the Church, one might assume that, being the Third Person of the Trinity, the Holy Spirit would have prominence in Christian theology throughout the history of the Church and in all corners of the church today. However, the doctrine of the Holy Spirit has been attacked often, not out of intentional distortion but due to ignorance and misunderstanding. Marcionism had issues not only with the recognized Canon of Scripture, omitting large portions of the Bible, but the movement's doctrines also failed to make any mention of the Holy Spirit. Montanism, conversely, focused all of its attention on the Holy Spirit. Montanus and his second-century disciples asserted that the Spirit was speaking new revelations through them—new, that is, in the sense of adding to Scripture, particularly about the coming of Christ and the responsibilities of the Church. The Holy Spirit, according to Montanists, continued to reveal new truths in addition to God's Written Word.[134] In other controverted moves, Mary Baker Eddy (1821 - 1910), the founder of the Church of Christ, Scientist, replaced the Holy Spirit with divine Science, which she also designated as the "Holy Comforter." Herbert W. Armstrong (1892 - 1986), founder of the Worldwide Church of God, argued that the Holy Spirit is a holy attitude shared by God the Father and God the Son. The Jehovah's Witnesses interpret the Holy Spirit to be God's active force to compel His servants to accomplish His will. The Way International ministry negated the separate personhood of the Holy Spirit was by describing the name as a title for God the Father, a "holy spirit" within believers as a gift given to believers upon their spiritual rebirth.[135]

Unfortunately, misconceptions concerning the Holy Spirit are widespread today and do not abate. One of the common popular misconceptions with regard to the Holy Spirit relates to how Christians refer to and think of Him. Many, typically in Protestant Evangelicalism, consider God the Spirit to be more of an impersonal force than an actual Person. When describing the Holy Spirit, believers often refer to Him as "It." Along the same line of thinking, the Holy Spirit is often practically considered to be a tool that Christians can use to increase their prosperity, enhance their spiritual abilities, or to grow churches. Yet, in Scripture, the Holy Spirit is referred to by male pronouns of "He" and "Him," as Jesus described the Spirit to His disciples (John 14:15–17, 26; 15:26), rather than by neuter pronouns such as "It." The Bible portrays the Holy Spirit as a Person who is grieved by sin and rebellion (Isa. 63:10; Eph. 4:30) and directs the actions of individuals (Matt. 4:1; Mark 1:12; Luke 4:1; Acts 16:6; 18:5). Furthermore, the Holy Spirit communicates with and through individuals (2 Sam 23:2; Ezek. 2:2; 3:24; Acts 1:16; 4:31; 6:10; 13:2; 21:4; 28:25). Thus, He is not an impersonal force to be used for any end whatsoever, but a Member of the Triune Godhead who desires to use His people for the glory of Christ.

---

134 Daniel Castelo, *Pneumatology: A Guide for the Perplexed* (London: Bloomsbury T and T Clark, 2015), 47.

135 Garrett, *Systematic Theology*, Vol. 2, 142-3.

Another popular error promoted within Evangelicalism (as separate from Pentecostalism) views the Holy Spirit as having only a minor role. According to this view, the Holy Spirit merely convicts Christians and possibly unbelievers of sin and heightens the corporate worship experience by making believers aware or more aware of His presence or of Christ's presence. Contrary to such limitation, the Holy Spirit has been involved in the major acts of God in history, including creation (Gen. 1:2; Job 26:13), the ministry of God's Hebrew prophets (1 Sam. 10:10; Neh. 9:30; Zech. 7:12; Eph. 3;5), the virginal conception of Christ (Matt. 1:20; Luke 1:34–35), the ministry of Jesus (Matt. 3:16; 4:1; Luke 4:1, 14), and the birth of the Church (Acts 2:1–41). The Holy Spirit inspired the writing of Scripture (Acts 1:16; 28:25; 2 Pet. 1:19–21), in which He empowered believers to perform extraordinary feats and fulfill leadership roles (Exod. 31:3; 35:31; Judg. 3:9–10; 6:34; 11:29; 14:6, 19; 15:14; 1 Sam. 11:6; 16:13). The Holy Spirit displays the spiritual fruit that emulates Christ's character (Gal. 5:22–23). Also, He guides His people to the truth (John 15:26; 16:13; 1 Cor. 2:10; 1 Pet. 1:22; 1 John 5:6). At times, the Holy Spirit displayed His miraculous power, such as transporting God's servant Ezekiel to Jerusalem (Ezek. 8:3) and to a valley filled with dry bones (Ezek. 37:1). Far from being limited, the Holy Spirit by Scripture's testimony has proven Himself fully God, fulfilling roles necessary to creation, human history, and to the existence and health of the Church.

Arguing for the existence and work of the Holy Spirit is largely the work of the polemicist rather than the apologist, because it is mostly those within the Church that distort the doctrine. Therefore, when defending the doctrine of the Holy Spirit, the appeal to the testimony of Scripture should be foremost. Scripture itself is the product of the Spirit. No text has inspired and changed lives more than the Bible. As discussed earlier, a safe assumption as to its divine inspiration can be made according to the lives the Bible has changed and its historical power and use. According to Scripture's self-attestation, of the Three Persons of the Trinity, it was the Spirit who had the role of inspiring God's Written Word (2 Pet. 1:19–21). The fact that the world has the Bible indicates that the Spirit exists. Not only does He exist, He is a Person, since only a person possesses the intelligent agency needed to inspire the writing of the Scripture.

Another product of the Holy Spirit is the Church. Beginning in Jerusalem, Jesus' disciples spread the Gospel throughout the city and extended its witness into the regions of Judea, Samaria, the eastern half of

Pneumatology

the Roman Empire, and then to the entire empire, and over the centuries, all over the world. Many explanations for this phenomenon have been offered, but the most plausible one is that God is behind this movement. God the Spirit, who birthed the Church, transforms the Church, sustains the Church, and empowers the Church; the Spirit is the only reason to explain the Church. An impersonal force or the spirit of Science cannot explain the history of the Church, only the Third Person of the Trinity, as the Bible, particularly Jesus in the Gospel of John, describes Him. Only the Spirit suffices for the changes that occur in individual believers and in the gifts given to the Body of Christ as a whole; only the Spirit can explain how simple-minded men such as Billy Sunday and Dwight L. Moody can become gifted preachers of the Gospel and affect changes in the lives of thousands of men and women.

Essential to Christian theology, the doctrine of the Holy Spirit completes the doctrine of the Trinity. Without studying what the Scripture says about God the Spirit, the believer is left in ignorance of the work of God in history, the origins of the Church, and the life that God desires His people to live. Ignorance of this doctrine often leads to unbiblical beliefs and a spiritually deficient life.

Pneumatology: The Indwelling by the Holy Spirit

The expression, "Ask Jesus into your heart," has become popular language to express what happens at conversion to evangelical Christians; in some sense, it signifies their conversion. The phrase is heartfelt, endearing, and completely unbiblical. Jesus does not indwell the believer when the believer converts; the Holy Spirit does. Upon conversion, God the Spirit enters the believer, and the believer enters into a close and intimate relationship with God. With the Spirit indwelling in the convert, He empowers believers to live obediently and serve in the Kingdom of God and brings them under conviction when they sin.

The strongest biblical evidence for the Holy Spirit's indwelling is found in Paul's writings. Repeatedly, the apostle stresses that God the Spirit exists within the follower of Christ (Rom. 8:9–11; 1 Cor. 3:16; 2 Tim. 1:14). Paul also describes believers (plural) as the "temple of God" (1 Cor. 3:16–19; 2 Cor. 6:16), which implies that Christians have been made holy by the God who lives within them. While Paul's letters provided the strongest affirmation, John 14:17 records Jesus as informing His disciples that the Holy Spirit will come and dwell within them. James 4:5 also affirms this truth. In Acts, Luke records numerous times when believers received the Holy Spirit (Acts 8:14–17; 9:17; 10:44–45; 19:2–6) or were filled with the Spirit (Acts 2:4; 4:8, 31; 6:3, 5; 7:55; 11:24; 13:9), signifying an indwelling by Him. Scripture consistently describes followers of Christ as living temples of God who have the Holy Spirit within them, particularly in the New Jerusalem when God again dwells with His people (Rev. 21:3, 22).

Evidence for God the Spirit's indwelling of His people exists within every converted individual. As noted earlier, the transformation of the converted testifies to the existence and work of the Holy Spirit within people. Further proof can be found in the spiritual gifts that the Holy Spirit endows upon each believer. The Spirit grants each believer at least one spiritual gift (1 Cor. 12:1–11; Eph. 4:11–16). Upon their conversion and their entry into the Church, Christians begin to participate in ministry in the context of their gifting in the local church and to their capacity to evangelize the community. While ministering and serving, new believers exhibit abilities that benefit the Church and glorify God. Gifts that were not evident prior to conversion, but manifest after submission to Christ, should cause one to pause before dismissing the notion of the indwelling by the Holy Spirit. Thus, the indwelling of the Holy Spirit is evident in the transformed lives of God's people.

Beyond the evidence of changed lives, verification of the indwelling of the Holy Spirit is found in the connection that believers have with God. Throughout the centuries, Christians have sensed a close connection with God, a togetherness or communion not merely related to the means of grace at table in the Lord's Supper. They have been led to act out compassion, speak words of comfort, share the Gospel, make amends for their wrongdoing, and worship in adulation because they have the inward conviction that God is guiding them. This testimony transcends culture and age in which those from various eras of history and cultures of the world acknowledge the same truth: they have a relationship with God. The indwelling of the believer by the Holy Spirit explains the testimony of an intimate relationship between God and His disciples. A distant God does not have a close relationship with human beings, and without the indwelling of the Holy Spirit, God and the believer might remain distant from each other. The indwelling brings an intimate connection between God and His spiritual child.

Pneumatology

The debate over the indwelling of the Spirit largely ensues between believers, specifically around the topics of holiness and the degree to which ordinary men and women can relate to the Holy Spirit. In this debate, there are two major Protestant traditions. Evangelicals largely see the Spirit's indwelling, which occurs upon conversion. Pentecostals differentiate between a person's initial baptism upon conversion (which some say is also a product of the Spirit) and a "second baptism" that happens when a believer allows the Holy Spirit to fill him or her in a "full" or entire way that did not occur upon mere conversion. Proponents for this second baptism, this filling by the Holy Spirit, point to occasions in Acts where certain converted individuals are believed to have received a subsequent filling (Acts 8:14–17; 19:1–6).[136] These passages are admittedly difficult to understand, but interpreting Acts in a completely prescriptive way for all Christians to operate under the same expectations and circumstances as the Church of the first century is impossible and places evangelical Christians and their Pentecostal fellow believers at an impasse if the former do not believe that the Spirit's inauguration in their life comes at a time later than their initial conversion. The Apostolic Age witnessed the writing of the New Testament, the birth of the Church, and the inauguration of the Great Commission. With the New Testament in the stage in which it was written, the Church possessed only the Old Testament, the teachings of the apostles in letters that were beginning to be circulated, and the Gospel message spoken by the initial leaders of churches and their acquaintances such as Apollos and Timothy, who in some ways inherited the message of the original disciples and Apostles. The powerful manifestations of the Holy Spirit recorded in Acts validated the Gospel. Upon the completion of the New Testament Canon, the Spirit was understood primarily to have spoken His truth through the Old and New Testament. The manifestations of the Spirit in filling believers are often primarily to be considered signs of the Apostolic Age, which has since come to a close with the death of John the Apostle at the end of the first century. This view is known as "cessationism," but the degree to which the Holy Spirit speaks to Christ's people cannot be entirely limited since, as noted above, we believe that the Spirit still indwells converts and sanctifies God's people in an on-going process of their developing a spiritual sense of God's power within them to allow them the fruit of the

---

136 Castelo, *Pneumatology*, 103-110.

Spirit (Gal. 5:22) and to abound in hope (e.g., Rom. 15:13) as Christ promised (John 10:10). Also, God cannot be limited, since He is all-powerful and all-knowing, and communicates certain attributes, such as divine love, to us at least partly by the Holy Spirit being a temple within us.

Often misconstrued and misunderstood, the doctrine of the indwelling and Holy Spirit sanctifying Christians and setting them apart for communion with Him is a wonderful truth of God's connection with the believer. The evidence of transformation, spiritual direction, and bestowing of gifts upon followers of Christ finds explanation with the Third Person of the Trinity inhabiting God's people.

Chapter 6

Anthropology

Historical Background:

In 1818, a novel was published that forever impacted horror fiction. Its title was Frankenstein; or, the Modern Prometheus; *written by Mary Shelley (1797-1853). Shelley's novel tells the story of a brilliant scientist, Victor Frankenstein, who discovers how to bring life to non-living tissue. He unearths remains of corpses from a nearby cemetery to construct a body, and after spending long hours obsessing over his experiment, brings this being to life. At the moment that the creature comes to life, Frankenstein is repulsed by its hideous features and flees.[137] Rejected by his creator, the creature also leaves Frankenstein's laboratory and soon discovers that the world hates him because of his deformed appearance. Thus begins his lifelong pursuit of revenge to destroy all that Frankenstein holds dear.[138] The creature leaves a path of death in his wake with the murder of Frankenstein's brother, friend, and his wife. Frankenstein now pursues his own design for revenge, determined to destroy his creation.[139] He follows the creature to the North Pole. By this time, his health is all but ruined. Rescued by a scientific exploration ship, Frankenstein ultimately dies, even though he is under the care of the captain of the ship.[140] Ironi-*

137 Mary Wollstonecraft Shelly and Percy Bysshe Shelley, *Frankenstein or the Modern Prometheus*, 2d ed. ed. Charles E. Robinson (New York: Vintage, 2008), 75–82.

138 Ibid., 160-168.

139 Ibid., 218-223.

140 Ibid., 228-240.

cally, Frankenstein's monster witnesses his creator's death, and full of guilt and remorse, vows to kill and dispose of himself so that the world would never know of his existence.[141]

Shelley's tale brings to mind questions about human beings and their existence. Frankenstein created life in a laboratory without any thought of instilling his creation with a soul or the process to do so. Frankenstein's creature began as an innocent being who eventually became corrupted, which contradicts Scripture's doctrine of original sin. The novel's representation of mankind presents a different picture than what the Bible describes as beings who are created in God's image. In her now-famous novel, Shelley propagated the popular understanding of humanity in her day and one that continues to be popular in secular cultures. Scripture presents a far different conception of humanity. A sound theology includes a proper understanding of the origins, identity, and purpose of man. Anthropology, in the field of theology, is the study of man and his relation to God.

Anthropology:
Humanity Created in the Image of God

Human beings, created on the sixth day of creation, are different from the rest of the created beings. Man, as Genesis 1:26–27 declares, was and is created in the image of God, known to many scholars and others by the Latin term *imago Dei*. This does not mean that God has the same physical appearance as human beings do, but that God endowed man with the ability to communicate with Him and serve Him; also, humans have the privilege to be stewards over the Earth.

The question, "What is man?" has been the subject of much discussion in religion and philosophy. In Greek thought, particularly in the writings of Plato (428 - 348 BC), humans were considered primarily spirit and their physical bodies foreign to their true nature, sometimes called the "form" of being human. Such a belief as Plato's is classified as idealistic anthropology, since Plato called such forms "ideas." Idealistic anthropology accepts the soul's immortality, but

---

141 Shelly and Shelley, *Frankenstein*, 241-245.

denies any possibility or sort of physical resurrection. Due to the dominance of modern humanism, the Renaissance idea of bodiless immortality began to be accepted beginning with the Enlightenment. With the later introduction of modern evolutionary theory as a motif influential in the social sciences, materialistic anthropology became popular. According to materialism, human existence is material only; all aspects, including mental, emotional, and even spiritual are the effects (or "epiphenomena") of the physical body. Marxism embraced this view, understanding humans to be the products of nature by what may be called "blind chance." Marxist thinkers also hold that man is not responsible to God because he was not created by God, but he was born into a society, the famous Marxian proletariat. Humans, then, are part of a social structure and, due to its materiality, the social structure has more importance than the individual. Later, behavioristic materialistic anthropology, influenced by B.F. Skinner, conceived of humans as products of their material environment. Therefore, they do not have value as individual beings but only as parts of a larger environment. Such materialistic anthropologies present humans in a very different way from the biblical doctrine that man is specially created by God and unique from the rest of creation. Similar to animals, man is a body, and nothing else matters or is a reality pertinent to human "decisions" that are (in actuality) determined anyway by material causal conditions and their conditioning of our "minds" (i.e. brains).[142]

Aside from Genesis 1:26-27, additional verses in the Bible identify mankind as being created in God's image. In the beginning of the first recorded genealogy of the Old Testament, Genesis reiterates that God created humans in His likeness (Gen. 5:1). After the Flood, the taking of human life was declared by God to be evil, because it was the ending of a life created in the image of God (Gen. 9:6). One of the most famous of David's Psalms exults in the fact that God created man and placed him in the honorable position of being slightly lesser than the angels and above all the animals that live on the earth and all the fish in the sea (Ps. 8:3-8). The New Testament reiterates the Old Testament themes of mankind being created in God's image. Paul declared this in his letter to Christians at Corinth when discussing the roles of men and women in the context

---

142 Anthony A. Hoekema, *Created in God's Image* (Grand Rapids: Eerdmans, 1986), 1-3.

of corporate worship (1 Cor. 11:7). James insisted that cursing any person should be classified as sin, since human beings were created in the likeness of God (Jas. 3:8–10). These passages have the common thread of describing humans as beings designed to be separate from the rest of creation on earth for the special purpose of serving the Lord.

The argument that man is an animal like all of the beasts of the earth fails to provide convincing or substantial proof of its claim. No other creature on the planet has established civilizations, written books on every field of science and every type of literature, invented technologies, and journeyed into outer space. Humans are decidedly different from animals in many ways far beyond appearance.

Superior intelligence alone cannot explain this difference. Mankind has not only advanced, but we have a history, a history of progression in all sorts of cultural areas. The chronicles of thousands of years of the rise and fall of nations point to a journey humans undertake to attempt to understand ourselves and the meaning of life. Each culture has its myths, folklore, theology, and philosophy that are either efforts (myths, folklore) to explain nature or profound investigations (theology, philosophy) into knowledge, truth, and ethical conduct. That search for meaning involves knowledge of the origin of life and the existence of the One who created life. Intelligence alone cannot account for mankind's search for meaning, but the fact that humans have been created to have a relationship with God does account for it. Throughout humanity's entire history, mankind has been an overwhelmingly religious species. No other creature on Earth performs religious rituals or participates in any semblance of worship of a deity. Only human beings involve themselves in such activities.

Like the evolutionary conception of humanity, the pantheistic model fails in its attempt to furnish a proper understanding of the nature of mankind and God. If humans are a part of God, or if God is an impersonal force present in everything in the universe, then it is difficult to distinguish between God and man. Instead of elevating man to godlike status, pantheism lowers God from being transcendent to being tied to the physical. Therefore, according to pantheism, God is, in some sense, material. However, if God is material, then He is limited and cannot be God, who is unlimited. Scripture, on the other hand, describes humans, not as being connected to God by identity or nature, but as connected by relationship (John 1:11–13; Heb. 11:6; Jas. 4:8; Rev. 3:20). A parallel can be found in the relationship between parent and child. The parent and the child are not the same, but they have an attachment in that they have a relationship. Likewise, humans can be connected with God through fellowship, but are not to be considered God or a part of Him.

Of all the creatures on the earth, humans are distinct. They possess intelligence, display moral obligations, develop preferences and distastes, fall in love, and spend time in worship. These characteristics and actions no other physical being on Earth has or does, simply because God created them with intent to commune with and serve Him as nothing else can. By God's grace, man is created in His image, and humans are designed to be in communion with Him and with each other.

Anthropology:
The Existence of the Soul

God created human beings with a soul. The soul is, in essence, the actual self of the person, which includes emotions, inclinations, passions, and thoughts. Most importantly, the soul makes humans spiritual beings. Through the soul, God communicates with human beings. Because of the soul, human beings exist after death.

In recent years, the strongest opponents to the existence of the soul have been physicalists, who accept a materialistic understanding of existence, with only matter and energy existing. In this view, humans consist of matter alone and do not have a nonphysical soul.[143] Within Christianity, two major points of view exist concerning the soul. Mind-body dualism acknowledges the traditional understanding that human beings have both body and soul. Some biblical Christians accept substance dualism in which the soul is distinct from the body and directs the body instead of being a property of it, as held by property dualism.[144] Some Christians embrace a form of physicalism (called Christian physicalism) that regards certain Scripture passages as compatible with physicalism; thus, such Christians reject the concept of an immaterial soul.[145]

---

143 Alex Rosenberg, *The Atheist's Guide to Reality* (New York: W.W. Norton and Company, 2011), 147.

144 J.P. Moreland, *Scaling the Secular City* (Grand Rapids: Baker, 1987), 78–80.

145 Ralph Stefan Weir, "Christian Physicalism and the Biblical Argu-

Thinking Rationally About Christian Theology
A Handbook on Polemics

From a biblical standpoint, a strong case can be made that both body and soul exist as two dualistic components. Moses, when instructing the Israelites before they entered the land of Canaan, told them that their purpose was to love and obey the Lord with all their heart, soul, and might (Deut. 6:5 ESV; cf. 6:5; 11:13, 18; 13:3; 26;16; 30:6, 10). By distinguishing between the heart and the soul, Moses signified that the soul did not merely represent human emotion, but the spiritual nature of man. Additional Bible verses use the same wording, and this implies a consistent theme (Josh. 22:5; 23:14; 1 Kgs. 2:4; 8:48; 2 Kgs. 23:3, 25; 1 Chron. 22:19; 2 Chron. 6:38; 15:12, 15; 34:31; Jer. 32:41; Acts 4:32). Jesus warned that one should not fear those who could destroy the body, but the One who could destroy the soul by sending it to hell (Matt. 10:28); by this comment, Jesus indicated that the soul exists after death and that a person is to be prepared for that eventuality. Jesus also partly echoes Deuteronomy, stating that the chief end of human beings is to love the Lord with all their hearts, minds, and souls (Matt. 22:37; Mark 12:30; Luke 10:27). The Apostle Paul wanted God to sanctify the Thessalonian Christians, bringing about the purification of their souls (1 Thess. 5:23); such a sanctification finds part of its meaning in the soul's connection with God and so demonstrates that there is a soul and that it can be intimately connected with God. Peter explained that, through faith, God brings about the salvation of souls (1 Pet. 1:8–9), revealing that the soul is the most important part of the person and in need of the salvation that God works. The Bible thus leaves no confusion with respect to the existence of the soul.

Tradition of the existence of the soul extends to the ancient past. Throughout most of mankind's history, humans have believed that they are more than mere walking bodies of flesh and bone. Humanity's disposition to religion is part of the reason for this, but it is not the only reason. Epistemologically, the acquisition of knowledge is impossible without a soul. Scientists can account for much of the knowledge that people accumulate through exposure to the outside world, but certain items, such as the abstract proofs of mathematics and unseen or conceptual physics components are known outside of experience. The profound sense of discernment between right and wrong seems to be an intrinsic part of being human, although not a spatial (or extended) part of

ment for Dualism" in *International Journal for Philosophy of Religion* 91(2022):115–22 https://doi.org/10.1007/s11153-021-09811-0 (accessed January 10, 2023).

the person. If all that exists is the material body, what part of the human body contains morals or has ideas of a nonphysical nature? Also, the ability to make decisions and to have abstract thoughts presents evidence that there exists within man a spiritual essence. The mere possession of a brain cannot sufficiently explain thought processes, just because it is physical. The brain under a physicalist model functions as the center of the nervous system and can enable bodies to react. However, to explain reasoning, higher thinking, and ethical values is difficult, because the use of higher reasoning, namely logic and the possession of ethical values, has a universal nature that humans around the world recognize, yet these are distinctly non-physical or not particularly identifiable as physical processes. Can brains, as mere physical matter, determine universal principles without having a soul, created in the image of God, who as *lógos* (John 1:1) is the Source of logic and absolute morals? Physicalism is difficult to sustain in the face of the aspects of life that humans deal with on a daily basis and often take for granted.

Physicians and medical researchers have catalogued numerous cases of out-of-body experiences when individuals have actually died and then reported what they witnessed after they were resuscitated. Many of these experiences enable the individuals to observe at an elevated level events "above" their bodies and to see "beneath" them what occurred in the room after their death. If the soul does not exist, observation should cease at the moment of death.[146] From the perspective of physicalist naturalism, nothing should occur after the body dies. However, medical documentation of out-of-body experiences appears to testify to post-mortal perception and interactivity. Such activity of the mind after death points towards the existence of the human soul.

Claiming that human beings are merely physical bodies without a soul is difficult to support. The religious nature of man is quite apparent, and there exists in humans knowledge and inclinations which they cannot simply have received from the world around them. Both phenomenological reports of perceptions after death and the religious tendency of humans to conceive of non-physical life, such as the possible relationship with God, who is a spirit, (John 4:24; cf. e.g., Gen. 1:2 and numerous other passages, and *Pneumatology*, above) support the idea of a nonphysical soul. People have souls, souls that are eternal and need salvation.

---

146 P.M.H. Atwater, *Near-Death Experiences: The Rest of the Story* (New York: MJF Books, 2011), 25-34.

Anthropology: Sin

Sin is any thought, spoken word, or action which displeases God, or the refraining from an action that God desires the individual to perform. Every human being commits sin, because every person inherits a sin nature at the moment of conception. Sin is the fundamental problem of humanity and prevents man's ability to pursue holiness and perfect fellowship with God by their own efforts. Sin is the reason for the corruption and wickedness of the world, and existence will not become whole until sin is removed from it.

One of the earliest perversions of the doctrine of sin came in the fourth century with Pelagius (c. 354- 418). Pelagius denied the universal affect of Adam's fall (Gen. 3:1-19) and believed that man could live sinless by his own efforts.[147] John Wesley believed in the debilitating affects of sin, but he rejected the impact of original sin on individuals. Because of the preventing grace from God, a person is not actually a sinner until he or she commits a sin. Thus, man is not condemned by an inherited sin nature, but by his own sins which he has committed.[148] Antinomianism argues a similar point to Pelagianism, but only after conversion. Once an individual converts, then the moral laws found in God's Word no longer apply. Reference to obedience does not apply to Christians who are free under the grace of God.[149] With the onset of moral relativism, contemporary society has moved away from the notion of sin. There are two different levels with respect to the denial of sin. The extreme level rejects any notion of sin or a concept of morality. Another level regards not all, but certain immoral indiscretions, such as fornication, lying, or laziness, as now acceptable, while others, like greed, adultery, and murder are still not tolerated. Unfortunately, the Church has had those who reject the biblical conception of sin, holding to popular perceptions of sin according to culture. Progressive Christianity has also taken a negative view towards the biblical concept of sin, with

---

147 Augustine, *The Deeds of Pelagius* 6. 16-19 in *Answer to the Pelagians, The Works of Saint Augustine: A Translation for the 21st Century,* trans. Roland J. Teske, ed. John E. Rotelle (Hyde Park: New City, 1997), 346-348.

148 R. Stanton Norman, "Human Sinfulness" in *A Theology for the Church,* ed. Daniel L. Akin (Nashville: Broadman and Holman, 2007), 456-457.

149 Robertson McQuilkin, *An Introduction to Biblical Ethics* (Wheaton: Tyndale, 1989), 80.

some progressive pastors even stating that humans do not inherit original sin and should not consider themselves sinners.[150]

From a biblical standpoint, one can peruse any book of God's Word and find clear verification of sin's existence. To begin with, Scripture defines sin as rebellion against God (1 Sam. 15:23; Job 34:37), the transgression against God's law (Jer. 44;23; Rom. 8:7; Jas. 2:9-10; 1 John 3:4), and anything that exists outside of God's righteous standard (1 John 5:17). As to the seriousness of sin, Scripture explains that God hates it (Ps. 11:5; Prov. 6:16-19; Zech. 8:17; Mal. 2:16; Rom. 1:18; Eph. 5:6) and brings judgment because of it (Gen. 6:5-7; Jer. 51:47; Ezek. 11:5-12; Rev. 18:1-24; 20:11-15). The Bible is quite clear as to sin's origins, describing its entrance into the world at the Garden of Eden, when Adam and Eve disobeyed God (Gen. 3:1-19). Because of Adam and Eve's disobedience, their descendants, entailing all of humanity (Gen. 3:20), inherited sin as part of their nature (Ps. 51:5; Rom. 5:12). Concerning its universality, God's Word states that all are sinners (Eccl. 7:20; Rom. 3:23), and no one can claim righteousness on their own (Rom. 3:10). Furthermore, not only do all people sin, but they sin thoroughly and are completely wicked (Ps. 14:2-3; 53:2-3; Isa. 64:6; Rom. 3:10-18). Sin is the cause of the separation of God and man, preventing a close, intimate relationship (Isa. 53:6; 59:2); the ultimate consequence of sin is death (Rom. 5:12; 6:23; 1 Cor. 15:56; Jas. 1:15). Due to the thoroughly wicked nature of man, he cannot save himself (Gal. 2:16; Eph. 2:8-9). When reading the pages of the Bible, one finds a comprehensive understanding of sin and its consequences.

Arguing for sin's existence often poses little difficulty. A large majority acknowledge that they possess faults and have committed what the Bible classifies as sin, including lies, lust, hate, covetousness, greed, harsh and blasphemous language, etc. Only those in complete denial would argue for their perfection. What many claim is that they are generally good in moral character. Unfortunately, this self-appraisal is the result of a failure to truly examine one's own misdeeds. Any serious self-assessment will reveal that one has committed numerous sins, more than most would care to admit.

A more fundamental issue is sin's universality. All human beings commit wrongdoings and have inclinations towards performing them.

---

150 Alisa Childers, *Another Gospel: A Lifelong Christian Seeks Truth in Response to Progressive Christianity* (Carol Stream: Tyndale, 2020), 87-8.

Selfish tendencies seem universal. How is that so? If humans are evolving, as naturalism holds, then why have humans not shed certain aspects of immorality over the millennia? In fact, there is no indication that sin is diminishing or that it will diminish in the near future. Mankind still has its faults, and that has not changed. The sins that men and women committed thousands of years ago are still being committed in the twenty-first century. Recent technological advancements have only introduced creativity to disobedience instead of improving man's ethical and spiritual state.

Even in this current skeptical age, the biblical concept of sin is impossible to deny. Because billions of human beings live on this Earth, sin everywhere abounds. In general, people know that they commit wrongdoings. Guilt often comes to those who commit moral errors. To remove sin from one's life by one's own effort is obviously impossible due to the strong evidence that no sinless individual currently exists on Earth. Even denial of sin fails to achieve the desired result, because those who deny sin's existence at times commit the most horrendous of sins that even the culture at large finds repulsive. Sin is the greatest problem that mankind faces, and mankind cannot rid itself of this problem. A Savior is needed to deliver humans from this problem called sin.

Chapter 7

Soteriology

Historical Background:

Charles Dickens' semi-historical novel, A Tale of Two Cities may be considered an early work of historical fiction. It weaves a captivating story of two men in the midst of the French Revolution at the end of the eighteenth century. In it, Charles Darnay, scion of the French aristocratic St. Evremonde family, leaves France to start a new life in England.[151] He eventually marries an English woman, Lucie Manette, and the couple have two children.[152] Meanwhile, Sidney Carton is a barrister, who, aside from his brilliant legal mind, wastes his life by abusing alcohol.[153] Although the two men live very different lives, by their appearances, they are nearly identical.

When the Revolution engulfs France, Darnay receives a plea for help from one of his family's servants. He travels to Paris to save the life of this servant, but is himself arrested, and being the heir of a notorious noble family, is ultimately sentenced to death.[154] Carton emerges out of his meaningless existence and travels to Paris to assist Charles Darnay and his wife, whom Carton secretly loves.[155]

---

151 Charles Dickens, *A Tale of Two Cities* (Salt Lake City: Project Gutenberg, 1994), 55-67, at URL https://www.gutenberg.org/files/98/old/2city12p.pdf, (accessed January 29, 2023).

152 Ibid., 167–169.

153 Ibid., 120–123.

154 Ibid., 216–226.

155 bid., 260.

> *Shortly before Darnay is sent to his execution, Carton visits Darnay in his cell, drugs him, and switches Darnay's clothes with his own, taking Darnay's place in prison.*[156] *As Darnay's family escorts an unconscious Darnay to safety, Carton mounts the platform of execution and is beheaded by the guillotine.*[157]
>
> *Carton sacrificed himself to save another man. He took on the role of a savior. Dickens's famous novel clearly has salvific overtones. It paints a picture of one who saves an individual from certain destruction. The Bible, likewise, is such a story, describing the long series of events in which God has worked both providentially and miraculously to save mankind.*

Soteriology, or the doctrine of salvation, places Christianity in a unique position among the faiths of the world. World religions generally require of their devotees that they do most, if not all, of the ethical work needed (but variously defined) to achieve some sort of spiritual salvation and receive a good afterlife. However, the New Testament states that it is impossible for one to save oneself because of the complete sinfulness of each person; such a condition strands the individual apart from a holy God, the Bible maintains. Biblical salvation, then, can only come through God the Son, who sacrificed Himself so that all who believe in Him can be forgiven of their sins and receive eternal life. This is the crux of Christianity, and even as it has been denied, rejected, and distorted over two millennia, this truth remains what differentiates the Christian believer, who, if he commits to defending his faith will find the soteriological doctrines to be under constant attack and will need to counter them to effectively share the Gospel.

Soteriology:
Grace

When contrasting Christianity with other religions and belief systems of the world, many differences surface. However, two major differences stand out more than any other. The first is that Christianity's tenets are

---

156 Dickens, *A Tale of Two Cities*, 307–313.
157 Ibid., 325–330.

based on historical facts: God's miraculous intervention to create and sustain the nation of Israel, the life and ministry of Jesus, the resurrection of Jesus, and the miraculous birth of the Church. Secondly, there are the doctrines of grace, which are based on a definition of "Grace" as unmerited or undeserved favor. God extends His grace by offering salvation to the undeserving through His Son's vicarious death and resurrection to any who would receive Him. No ritual or achievement can earn eternal salvation. It is a gift from God.

If any doctrine is more difficult to understand than God's eternality, the Trinity, and Christ's dual nature, it is the doctrine of grace. Receiving forgiveness for every sin and the gifts of salvation and eternal life without any human effort baffles the mind. For that reason and due to Satanic obfuscation and inspiration, a majority of faiths reject any concept of grace. Islam holds to the Five Pillars and obedience to Allah. If one's good deeds outweigh one's bad deeds on an eternal scale, then one will enjoy eternity in Heaven. Buddhism teaches that, through an individual's own efforts to overcome craving, a person can achieve enlightenment. Cults are no different. The Latter-Day Saints stress striving for moral perfection and following the official practices and rituals so that they may achieve divine status to rule over a planet. Scientology encourages its adherents to perform the process of removing the negative memories they call "engrams." This process, called "auditing," is considered the first step to realizing one's potential as a powerful alien being and reaching self-actualization. Tragically, many who attend Christian churches also believe that they must earn their salvation by church attendance, abstaining from sin, participating in communion, and being baptized. Certain denominations or Church branches, such as Roman Catholicism, Anglicanism, Lutheranism, the branch of Anglicanism known as the Episcopal Church, the Disciples of Christ, and the Christian Church stipulate that salvation is granted only to those who participate in baptism.[158] Conversely, others who have a superficial understanding of the Gospel misunderstand grace as an automatic forgiveness on the part of God without the need for repentance or submission to Christ as Lord. This ignores the seriousness of sin and the effects of its total corruption upon each person. If this was the actual meaning of grace, then there would have been no need for Christ to atone for sin (Luke 24:46–47). Whether

---

158 B. F. Smith, *Christian Baptism* (Nashville: Broadman, 1970), 149-51.

coming from an emphasis on works for salvation or a misunderstanding of grace to be an overlooking of sin, any distortion to grace is a rejection of grace, as is illustrated by these equations:

$$Grace$$
$$=$$
$$salvation\ provided\ by\ God$$
$$+$$
$$purchased\ totally\ by\ His\ effort$$
$$+$$
$$removal\ of\ sin\ by\ God$$

$$Grace$$
$$\neq$$
$$eternal\ life\ gained\ by\ human\ effort$$

$$Grace$$
$$\neq$$
$$eternal\ life\ provided\ by\ God$$
$$+$$
$$human\ effort$$

$$Grace$$
$$\neq$$
$$eternal\ life\ provided\ by\ God$$
$$+$$
$$dismissal\ of\ sin$$
$$-$$
$$need\ for\ the\ removal\ of\ sin$$

Grace, while difficult for the human mind to comprehend, is found throughout the Bible. According to Scripture, two kinds of grace come from God. Common grace, the gift of life and the resources to enjoy and prosper in th at life, is given to the population of the world in general (Ps. 145:9; Matt. 5:45; Luke 6:35-36; Acts 14:16-17). Special grace is bestowed to those who call upon the Lord for salvation. In the Old Testament, God's special grace is bestowed at His pleasure (Ex. 33:17; Ezra 9:8), and God pleases to give grace to those who by faith live in obedience and righteousness (Ps. 84:11; Prov. 3:34). Knowing this, Moses pleaded with God to offer His grace to the Israelites despite their rebellion (Exod. 33:12-16; 34:9). The New Testament explains the means of grace through Christ's sacrificial death and His resurrection (Rom. 5:14-21; Ep. 1:7; John

1:14-17). The perfect summary of this doctrine is found in Paul's letter to Ephesus, where he explains that the Ephesian believers received their salvation through the grace of God (Eph. 2:8-9). Since it is from God, grace is greater than sin and nullifies its corruption and consequences (Rom. 5:20; 6:14). Aside from the specific mentions of grace, the Bible, overall, gives a narrative of God's showering of His grace for the ultimate purpose of the salvation of the inhabitants of the world, from the call of Abram (Gen. 12:1-3) to the creation of a perfect new heaven and a new earth which God will establish in the future (Rev. 21:1-27).

Defending the doctrine of grace entails the awareness of the seriousness of sin and the nature of God. As described earlier, sin corrupts every person thoroughly, so thoroughly that no person can save herself. Despite the efforts of an overwhelming majority of the world's religious systems, sin has not been eradicated from the world, nor has any individual reached a sinless state by performing a prescribed method of spiritual acts by their own efforts. Clearly, man cannot save himself. He must have outside assistance. Such assistance would require intervention from One who is not human and is sinless. Only one such Person exists, and that is God.

Grace is also consistent with the nature of God. God is good (Ps. 27:13; 34:8). Therefore, a good God would naturally bestow grace, a grace that is completely undeserved and unearned and a grace that mankind so desperately needs. The grace God offers comes with a price,, a price that He paid Himself (Rom. 5:8; Eph. 2:8-9). For those who claim that the necessity of believing in Jesus Christ and submitting to Him as Lord and Savior is not true grace, they are ignoring the terrible price the Son of God paid through His death by crucifixion. It was a price that God did not have to pay, but that He did pay out of His love for the people He created (John 3:16; Eph. 2:4; 1 John 4:10). Grace must be God's way, because it is the only way (John 14:6; Acts 4:12); grace is God's gift and, as such, His to dispense.

Perhaps the most beautiful concept in Christian Theology is grace. God the Father sent God the Son, who willingly sacrificed Himself to atone for the sins of mankind. This sacrificial act was done, not because humanity performed great deeds to earn Christ's atonement. No, this act was a display of divine favor motivated by love for beings that did not love Him. That act and the salvation to which it is connected is grace. It is a grace that no human being can fully fathom, but a grace that is real and available to all who accept it.

Soteriology:
Salvation

Through the work of Christ, an individual becomes a follower of Jesus Christ by repenting from his sins, by accepting[159] Him as Lord and Savior, by trusting in Him, and by belief in His death and resurrection. At the moment of his acceptance of Christ, the individual is forgiven of sins and receives eternal life. This is what the Bible calls "salvation," but, through most of the history of the Church, this understanding of salvation has not been the one most accepted.

As with the doctrines of the Trinity and the Deity and Humanity of Christ, salvation has long been assailed by unbiblical distortions. The war against biblical salvation began with Judaizers during the first century, arguing that individuals must first accept the physical signs of conversion to Judaism before committing to Christ in order to be truly converted (Acts 15:1; Gal. 2:4, 11–13). A heresy that has persisted as a thorn in the side of Christian orthodoxy is universalism, a false teaching that dates back to the second century with Origen (c. 185 – c. 253) and states that all persons who have ever lived on Earth will eventually enjoy eternal salvation.[160] A modern version of this belief regards all humans as saved presently and not over a long process of many years, as Origen believed; one such modern view was popularized by Rob Bell, among others.[161] Universalism was not the only distorted view of salvation in the first years of the Early Church. Pelagianism, with its denial of original sin and the universality of Adam's fall, asserted that the first man provided only a bad example, and one could be rescued through discipline and personal piety. One can then live a sinless life without the need of Christ's salvation.[162] A softer, but equally heretical version of this view is semi-Pelagianism, which states that salvation through Jesus, plus good works such as baptism and accepting communion, saves the individual. The Medieval Church

---

159 Sincere Christ-followers differ on the meaning and source of this acceptance of Christ's sacrifice; cf. *The Sovereignty of God* and *The Atonement*, above, and the statement just below on biblical salvation "through faith."

160 Origen, *On First Principles*, III, VI, G. W. Butterworth, trans. (New York: Harper and Row, 1966), 250-1.

161 Rob Bell, *Love Wins*, (New York: Harper, 2011), 183-90.

162 Augustine, *The Deeds of Pelagius*, 6. 16-19, 346-348.

embraced semi-Pelagianism, and that heresy dominated the theological landscape without challenge until Martin Luther (1486-1546) inaugurated the Protestant Reformation. As noted earlier, pluralism considers several religions as equally truthful and offering a viable path to an enjoyable afterlife. Pluralists such as philosopher of religion and theologian John Hick (1922 - 2012) rebuff the idea that Jesus is the only way to salvation in that other faiths appear to have alternate versions of transformative salvation that may be acceptable to God.[163] James H. Cone (1938 - 2018), progenitor of Black Liberation Theology, spurned the idea that Jesus died for the sins of the world so that man can receive forgiveness of sins and a place in heaven, claiming such as being a product of "white Christianity." Cone advocated a salvation that stressed liberation from earthly oppression.[164] A more recent alternative to biblical salvation is inclusivism. Adherents of this doctrine such as Clark Pinnock (1937 - 2010) falsely claim that Jesus saves individuals though they might not have specific knowledge of the Gospel. Though they might not be aware of it during their earthly life, they can be saved through Jesus' crucifixion and resurrection.[165]

Biblical salvation, exclusively offered by grace, through faith in Jesus Christ, is the only view represented in the New Testament. Statements from Jesus (John 14:6) as well as Luke's Acts record of apostolic preaching (e.g., Acts 4:12) reveal that the original teaching concerning salvation

---

163 John Hick (John Harwood Hick), "A Pluralist View" in *Four Views on Salvation in a Pluralistic World*, eds. Dennis L. Okholm and Timothy R. Phillips (Grand Rapids: Zondervan, 1996), 43-44 (Hick is also justly famous for advancing the notion of "eschatological verification," i.e., that at the end, humans will know the truth about God experientially rather than by truths told them by revelation or by theologians, as today!).

164 James H. Cone, *A Black Theology of Liberation*, 2nd. ed. (Maryknoll: Orbis, 1986), 126-8.

165 Clark H. Pinnock, *A Wideness in God's Mercy* (Grand Rapids: Zondervan, 1992), 153-72. Pinnock even offers the possibility of salvation postmortem for those who did not have the opportunity to be exposed to the Gospel, which may seem to solve one sort of theological problem only to open theology to a host of others around the notions of what is justice and whether God properly sanctions unjust acts such as those in the holocaust that have mainly earthly but incredibly long-lasting and severe consequences for its victims.

declared that salvation came through Jesus alone, by grace alone, through faith alone. Additional passages in the New Testament, particularly in the letters of Paul (Rom. 1:16; 1 Thess. 5:9; 2 Tim. 2:10; 3:15), denote that salvation comes through Jesus. Paul also explains how one can receive salvation by believing and trusting (or accepting) that Jesus is Lord and God and affirming the validity of His resurrection (Rom. 10:9-10). Peter's sermon at Pentecost stressed the necessity of repentance of sins for salvation (Acts 2:37-38). Another significant component of salvation stressed in the New Testament is submitting to Jesus as Lord of one's life (1 Cor. 11:3; Eph. 5:22; Jas. 4:7; 1 Pet. 5:6). A study of the New Testament not only substantiates the existence of spiritual salvation, but explains the means of salvation and the path to it.

Both Paul and the writer of Hebrews explains the logic of the exclusivity of Christ. Philippians 2:5-11 and Hebrews 2:1-10 detail the sacrifice of the Son of God to secure eternal salvation for sinners. God the Son became fully human and lived in the humblest of circumstances to die, in obedience to the Father, the most humiliating and excruciating death by crucifixion. Such a sacrifice from God Himself not only demonstrates how amazing is the salvation that Jesus Christ offered to sinners, but that if such a sacrifice was made, then it would necessitate that this is the only means of eternal salvation for humanity; otherwise, such a death is empty of meaning. Only if God did not need to die is pluralism plausible as a belief. Furthermore, pluralism assumes the similarity of many of the major religions of the world, which, upon close examination, is simply a false assumption. Though the study of Comparative Religion argues for the similarity of the world's belief systems, the world's religions are far more different from each other than similar. Muslims worship the one deity, Allah, while Hindus state that 330 million gods exist. Buddhists advocate for the Eightfold Path in the pursuit of enlightenment and nirvana, but with Taoism, the individual must align oneself to the *Dao* to be spiritually transformed.

The religions of the world are very diverse, and Christianity stands out in its uniqueness in two major respects. First, Christian beliefs are based on the historical; revelation is recorded in the Bible and is validated by ancient documents outside of Scripture and by archeological evidence. If the events in the Bible did not occur or its claims are not true, then Christianity would be false and could not function as a sustainable belief system, as Paul at least partly reasoned in 1 Corinthians 15:12-

19. Secondly, Christian salvation is based on the concept of grace, the unmerited favor of forgiveness of sin and eternal life bestowed upon those who follow Jesus Christ. No other belief system has this doctrine of a grace awarded unmerited to sinners by a just, righteous, holy, and loving God with whom He is in communion. Grace recognizes the seriousness of sin and emphasizes the immeasurable wonder of God's undeserved favor to forgive sin through the vicarious death of His Son. While universalism stresses the love of God, it ignores the seriousness of sin. As was shown earlier, sin's existence is self-evident. Therefore, universalism fails as a belief in that it denies reality. Pelagianism and semi-Pelagianism also diminish the seriousness of sin in the claim that the believer can live a life of righteousness through human effort to achieve or partially achieve salvation. If salvation through human effort were possible, which it is not, then Christ's death would not have been necessary. As one writer put it, it is of equal consequence to miss a train by a minute as by an hour—and human effort will always miss the train of God's undeserved grace.

Every person needs the salvation that can only come through Jesus Christ. Heresy has so distorted this doctrine that many who regularly attend church are completely ignorant of what true salvation is and how one may receive it. It is for true believers to inform their lost friends, neighbors, co-workers, and those in works-based religions and churches of the content and path to biblical salvation.

Soteriology: Justification

At the moment of salvation, the status of the converted individual is dramatically changed. Christ's atoning work on the cross positions the new believer into right standing before God the Father to be included among the righteous. That is not to say that believers become sinless at the time of conversion, but that God, through His grace and mercy alone, looks upon His adopted children as people who live and serve according to His will. This is the doctrine of justification by faith alone.

Like other doctrines in the discipline of soteriology, justification has been on the receiving end of attempts to pervert Christian theology. Early antagonism towards justification arose due to misunderstanding of the doctrine, notably lessening God's grace in giving the gift of salvation.

Theophilus of Antioch (ca. 120 – 190) held that justification signified that humans could save themselves, since God had granted them full autonomy.[166] Similar to Theophilus's heretical view, Pelagius regarded a person as having the ability to choose based on his own free will to live righteously; such a view dispenses with the need for justification by God, since man was created just.[167] The later modification, semi-Pelagianism, recognized the need for God's help in being brought into a right standing before Him.[168] However, semi-Pelagians equally emphasized the role of believers working alongside the Lord to perfect their salvation.[169] Thomas Aquinas continued in this tradition in the Middle Ages by emphasizing that good works perfect faith due to the fact that free will is inherent in man's nature and must have an active role in his salvation.[170] Good works, according to Aquinas, not only have efficacy for one's own salvation in the present life but also for the one who finds himself in Purgatory and must be cleansed of their sins before going to heaven.[171]

Developments in the last century have attempted to position justification less from a belief about the eternal consequences of sin and rather as liberation from evil and oppressive ideologies in the present. Jürgen Moltmann (1926 –) scorned the traditional understanding of justification, declaring the impracticality of convincing individuals of their sinful state in the eyes of God. Rather, Moltmann argued that justification signifies God's concern for justice in His identification with the oppressed, whether politically, economically, or culturally, and His desire to correct the oppressor. Therefore, according to Moltmann, true justification does not bring an individual into a rightful holy state before God so that a saved person may relate to God, but brings

---

166 Theophilus, *Ad Autolycum*, trans. Robert M. Grant (Oxford: Clarendon, 1970), 2.27, 71.

167 Pelagius, "Letter to Demetrias" in *The Letters of Pelagius and His Followers*, ed. and trans. B.R. Rees (Woodbridge: The Boydell Press, 1991), 3.2, 38.

168 John Cassian, *Conference Three: The Three Renunciations* in *John Cassian Conferences*, trans. Colm Luibheid (New York: Paulist, 1985), *16*, 95–6.

169 Ibid., *19*, 97–8.

170 Thomas Aquinas, *Summa Theologica*, trans. Fathers of the English Dominican Province, (1947), 2.1.113, (accessed April 15, 2023 at URL https://www.sacred-texts.com/chr/aquinas/summa/index.htm).

171 Ibid., Appendix 2.

justice to those living under tyranny.[172] An alarming issue facing the Church in the twenty-first century centers on the widespread acceptance of sexual immorality. According to persons of this perspective, a believer can identify with a sinful lifestyle, particularly homosexuality, as long as he does not act on it and remains in a "celibate" lifestyle.[173] Such a position flies in the face of the Scripture's understanding of the believer's new identity in Christ, in which he no longer identifies with sin but in a new life of holiness through the Savior's atoning work. Thus, the true Christian believer is a new creation in Christ (2 Cor. 5:17).

Despite numerous distortions throughout history, justification by faith alone is well-represented in the New Testament. Jesus promised that on the day of judgment, many will be condemned, but others will be acquitted (Matt. 12:36-37). He explained further in the parable of the Pharisee and the publican that the tax collector who acknowledged his sins and begged God for mercy was justified rather than the Pharisee who declared his own worth before God (Luke 18:9-14). By far the most extensive explanation of justification comes from Paul. Some of his letters establish the fact of justification through God's grace by simple affirmation (1 Cor. 6:11; Phil. 3:7, 9; Titus 3:7). When writing to the churches at Rome and Galatia, however, Paul more extensively dealt with the doctrine. Correcting the church in Galatia, the apostle wrote that justification came through faith in Christ and not through works (Gal. 2:16-17; 3:24). To the Christians in Rome, Paul conclusively demonstrated that no one possessed righteousness on their own or through their own effort (Rom. 2:1-24; 3:9-18). Abraham himself exemplified a life of faith rather than being justified by his works (Rom. 4:1-25). Therefore, righteousness comes through faith in and by Jesus Christ (Rom. 3:21-22, 28). Justification by faith for believers is possible only because of Jesus' death on the cross (Rom. 3:23-25; 5:6-9) and His resurrection; those who come to Jesus through faith will be reconciled to God the Father and have a relationship with Him (Rom. 5:10-11). Though his letter has confused many throughout Christian history, James focused on justification and

---

172 Jürgen Moltmann, *The Spirit of Life* (Minneapolis: Fortress, 1992), 125-8.

173 Sarah Pulliam Bailey, "Gay, Christian and...celibate: The changing face of the homosexuality debate," in *Religion News Service*, August 4, 2014 (URL https://religionnews.com/2014/08/04/gay-christian-celibate-changing-face-ho-mosexuality-debate/ accessed April 15, 2023).

its relationship with good works (Jas. 2:18–26). Taking James' words about works in proper context, good works do not earn justification, but they demonstrate that a person has valid faith (Jas. 1:22–25). Thus, a careful reading of the New Testament finds plenty of passages affirming justification by faith for all believers.

Distortions of the doctrine of justification occur when the seriousness of sin is lessened or when the efficacy of human effort for salvation is exaggerated, e.g. achieving justification, in full or in part, by a human effort. This view is premised on sin not entirely causing human depravity. However, such a doctrinal stance is nonsensical since the slightest acquaintance with humans at the earliest stages of life proves our stubborn selfishness. Our courts and prisons are full of contrary examples of depravity. By definition, justification signifies one brought into a right standing with God. Humans, with the exception of Christ, have failed to live lives that would ever come close to representing perfection and therefore never approach self-justification. Furthermore, justification implies a certain standard set by God. Acknowledging that such a standard exists is within reason, because humans can conceive of perfection as a principle. Yet, self-justification presents the contradiction of accepting a standard established by God but not requiring God's salvific power to meet this standard. If God is not needed fully or partially to reach perfection, then why is there a need to meet His standard and why, for that matter, does one need God in the first place? The attempt to bring oneself into right standing is the nonsensical position that acknowledges the necessity of God and the salvation He offers but requires man necessarily to save himself.

There is a tendency among individuals to believe that they can dramatically improve themselves. Indeed, improvements by one's own efforts are possible, such as healthier living, adopting better work habits, and showing more consideration to others, but self-improvement has its limitations. Individuals only achieve so much by themselves. They require assistance from others to accomplish many things in life, including getting married and starting a family, performing complicated medical procedures, and receiving formal training and education. If such important endeavors require more than the individual, then spiritual salvation, the most important and a far more complicated consideration than the above-mentioned endeavors, necessitates assistance. Since it is common knowledge that humans are not perfect, then only One who is perfect can provide the help needed to bring them into acceptable standing. The fact that all of the work done to provide for justification came by Christ's efforts, namely the incarnation, atonement, and resurrection, then the notion of human effort in assisting in any way in justification is redundant and absurd.

Justification is an amazing doctrine that declares that followers of Christ are made instantly accepted in the eyes of God the Father because of the work of His Son. Tied to the doctrine of grace, justification declares the great news that those who commit to follow Jesus will be brought into a position of vindication and absolution of their sins through no effort of their own.

Soteriology: Sanctification

Conversion is not the end of a believer's spiritual journey; rather, it is only the beginning. As the Holy Spirit indwells each believer, He works to direct and correct that disciple to become a godly and obedient individual. This is the process of sanctification, wherein the Holy Spirit makes the believer holy so as to become like the ultimate example of holiness, Jesus Christ.

When examining religious systems around the world, one finds various forms of spiritual growth processes that start with a beginner phase and progress to a higher level of maturity. Within Mahayana Buddhism for example, the Eightfold Path presumably offers the way to enlightenment for all adherents.[174] Jains believe that their Five Vows lead to spiritual awakening.[175] Within Christianity, there are two major aberrant views. From the Wesleyan and Holiness traditions there is sinless perfectionism or entire sanctification. Derived from John Wesley's (1703 - 1791) thought, this view is the conviction that Christians can reach a level of sanctification that involves complete freedom from willful sin,[176] thus resembling the view of works in other religious traditions. Another view, an extreme conversionist position, argues that upon the

---

174 Jack Maguire, *Essential Buddhism*, (New York: Pocket Books, 2001), 90–95.

175 Irving Hexham, *Understanding World Religions* (Grand Rapids: Zondervan, 2011), 234–5.

176 John Wesley, *Thoughts on Christian Perfectionism* in *The Works of John Wesley* vol. 13, eds. Paul Wesley Chilcote and Kenneth J. Collins (Nashville: Abingdon, 2013), 13:5.2–20, 61.

initial conversion of a person, the individual has been transformed to the point that no additional spiritual growth is needed. The believer's task is simply to await death or Christ's Second Coming. One of the most recent distortions of sanctification is the product of the Torahism or the Hebrew Roots Movement; its adherents stipulate that a believer must observe the Sabbath, eat only kosher foods, observe the Levitical feasts, and be circumcised to be in obedience to God, despite the New Testament's insistence that Christ's sacrificial death ended requirements for ceremonial Torah observance (Gal. 2:11–21).[177] A common adversary of sanctification is willful indifference. Too many Christians congratulate themselves on their having "walked forward," their baptism, and church membership, and have no interest in serious spiritual growth. Tragically, today's pulpits rarely address the need for sanctification, and its absence from the spiritual life of local congregations is in itself a heresy.

Biblically, the idea of God making individuals, places, objects, and even certain days holy begins in the Old Testament. God commanded the sanctification of Aaron and his sons to commission them to serve in the role of the priesthood (Ex. 28:1–43; Lev. 21:1–24). He commanded sanctification for the brazen altar of sacrifice for the Tabernacle as well (Exod. 29:36–37). Leviticus 11:44 begins a series of biblical commands to be holy ("For I am the Lord your God. Consecrate yourselves therefore, and be holy, for I am holy...." ESV; see the earlier discussions of God's communicable and non-communicable attributes). The Sabbath Day was sanctified as holy to God (Neh. 13:22). At other times, Levites, families, and even the entire nation were instructed to go through a process of sanctification before beginning a certain task or fulfilling a particular role (Josh. 3:5; 7:13; 1 Sam. 16:5; 2 Chron. 29:5). Sanctifying oneself was also closely connected to repentance (Joel 2:12–17). In the New Testament, all believers must actively participate in and seek sanctification, a process that only God can complete within each believer (1 Cor. 1:26–31; 1 Thess. 4:3–5). Jesus Christ is the One who sanctifies His people by His atoning sacrifice (Eph. 5:25–27; Heb. 13:12). Yet sanctification does not occur in an instant, but is a process requiring the work of the Holy Spirit within the believer (2 Thess. 2:13; 1 Pet. 1:1–2). Hardly a minor subject in the Bible, Scripture describes sanctification as a necessity in the life of God's people.

---

177 R. L. Solberg, *Torahism*, rev. ed. (Franklin: Williamson College Press, 2022), 14–21.

Soteriology

It is a difficult task in our contemporary age to argue for the sanctification of believers. With modern conveniences, most individuals love instant gratification and may despise anything that requires a process. Sanctification is often not looked on favorably because it is a lifelong process that carries over into our eternal life with God. However, the seriousness of the sinful condition within every person should convince every Christian that he has not arrived at a state of perfection. Christians, despite our transformation, are still sinners (1 John 1:8, 10). Claiming that sanctification is not needed entails claiming that one has reached the point in which he no longer sins. Often, when extolling a devout Christian who exemplifies all of the characteristics of godliness described in Scripture (Gal. 5:22–23; Eph. 5:8–10), that same person will confess that she has shortcomings and recognizes a degree of room for improvement. The reality of sin demonstrates the need for sanctification.

Sanctification mirrors the process of natural life. The lifespan of every human is a journey to maturity. At birth, a child cannot eat on his own, walk, or even crawl. But as he gets older, he learns to feed himself, crawl, and eventually walk. Over time, the child learns to read and process information, drive a car, and even live on his own and support himself. This is the normal process of life for human beings. The fact that the Christian life necessitates a maturation process or journey should not be a surprise, since the God who created life is also the Author of spiritual rebirth and our subsequent walk toward completeness, our goal of living with God. Therefore, upon the conversion of a believer, he or she begins a path of spiritual growth, a path that requires the supervision and inner work of the Holy Spirit.

When sanctification is no longer a priority for Christians, the Church is in crisis. Without the commitment to grow in Christ, the Church will fail to demonstrate that lives are transformed by God, and she will not effectively continue to evangelize non-Christians. Sincere believers desire to please God and want to grow spiritually. A church that does not aspire to grow spiritually appears to the world as nothing more than another community or social organization whose members enjoy one another's company. The unsaved will find little that attracts them to the Christian life if all they observe are individuals who claim to follow Jesus and yet demonstrate little-to-no growth as they walk with Christ during their lives.

Soteriology:
Glorification

Sanctification is the process whereby God continually draws believers closer and closer to godliness; glorification is the end goal of sanctification. Glorification occurs with the resurrection of believers. With the resurrection, followers of Christ will receive eternal bodies free from corruption and sin. At that time, God's people will be able to serve Him in perfect obedience with tireless energy throughout all eternity.

The destiny of mankind has always been of interest to cultures throughout history. Most world religions have proposed some sort of destiny for human beings. Hinduism declares that individuals can achieve *moksha* or "release" from the suffering of existence.[178] Buddhists strive for *nirvana*—when the liberation from ignorance, attachment, and negative emotions brings about the end of all suffering.[179] With the advancements of technology at the close of the twentieth century and into the twenty-first, hope renewed for highly-sophisticated artificial intelligence and robotic engineering to bring about some sort of a post-human existence. Post-humanism, according to some futurists, will enable humans to live in artificial bodies and extend life indefinitely.[180] Much confusion concerning existence after death is also found among Christians. Emmanuel Swedenborg (1688 – 1772) believed in an afterlife but not in glorification. No major change in personality or lifestyle took place. Instead, individuals lived in the afterlife in a way similar to their life on earth, even sleeping and marrying.[181] Others have accepted a view of eternal life called Christo Platonism. Originating from the teachings of Philo of Alexandria (ca. 20 BC – 50 AD) and Origen, who believed that

---

178 Vadsudha Narayanan, "Hinduism," in *Eastern Religions*, ed. Michael D. Coogan (Oxford: Oxford Univ. Press, 2005), 93.

179 Lama Zopa Rinpoche, *The Four Noble Truths: A Guide to Everyday Life*, ed. Yeo Puay Huei, (Somerville: Wisdom Publications, 2018), 132.

180 Nenad Vertovsek & Ivana Greurgic Knezevic, Philosophy and Consciousness in the Future: Cyborgs and Artificial Intelligence waiting for Immortality, *In Media Res* 9(2020):16 (URL https://doi.org/10.46640/imr.9.16.3 accessed January 14, 2023).

181 Colleen McDannell and Bernhard Lang, *Heaven: A History* (New Haven: Yale University, 1988), 186.

the ideal state of humanity existed apart from physical bodies, Christo Platonism argues that eternal life for Christians consists of a permanently disembodied state.[182] Accepting the Christo Platonic ideal for eternal life, Christians have focused on life without their bodies as their final state of existence. The New Testament, however, describes a far different future, a future resurrection.

On several occasions, the New Testament writers look to the hope of their future glorified state. Paul described glorification as the transformation of humble bodies into bodies similar to Christ's after His resurrection (1 Cor. 15:35-49; Phil. 3:20-21). John stated the same in his letter (1 John 3:2). This transformation occurs in an instant when Christ claims His Church (1 Cor. 15:50-55; 1 Thess. 4:16-17). Paul further explained that with their glorified bodies, believers will see God face-to-face (2 Cor. 3:18; Col. 3:4; 1 John 3:2). All that glorification entails is summed up by Paul's assurance that every believer will experience God's completing work motivated by His faithfulness (Phil. 1:6).

Those who accept a form of glorification that is not the biblical version would do well to study the Scriptural passages that deal with the eternal future of believers. Believers should desire to conform their doctrines to Scripture rather than to sources inspired by unbiblical worldviews. This includes beliefs related to eternity. To accept the reality of eternal life, but not refer to the Bible as the main source of our knowledge of it leads to serious doctrinal distortion.

Like many Christian doctrines, glorification strikes the skeptic as complete fiction. It is dismissed as one among many mythical hopes concerning life after death found among the religions of the world, which are summed up in "the Communist gibe about 'pie in the sky' and similar thrusts suggesting that Christians deal with the shadowy 'spiritual' values, and refers all insoluble 'real' difficulties to an imaginary Heaven."[183] However, in a theistic worldview, glorification makes perfect sense. God, who created the world, shows concern for His creation, specifically those created in His image, and He interacts with His creation and would logically be concerned about the eternal destiny of it. In a theistic worldview, God consistently and constantly maintains the existence of the universe and its inhabitants. To

---

182 Randy Alcorn, *Heaven*, (Carol Stream: Tyndale House, 2004), 52-3.

183 Cf. J. B. Phillips, "Ground for Hope" in *New Testament Christianity* (New York: Macmillan, 1956), 50.

abandon humanity at a certain point, after showing considerable care for our eternal survival, would not be consistent with God's nature, as He has previously demonstrated by His Son.

Furthermore, human beings know of the concept of perfection. Mentally, they understand what human perfection is despite the fact that they have not seen it, aside from the descriptions of Christ when He ministered on Earth. Many individuals spend their lives with the misguided but well-meaning goal of self-improvement, striving for perfection. That humans have never achieved perfection suggests the need for God to accomplish this goal. Since humans know of the concept of perfection, it is plausible to believe that such a state exists for humanity.

Through the records of the many instances of conversions to Christianity, family and friends noticed remarkable transformations of behavior and character on the part of the converted. Glorification represents the final and complete transformation of the believer. The initial changes in individuals who have accepted Christ are signs of the reality of glorification. Believers long for the day when they will no longer sin and will live in perfect obedience to the Lord God. That state of perfection is glorification. It is not the end result of human effort, but it is a gift from God, a gift that His people will enjoy for eternity.

Soteriology:
Eternal Security

At the moment of conversion, the individual who has accepted Christ begins on a path that will always keep him or her in the status of remaining saved. Such a dramatic change has occurred by the work of the Holy Spirit, that the believer would never want to return to a pre-converted state. The doctrine has been called many things, the oldest being "perseverance." Baptists typically call it "eternal security," while some theologians, such as James Leo Garrett, term it "abiding in Christ." The doctrinal foil for eternal security is the belief in the possibility of apostasy or "falling away." Apostasy represents the idea that Christians can turn away from the faith and reject Christ as Savior and Lord, changing their status to being an unbeliever. Two different opinions have arisen over the years concerning how one falls away. One states that this happens only due to a willful rejection of Christ on the part of the believer. Another believes that the falling into a sinful lifestyle without repentance will lead to the loss of salvation.

Historically, Roman Catholicism has long warned its followers of the possibility of apostasy, and the Seven Sacraments were a safeguard, not only to ensure initial salvation, but to keep Christians saved. With regard to the great theological debate between perseverance and Christian apostasy, the great opponent to eternal security is Arminianism. Initiated by Jacobus Arminius (1560 – 1609), the system countered John Calvin's understanding of the atonement; it subsequently was embraced (on the whole) by many branches of Protestantism including Methodism, Wesleyanism, and Pentecostalism. There are three major positions within Arminianism in relation to apostasy or falling away. The Classic Arminian position holds that apostasy occurs when a believer makes a decisive rejection of Christ.[184] For those in the Wesleyan tradition, unrepentant sin and willful disobedience leads to the loss of salvation.[185] Others, such as noted NT scholar I. Howard Marshall (1934 – 2015) believe the loss of salvation can possibly occur but that most Christians will persevere in their salvation.[186]

Advocates for eternal security point to several passages which strongly suggest that, after conversion, salvation lasts eternally for any individual who is truly saved. In John's Gospel, Jesus promised that anyone who comes to Him will never be "cast out" (John 6:37). Later, in the same Gospel, Jesus told His disciples that no believer would perish and that no one could remove a believer from His or His Father's hand (John 10:28-29). Assuring the Roman congregation, Paul declared that nothing could separate Christians from the love of Christ (Rom. 8:35-39), implying that believers have an eternal relationship with God. Later, stating it plainer, Paul described every gift of God as never being revoked (Rom. 11:39). Clearly, salvation was included among God's gifts to His people. Elsewhere, Paul described those who have accepted Christ as having been

---

184 Stephen M. Ashby, "A Reformed Arminian View," in *Four Views on Eternal Security*, ed. J. Matthew Pinson, Counterpoints: Bible and Theology, ed. Stanley N. Gundry (Grand Rapids: Zondervan, 2002), 181.

185 Robert E. Picirilli, *Grace, Faith, Free Will, Contrasting Views of Salvation: Calvinism and Arminianism* (Nashville: Randall House, 2002), 207.

186 I. Howard Marshall, *Kept by the Power of God: A Study of Perseverance and Falling Away* (Minneapolis: Bethany Fellowship, 1969), 209-10.

sealed by the Holy Spirit, who guarantees their salvation (2 Cor. 1:22; Eph. 1:13-14). Paul made similar assurances to the church in Philippi, where he promised that God, due to His faithfulness, would complete their salvation (Phil. 1:6). Echoing Paul, Peter wrote that the eternal salvation God gave to His believers could not disappear, because the disciples of Jesus were kept in God's power (1 Pet. 1:4-5). Thus, several New Testament passages support an understanding of an eternal salvation for all believers that no one can remove or destroy.

The argument against eternal security is twofold. First, Scripture seems to indicate that some believers do fall away, resulting in a change back to an unsaved state. Second, there appear to be instances where Christians, on occasion very well-known Christians, renounce the faith or descend into such an immoral state that they can no longer be called Christian.

Passages that impress on the reader the possibility of apostasy can be considered warning passages. God inserted such verses in His Word to challenge believers to examine their own salvation so that they will be certain that they are truly converted. Though some may deem this reason for such passages as excessive, they should keep in mind that there is no clear instance in the New Testament of a follower of Jesus Christ committing apostasy. More importantly, to interpret "apostasy" passages as warning passages indicates the existence of false conversion. False conversion is the misconception of individuals who give a shallow consent to the Christian faith without making a true commitment to becoming a disciple of Jesus Christ. Some have pointed to Simon, the Samaritan magician as a prime example of a false conversion (Acts 8:9-13, 18-24).[187] Certainly, Jesus' parable of the sheep and the goats strongly suggests the existence of individuals who consider themselves believers when, in fact, they are not (Matt. 25:31-46). Jesus also warned that not all who call Him "Lord" are truly His disciples (Matt. 7:21). False conversion is not a popular topic for preaching in evangelical congregations, and the resultant absence of such teaching has brought serious spiritual harm to

---

187 Henry C. Thiessen, *Lectures in Systematic Theology*, (Grand Rapids: Eerdmans, 1949), 357. Norman L. Geisler, "A Moderate Calvinist's View," in *Four Views on Eternal Security*, ed. J. Matthew Pinson Counterpoints: Bible and Theology, edited by Stanley N. Gundry (Grand Rapids: Zondervan, 2002), 91. Both Thiessen and Geisler consider Simon's "conversion" to be nominal, not demonstrating true repentance or obedience to Christ.

the Church. How many people have had some emotional experience at a Christian youth camp or a special evangelistic service and mistakenly believed themselves converted? Local congregations often fail to disciple and instruct new members on the meaning and significance of becoming a follower of Jesus Christ, and the outcome is what believers are witnessing today: teenagers subsequently leaving the faith after their first year in college and celebrity former "Christians" publicly denouncing the faith they once claimed to follow.

From a more academic perspective, critics of perseverance accuse the doctrine of being a vogue doctrine or a doctrine that was not embraced by the Apostles or the Early Church, but was accepted by certain circles in Christendom much later in history . Instead, John Calvin (1509 - 1564), his critics claim, invented the doctrine during the height of the Reformation. Calvin unquestionably advocated for the doctrine and popularized it to the effect that many Protestant Christians accepted it.[188] However the Early Church Father, Augustine of Hippo (354 - 430), laid the foundations for eternal security, declaring that believers persevered in their relationship with God through Christ. However, he did not believe in the assurance of salvation, which is a key doctrinal component of perseverance in later models.[189]

The biblical doctrine of eternal security has been studied, discussed, and debated over the centuries. It stands alongside such doctrines as the Trinity, the two natures of Christ, and His Second Coming as the subject of fierce debates. Some doctrines have a longer history of development because they were the center of major controversies and drew the attention of many leaders, biblical scholars, and theologians. At a time when the Church was under severe persecution and debating the very nature of the deity of Christ during her first three centuries, eternal security was not primarily an issue that surfaced for discussion amongst the early Christians. This fact does not make eternal security an uncertain doctrine.

---

188 John Calvin, *Institutes of the Christian Religion*, 2, 3, xi-xii, trans. Henry Beveridge (Peabody: Hendrickson, 2008), 186-188.

189 Augustine, *On the Gift of Perseverance*, 1.3, ed. Philip Schaff, trans. Peter Holmes and Robert Ernest Wallis, *A Select Library of the Nicene and Post-Nicene Fathers of the Christian Church* (Grand Rapids: William B. Eerdmans Publishing Company, 1971), 527.

Thinking Rationally About Christian Theology
A Handbook on Polemics

Though it has a large number of detractors in the Church, eternal security is based in rationality. Its rationality is tied to the nature of God and the nature of conversion. God, as an eternal, omnipotent, and omnibenevolent being, offers the gift of salvation to those who accept Him as Lord and Savior. It would be unreasonable to consider a gift from an eternal and omnipotent Being one that would not last forever. The nature of conversion is such that God transforms the believer into an entirely new person (2 Cor. 5:17). Biblically, it is nonsensical for a spiritually transformed person, who has been radically changed by the Author of salvation, to want to return to his pre-converted state. If such a thing is possible, one might conclude that God is not omnipotent and true conversion to be impossible. With conversion, God provides assurance of salvation (1 John 5:13). God's assurance to His true believers, whether a person of faith for an hour or for many years, would be nonexistent if apostasy were truly possible. Apostates, such as those seeds planted in the rocky soil beside the path, are more likely never to have been planted firmly at all, "since they had no depth of soil. But when the sun rose, they were scorched. And since they had no root, they withered away" (Matt. 13:5b–6 ESV). Such an eventuality Jesus Himself explains a few verses later: "As for what was sown on rocky ground, this is the one who hears the word and immediately receives it with joy, yet he has no root in himself, but endures for a while, and when tribulation or persecution arises on account of the word, immediately he falls away" (Matt. 13:20–21 ESV). Related to the nature of conversion is the nature of salvation itself. Salvation comes only to individuals through the grace of God (Eph. 2:8–9). Apostasy requires the believer to maintain her salvation so that she will not fall away and also to be able to convert again if she indeed falls away. This kind of effort betrays its rootedness in salvation by works, a completely unbiblical teaching.

No super-persuasive argument exists to put an end to the debate between eternal security and the possibility of true believers becoming apostate. But several New Testament passages indicate security's truthfulness, and reasonable consideration of the doctrine demonstrates its rationality. Passages that seem to indicate otherwise are better understood by considering the reality of false conversion. Eternal security is a gift from God who bestows grace upon His people, a doctrine definitely to be believed and cherished.

Chapter 8

Ecclesiology

Historical Background

Although he could have enjoyed the peace and comfort of his prestigious post as professor of theology at Union Theological Seminary in New York, Dietrich Bonhoeffer (1906-1945) chose to minister to his people living under the oppressive regime of Third Reich Germany.[190] During this tumultuous time, much of the established Church in Germany either fully supported, demonstrated reluctant compliance with, or did nothing to oppose the Nazi government. The supporters of Nazism in the Church were known as German Christians and, with Adolf Hitler's rise to power to usher in the Nazi control of the government, they did not oppose Hitler's installment of a Reichbischof over all Protestant denominations and churches in Germany.[191] Bonhoeffer, along with Martin Niemoller (1892 – 1984), Karl Barth, and some few others recognized that to comply or to do nothing to stand in the way of Hitler and his government would be completely unbiblical. Therefore, they established the Confessing Church, an opposition Christian movement of pastors and churches that refused to be under the control of the Third Reich.[192] This protest led to the arrest and imprisonment of hundreds

---

190 Eric Metaxas, *Bonhoeffer: Pastor, Martyr, Prophet, Spy,* (Nashville: Thomas Nelson, 2010), 328–46.

191 Ibid., 157.

192 Ibid., 222–6; The writing of the Barmen Declaration in May 1934 initiated the Confessing Church.

> of pastors. Bonhoeffer and Niemoller were eventually arrested and sent to concentration camps, and Bonhoeffer was eventually executed by hanging.[193] Today, Bonhoeffer and Niemoller, along with other members of the Confessing Church, are looked to as heroes. However, they were clearly in the minority of their day during the zenith of Nazi control. What convictions led to such sacrifice?
>
> One of the leading convictions that compelled the Confessing Church to action was the biblical doctrine of the Church and its purpose. Hitler conceived of the Church as a branch of government designed to demonstrate complete loyalty and encourage the citizens to be equally obedient. Scripture plainly prescribes another identity and purpose for the Church. The doctrine of the Church, called "Ecclesiology," is often considered not nearly as important a doctrine as the Doctrine of God, Christology, and Soteriology. Yet, one discovers the importance of Ecclesiology when the definition of the concept of the Church is distorted and Christianity itself becomes redefined. Bonhoeffer and his allies understood this and were willing to die for it. Therefore, any distortion of the doctrine of the Church can also be called heresy. Perhaps historical theologians will one day label as great heresy the late twentieth and early twenty-first century undermining of the biblical definition of the Church. Christians must be prepared to confront this heresy.

Ecclesiology:
The Priesthood of Believers

When an individual experiences conversion, she gains access to a relationship with God the Father through Christ. She also becomes a member of God's body of believers, and it becomes her responsibility to live in service and obedience to God throughout the rest of her life. The priesthood of all believers includes these three aspects: relationship, service, and obedience. All believers receive this privilege and responsibility.

The enemies of this doctrine come from two very different segments of Christendom. One outright denies the priesthood of all believers.

---

193 Metaxas, *Bonhoeffer: Pastor, Martyr, Prophet, Spy*, 530–2.

Ecclesiology

Those who do so hail from hierarchical denominations that have a fixed structure of leadership and a clear distinction between priesthood and laity. By the time Christianity entered the Middle Ages, the clergy were elevated to higher spiritual status.[194] The Donatist schism, beginning in the fourth century, began over the protest of the consecration of Cæcilianus because one of the consecrating bishops was under suspicion of committing apostasy under persecution. The tradition that the validity of the Church's ordinances depended on the personal holiness of the church leadership signified how elevated the clergy had already become in Christianity.[195] Even today, Roman Catholicism encourages confession to a priest to receive absolution from sins. This distinction is not found only in Catholicism. Protestant denominations have several models for ministry, and not all of them are biblical. The Reclusive Scholar model regulates the pastor, confining him to a ministry of solely studying in preparation for preaching and teaching and completely ignores any ministry needs, such as evangelism, grief counseling, and encouragement of the sick. In this role, the pastor functions more as an isolated ascetic who only comes out of his cloister to impart a few words of wisdom and then returns to his seclusion. At the other extreme is the Chaplain model; such a pastor neglects the role of teaching to minister to the congregation, who feel loved and appreciated but often do not grow. Another popular model is the Event Coordinator, in which the pastor's main responsibility is to conjure up activities that will increase church attendance and bring success and recognition to the congregation. For the CEO Visionary model, the pastor leads the local church or often a network of churches as the president of an organization. He is the genius of the company, and without him the organization will fail. Therefore, he is elevated to a status far above the "average" Christian, is virtually untouchable, and needs (or has) little accountability. In all of these models, the pastor is considered to be a special class of Christian who alone does the work and alone can enable the local church to maintain spiritual health.

An objective study of the New Testament indicates that every Christian is part of a priesthood (1 Pet. 2:5–10; Rev. 1:16). Serving as priests, believers

---

194 Earl D. Radmacher, *What the Church is All About* (Chicago: Moody, 1972), 55–56.

195 François Decret, *Early Christianity in North Africa*, trans. Edward L. Smither (Eugene: Cascade, 2009), 103–4.

have a high priest, who is Christ (Heb. 7:11–28; 9:11–15). As priests, believers are given full access to God and the opportunity to serve Him (Rom. 5:1–2; Eph. 2:17–19). A division between the clergy and the laity diminishes the important doctrine of grace. Grace stipulates that all followers of Christ have equal standing before God, because God equally bestows grace to all who receive Him, and all who receive Him are equally undeserving of His grace (Rom. 12:3–8; Gal. 3:26–29). Included into the priesthood of God with access to the Father, believers are granted the privilege of service and perpetual worship (Phil. 3:3; Heb. 9:14). Thus, when individuals accept Jesus Christ's offer of salvation, they enter into a position of honor created by God Himself so that His people may live lives that glorify Him.

Aside from the denial of the priesthood of believers, there is also a distortion of this belief. The more progressive wing of Christianity suggests that the priesthood of believers entails the complete freedom of Christ's followers to believe whatever they desire. This claim is erroneous. A priest can only serve in that role if he faithfully propagates the teachings of his faith. Absolute doctrinal freedom is logically flawed, because if any belief is approved from any source regardless of its alignment with Scripture, then Christianity cannot be distinguished from any other belief system. Furthermore, if such a practice of doctrinal freedom were universally adopted, Christianity would eventually cease to exist as a faith.

Another distortion comes from those ensnared in the Word of Faith (or Prosperity Gospel) movement. From this perspective, those who have converted to Christianity have been elevated to a special status that endows them with certain divine abilities. These abilities can be succinctly summarized in two words: wish fulfillment. If a believer has enough faith, anything he or she desires (health, wealth, influence, uninterrupted happiness) can be his or hers. This heresy has wreaked havoc within evangelical Protestantism. True believers are servants who wish to please their Master and develop as they grow in their relationship with Him. Their desires conform to His will for their lives.

Ecclesiology:
The Necessity of the Church

At Pentecost, the Holy Spirit gave birth to the living Church. According to Luke's history of the first decades of Christianity, the faith did not operate apart from the Church. All missionary activity and the growth of the faith occurred in the context of the Church (Acts 2:1–47; 8:4–8; 10:34–48; 13:1–3). The Church is the means by which the followers of Jesus Christ make disciples, worship with fellow Christians, and continue on the path to spiritual maturity.

During much of its history, the Church has been regarded as the legitimate movement of Jesus' disciples, a movement initiated by Christ. This idea, however, came into question in the twentieth century. Maurice Goguel (1880 – 1955) denied that Jesus ever intended for His disciples to form a Church, since Jesus believed His return would be soon. The Church, then, came out of the disciples' efforts to continue after Jesus' crucifixion.[196] Lloyd M. Graham, in his acerbic diatribe against Christianity, claimed that the Church did not originate from the plans of Jesus, nor did Peter, claimed by the Catholic Church as its first Pope, even exist as the Scriptures described Him.[197]

A widespread notion among many who call themselves disciples of Jesus is that the Church is no longer necessary. A combination of radical individualism and privatism has influenced many in the West to regard worship solely in a noncommunal way, apart from koinonia. Arguing for the full autonomy of individuals and for its deeply personal nature, many regard worship as an activity that is best done alone with God. Advances in technology, which allow people to view worship services on their computers via live streaming or recordings, provide additional excuses to eschew meeting with fellow believers.

It would be difficult to study the New Testament divorced from any conception of the Church. Luke records the very birth and early days of the Church in the Book of Acts (Acts 2:1–47). Only a short gap of weeks occurred between the conclusion of Jesus' ministry at His ascension (Luke 24:50–51; Acts 1:9) and the inauguration of the Church by the Holy Spirit at Pentecost (Acts 2:1–4). Christ ministered forty days after His crucifixion and resurrection, which occurred at Passover (Acts 1:3), and Pentecost or the Feast of Weeks occurs fifty days after Passover (Lev. 23:15–16; Deut. 16:9–10), as still reflected in today's worship calendar. The brief intermission between the two events strongly implies intention and planning on the part

---

196 Garrett, *Systematic Theology*, 2:464.

197 Lloyd M. Graham, *Deceptions and Myths of the Bible* (New York: Citadel, 1975), 439–41.

of the Godhead. Concerning the additional literature of the New Testament, many of the letters were written specifically to local congregations (Rom. 1:7; 1 Cor. 1:2; 2 Cor. 1:1; Gal. 1:2; Eph. 1:1; Phil. 1:1; Col. 1:2; 1 Thess. 1:1; 2 Thess. 1:1). Aside from, this Jesus expressly stated to His disciples and directly to Peter that He planned to establish the Church (Matt. 16:18). Though many individual Christians are mentioned in the New Testament, they are understood to be part of a larger context of believers. This is evident in the personal greetings and acknowledgements found in a few of Paul's letters. The persons mentioned are members of local churches (Rom. 16:3–16; Col. 4:15, 17; Phil. 1:1–2). Essentially, the New Testament is a series of writings to, for, and about the Church, and it is strong evidence that the body of believers was created by God and was part of His plan all along.

Much of the strength of the argument against the Church involves the many abuses over the centuries by leaders who took on the role of political potentates rather than propagators of the Gospel of Jesus. From the excesses of the Crusades to the Spanish Inquisition and to the more recent cases of the abuse of children and women by clergy, one can easily observe that very disturbing crimes have been committed in the name of God and His Church. True Christians must wonder if those who committed such crimes could even be considered to be actual followers of Jesus. Even in defense of the Church as a whole, no Christian should dismiss these instances as minor or insignificant. Christians should be the first to admit and condemn these horrific acts. However, these crimes and immoral actions are abuses that do not represent her purpose or true function, as God established it. It is also logically inconsistent to condemn a world-wide institution on the sole basis of the abuses committed by a segment of it. If one hospital mistreated patients, few would suggest that all hospitals are evil and therefore, must be closed. Hospitals have a necessary function and are a benefit to the community. Biblical and faithful churches have a necessary functionality that benefits the community. Local congregations minister to the poor, operate private schools, provide marriage and family counseling, and comfort the grieving. The absence of a biblical church that loves and ministers to its members and community would be painfully felt.

It should also be remembered that the Church's primary function is to make disciples (Matt. 28:19–20; Acts 1:8). There is no means, biblically or conceptually, otherwise available for the spread of the Gospel. Spreading the Gospel and helping Christians to mature spiritually is God's expectation for His people, and all of His people should desire to be a part of the means of fulfilling that expectation. No other institution can fulfill the Great Commission. Ministries of all kinds exist besides the local church, but only as partners with the Church as a whole, working alongside the local Church (and thus called "parachurch" ministries) and often under the Church's direction. True Christian ministries were born within the context of the Church, and without the Church they would not have existed. The Billy Graham Evangelistic Association, for instance, works with local churches during Crusades so that their evangelistic events can be successfully promoted and so newly converted believers can be properly discipled.

No one should discourage private, individual worship. Prayer and Bible study should be incorporated as a regular habit in believers' daily lives. There are many instances of this type of worship occurring in Scripture. Jesus, in fact, modeled this form of worship. But there is much to be said in favor of corporate worship or worshipping alongside fellow believers as a community and being part of that community; Hebrews 10:25 is but one such NT witness to the importance of meeting together in these last days. Because we are sinners, believers need accountability and need correction when they sin. We need to be challenged to grow further in our devotion to the Lord. We need support from one another when tragedy strikes and mutual aid is required. Anyone who does not recognize this is so much the poorer in his faith. When an individual accepts Christ as Savior and Lord, he is instantly born into the Church. Despite her imperfections, the Church was created to be God's instrument to evangelize an unsaved world and to be an enormous benefit to her members. When a community of believers expresses sincere devotion to the Lord, behaves in a Christlike manner, and demonstrates love for one another and compassion for unbelievers, it represents God's plan for the Church. Would that every church followed this example so that the word, "church," would not leave a bitter taste as it does for so many.

Ecclesiology: Defining the Church

As the *ekklesia*, or the assembly of God's people, the Church consists of those who have accepted Christ as Savior and Lord and thus are spiritually born into the community that is the people of God, His saints and followers.[198] They gather to worship the Lord, observe the ordinances, and grow spiritually as disciples of Jesus Christ. This is the Church, and this definition for God's people is found in several key passages in the New Testament.

Controversy over the Church as a doctrine did not arise until Christianity became legal in the Roman Empire at the declaration of Constantine (c. 272 – 337) at the Edict of Milan in 313 and when it became the state religion under Theodosius (347 – 395) in 381. At this turning point in history, the Church came to be identified with the Roman Empire. Leaders of the Empire began to exert their influence upon the Church, particularly in doctrinal matters, and the Empire's citizenry were affiliated with the Church as members without personal commitment. Even after the Empire's demise in 476, the Church still exerted power, even over other nations and their rulers. Such power continued throughout the Middle Ages and existed unchecked until the sixteenth-century Protestant Reformation. In Europe, from the fourth century until the sixteenth, the Church was not defined so much as God's people gathered for worship and living in service to Him than as an authoritarian regime exerting control over people and nations.[199]

The Protestant Reformation helped to bring the Church back to its biblical definition, but the Church's association with the State was more difficult to change. As such, a state church exists in many nations around the world today, including the so-called Protestant countries of Europe that have long since strayed from their evangelical roots. In such circumstances, every citizen in good standing is commonly regarded as a member of the state church, regardless of conversion experience or an active and growing faith. This is how the Anglican Church has for centuries operated in the United Kingdom. Though the concept of the state church initially began with its intent to be involved in the life of the citizen of the state from birth to death and has done an excellent job of incorporating new members, the state church has done a poor job of making true converts. With skepticism holding sway in Europe in the eighteenth century, liberalism sweeping through Europe and the United States in the eighteenth and nineteenth centuries, and secular

---

198 Johannes P. Louw and Eugene A. Nida, eds., *Greek English Lexicon of the New Testament*, 2d ed. (New York: United Bible Societies, 1989), 126.

199 Allison, *Historical Theology*, 572.

humanism proceeding virtually unchecked through the Western World in the twentieth century, the state church moved away from identifying as a body of believers to functioning as an institution that merely maintained traditional ceremonies. Today, the structures reserved for worship in state churches largely have the function of museums, such as the Anglican cathedral in Liverpool, England, with only a handful of individuals gathered for worship services. Few objective church historians will deny that the state church has failed to fulfill Christ's mission for the Church, teaching His truths and discipling people as in the Great Commission.

The twentieth century brought new developments and challenges to the Church. One of those challenges was the ecumenical movement. Concerned over division, several Protestant denominations, and later the Russian Orthodox Church and Roman Catholic Church, formed the World Council of Churches (WCC) in 1948. Rather than promoting biblical doctrine and the furtherance of the Gospel, the WCC membership gave their approval to liberation theology and the socialist agenda. In fact, doctrine and evangelism were deemed minor concerns for the WCC, inciting a negative reaction from American evangelicalism.[200] Another challenge came from the megachurch movement. The megachurch upended a more traditional understanding of the local church. Embracing principles from successful business models, innovative but misguided pastors redefined church success as drawing large crowds to weekly religious services and gaining national and international renown and recognition. In so being redefined, churches became known as a mass of individuals that associated themselves with a local, often nominally-Christian organization. Worship services were transformed into religious entertainment that made brief references to Christianity, with sermons closely mirroring motivational speeches. Discipleship, as a biblical practice, became so diluted that it eventually became synonymous with mere church attendance.

Such redefinitions of the doctrine of the Church as occurred in the latter half of the twentieth century were difficult to counter. Proponents of these concepts pointed to their validation by large numbers, massive facilities, and numerous ministries. Yet, cracks in the seemingly unassailable castle of the numbers of people reached by "the successful church" began to show after this model reached near-universal approval.

---

200 Allison, *Historical Theology*, 584.

One such crack has been the growing ratio of unbelievers to believers in the culture, despite the dramatic increase of large membership churches. Another crack (and equally disturbing trend) is the epidemic of doctrinal ignorance of even the most basic tenets of the faith among those who designate themselves as "born again Christians." In short, the new and supposedly successful re-conception of the local church prevented the Church as a whole from discipling and fulfilling the Great Commission, and the Churches that embraced this definition were not, in fact, much like churches at all.

Aside from these problematic redefinitions that have surfaced within the Church's own walls, cult movements outside the Church have offered their own version of the body of Christ.[201] Typically, cults that have broken from Christianity seek to correct the abuses of the Church and the doctrine of the Church. Therefore, those within a particular cult movement regard only themselves as the true Church, while those without are thought to be false. Thus, when one seeks to discover, outside the pages of the New Testament, the definition for the Church and for local churches, one may receive several conflicting answers.

A thorough examination of the New Testament furnishes a solid definition of the Church: the body of Christ. The first major book that deals with the subject of the Church in great detail is Acts. As the sequel to the Gospel of Luke (Acts 1:1), Acts covers the history of the Early Church following the ministry of Jesus. In Luke's description of its origins, the Church only grew when God added to it with the conversion of people (Acts 2:47; 5:14). Similarly, when describing the work of the Holy Spirit in Antioch, Luke records that the disciples of Jesus first came to be called, "Christians" there (Acts 11:26). In this verse, the disciples were equated with the Church, as well as being Christians. With this one verse, the makeup of the Church is unquestionably declared as consisting of followers of Jesus Christ. One of the greatest discourses on the nature and purpose of the Church is found Paul's first letter to the Corinthians. On two occasions in that letter, Paul refers to the church in Corinth as composed of "saints," (1 Cor. 1:2; 14:33) and he further describes the churches in Galatia as consisting of "saints" (1 Cor. 6:1). Discussing the

---

201 In the following ecclesiological discussion, "body" of Christ is not capitalized, to avoid confusion with the tradition of capitalizing Christ's Body in writings about communion or the Lord's Supper.

issue of unity within the Church, Paul calls it the "body of Christ"; the apostle directly states that this body is composed of many members that are the Christians to whom he was writing (1 Cor. 12:12-31). Paul echoes this sentiment, albeit much more succinctly, in his letter to the Romans (12:4-5). To the church at Ephesus, he describes the church as a "household" that consists of "members" who are "saints" set apart and chosen (Eph. 2:19-22). So, a number of New Testament passages provide a clear definition of the "invisible" or universal Church as including all people in various local assemblies of faithful followers of God, who are committed to serving Him as Lord.

Any definition of the Church that differs from the understanding that it is the body of converted and obedient Christ-followers commissioned to proclaim the Gospel and make disciples by teaching Christ's commands to people is an unbiblical and heretical definition. Two major motivations are the source of redefining what and who the Church is, i.e., power and convenience. Those seeking power redefine the Church to use it as a means of control. One must meet the unscriptural demands of the cult leader, institution, or movement to be accepted as a member of the "True Church." For convenience's sake, others redefine the Church by making the meaning of membership so shallow and ambiguous that it requires little to be considered a part of a local congregation or of the Church universal. Having convenience as a motivation comes in two separate forms. Liberal Protestantism jettisons core doctrines, such as the inerrancy of Scripture and exclusive salvation through Jesus Christ, in the attempt to keep its relevancy in an increasingly secular culture. Many contemporary evangelical churches have shied away from emphasizing radical discipleship, commitment, spiritual and moral obedience, spiritual growth, and sacrifice to make Christianity appear casual and comforting. The watering down of the meaning of serving in the body of Christ has been used as a tactic to lure the unchurched into attending services and increase attendance numbers, as validation of the power or popularity of local or regional leaders.

At its birth in the first century, the Church was known as the committed followers of Jesus Christ who actively fellowship together, make disciples, and serve the Lord. All other subsequent definitions are departures of the biblical concept. True churches seeking to be obedient to the One who created the Church Universal understand this fact.

Ecclesiology:
The Great Commission

Before He ascended, Jesus gave His disciples their mission and purpose while they lived on this Earth. All disciples are to make additional disciples by spreading the Gospel or "Good News" and inviting unbelievers to accept that they are sinners in need of salvation, acknowledge that Jesus the Son of God died on the cross for their sins and rose again, and follow Him. This is what has been called "the Great Commission" by Christians for hundreds of years.

Even the sharing of the Gospel, a hallmark of the Christian faith since its inception, has been subject to rejection and distortion. One type of distortion has occurred in the context of sharing the Gospel to cultures of worldviews vastly different from a biblical one. In this situation, some missionaries have adopted a form of syncretism. Syncretism is the combining of two or more religions to form a completely different belief system. What emerges is often called Christianity, but it is actually something quite different.[202]

Other heresies present obstacles to sharing the Gospel. Universalism undermines the necessity of evangelism, since all people would eventually be saved or, according to modern universalism, every person in the world has already received salvation. Therefore evangelism is unnecessary or merely involves the sharing of the fact that one is already saved. Pluralism considers any religion that holds to some believe in salvation and religious transformation to be a legitimate way to salvation.[203] A version of inclusivism related to evangelism is the belief known as the "wider hope." Some have considered a belief in God based totally on natural theology for those who live in remote regions far from any possible exposure to the Gospel to be sufficient for salvation. Therefore, those acknowledging the unknown god are saved without knowledge of Jesus and His death and resurrection.[204]

---

202 Kevin Greeson, "Effective Bridging and Contextualization," in *Discovering the Mission of God*, eds. Mike Barnett and Robin Martin (Downers Grove: InterVarsity, 2012), 424.

203 Hick, "A Pluralist View," 45.

204 C. Gordon Olson, *What in the World is God Doing?* (Cedar Knolls: Global Gospel Pub., 1994), 38.

Ecclesiology

A heresy arising from an alternate theological perspective is Hyper-Calvinism. Hyper-Calvinism had a significant influence on reformed Congregationalists and Baptists in England during the seventeenth and eighteenth centuries, arguing that God had already chosen and eternally saved the elect. Hence, it was offensive to proclaim the Gospel to people who were already saved or predetermined to be eternally damned.[205] At the turn of the twentieth century, liberal Protestantism in the United States embraced the Social Gospel. Pioneered by Walter Rauschenbusch (1861-1918), the Social Gospel directed its attention towards needs in society in which the Gospel is actually defined as bettering the community and civilization through social action instead of personal salvation through Christ's atonement and resurrection.[206] Much of Progressive Christianity has adopted a variation of the Social Gospel as the true purpose and message of the Kingdom of God. A phenomenon that arose in the twentieth century and still continues, the Prosperity Gospel stresses that salvation through Christ did not only entail a spiritual dimension of forgiveness and eternal life, but also extended to material possessions. Those believers who live in obedience to God will enjoy financial blessings and even strong physical health.[207]

Currently, the dominant motivator for neglecting to proclaim the Gospel message has less to do with unbiblical belief than with unbiblical behavior: apathy. A vast majority of Christians in the West are so fixated on acquiring possessions, preferring the world of entertainment over the world of reality, and pursuing ephemeral conceptions of happiness that they take little thought to evangelize the lost. The widespread apathy of the Church, particularly in the West, is one of the main factors for this civilization's spiritual decline.

From a biblical perspective, ample support for sharing the Good News is found in Scripture. Beginning with the ministry of Jesus, a strong emphasis was placed on sharing the Gospel and making disciples. Jesus told His disciples that they were the light to the world (Matt. 5:14). He

---

205 David J. Engelsma, *Hyper-Calvinism: The Call of the Gospel*, Rev. ed. (Grand Rapids: Reformed Free Publishing Association, 1994), 16-17.

206 George M. Marsden, *Fundamentalism and American Culture*, 2d ed. (Oxford: Oxford University Press, 2006), 91-92.

207 Donald W. McCulloch, *The Trivialization of God: The Dangerous Illusion of a Manageable Deity* (Colorado Springs: Navpress, 1995), 43-46.

stated that pursuing the lost and saving them was His purpose (Luke 19:10). Before He ascended, Jesus explained His expectations for His followers to make disciples (Matt. 28:19-20; Acts 1:8). Jesus also reminded His disciples of the lostness of the world and that workers were needed to share the Gospel (Matt. 9:37-38). After Jesus' earthly ministry, the Early Church consistently spread the Gospel throughout the eastern Roman Empire (Acts 13:4-12; 14:1-28; 16:11-34; 17:1-34; 18:1-16; 19:1-20) and to Rome itself (Acts 23:11; 28:17-31; Rom. 1:7). The history of the Early Church in the Book of Acts portrays obedient believers as those who actively shared the Gospel (Acts 2:14-40; 3:12-29; 6:7, 8-9; 8:5; 9:20; 6:2-23;28:30-31). In his letters, Paul first instructed believers on the content of the Gospel, stating that anyone who desires to accept Christ must acknowledge Jesus as Lord, believe in His resurrection, and call upon Him to receive salvation (Rom. 10:8-13). Paul also emphasized the central importance of evangelism in his ministry as well as in the ministry of every believer (Rom. 1:14-17; 10:14-21; 1 Cor. 2:1-5; 9:15-23; 2 Cor. 5:18-20; 2 Tim. 1:8-12; 4:1-5). When looking at the New Testament in its entirety, one can see that it functions as a presentation of the Gospel of Jesus Christ, since the Gospels contain detailed descriptions of Jesus' identity, life, teaching, ministry, death, and resurrection (Matt. 1:1-28:20; Mark 1:1-16:8; Luke 1:1-24:53; John 1:1-21:25), and other books, mostly letters, give in-depth explanations of the beliefs of Christianity (Rom. 1:18-28; 2:1-3:26; 5:1-6:23; 10:4-13; 1 Cor. 2:6-16; 11:1-34; 12:1-31; 15:1-57; 2 Cor. 5:1-11; 10:1-6; Gal. 1:6-10; 2:11-21; 3:1-29; 4:1-7; Eph. 1:7-14; 2:1-22; 4:1-24; Phil. 2:5-11; 3:17-21; Col. 1:9-23; 2:1-23; 1 Thess. 4:13-18; 5:1-10; 2 Thess. 1:3-10; 2:1-12; Heb. 1:1-14; 2:5-18; 4:12-16; 6:1-20; 7:20-28; 8:7-13; 9:11-28; 10:11-18; 11:1-3; Jas. 2:14-26; 1 Pet. 1:3-12; 2;1-10; 3:18-22; 2 Pet. 1:16-21; 2:8-13; 1 John 2:3-29; Rev. 19:11-21:27). Therefore, the New Testament contains both direct instruction concerning the sharing of the Gospel and making disciples as well as many examples of the fulfillment of the Great Commission.

The subsequent history of the Church after the New Testament details the spread of Christianity to western and northern Europe, Asia, North and South America, and sub-Saharan Africa. From various corners of the world, Christian communities exist because disciples of Jesus conveyed the truth of the message of salvation to the unsaved. Christianity's success came through the work of the Holy Spirit as He used Christians to share the Gospel. If the Church took the position of hyper-Calvinism, which is sometimes deterministic (denying that persons exercise any choice with regard to the Gospel), then it not only may have failed to spread, but it may likely have died out within one to two generations.

Examining the actual content of the Gospel reveals an incredible message for all of mankind. Every human being who thought themselves accursed by the standards of the law and thus believed themselves to be destined to spend an eternity in suffering can escape that punishment by believing in and submitting to Jesus Christ, who died for the sins of the world and rose from the grave. Those who submit to Christ will spend an eternity with the Lord in joyful service and worship. No message on earth is greater than this. So great a message is the Gospel that it must be shared to those who have not heard it, not for proselytizing, as the Jewish leaders of Christ's day (Matt. 23:15) believed, but to invite people openly and sincerely to become a part of the "household of faith" (Gal. 6:10). Those adhering to different belief systems, such as atheism, Buddhism, and Islam, should acknowledge that those sharing the message of Jesus Christ betray only an enthusiasm that Christians have for their faith, just as atheists, Buddhists, and Muslims often betray an enthusiasm for their own faith. Christian enthusiasm for the Gospel should not be offensive but rather winsome and inviting to others to join us in accepting the love of God demonstrated to the world through Christ (John 3:16). It is perfectly reasonable that when one believes and accepts the Gospel, he or she will want others to know about it.

Chapter 8

Angelology

Historical Background:

One of the strangest heretical movements of the ancient world was Manichaeism. Founded by Mani (216 – 274), a Persian, Manichaeism advocated extreme asceticism with the practice of celibacy, poverty, and the consumption of vegetables alone for food. Doctrinally, the Manichees espoused several beliefs contrary to orthodox Christianity. Embracing Docetism, they denied the Incarnation of Christ, believing Him to be divine and merely appearing human.[208] Curiously, Manichaeism was also influenced by pantheism, accepting that every piece of fruit that hung from the tree represented Christ's atonement, and therefore, Christ was actually in each fruit.[209] Thoroughly Gnostic, Manichaeism also rejected the entire Old Testament, because they regarded Yahweh as a separate being from God the Father in the New Testament.[210]

Beyond these theological aberrations, what made Manichaeism so unusual was its elaborate mythology. Inspired by the Zoroastrian-

208 Augustine, *The Confessions*, 5.20, trans. Maria Boulding (New York: Vintage, 1997), 91.

209 Peter Brown, *Augustine of Hippo: A Biography*, 2nd ed., (Berkeley: University of California Press, 2000), 41-42.

210 John J. O'Meara, *The Young Augustine*, 2nd ed. (New York: Alba House, 2001), 52-6. Augustine, *Confessions*, 5.21, 91-2. The Manichees also cast serious doubt on the reliability of the New Testament, alleging its corruption, particularly in the life and ministry of Jesus.

ism of Mani's homeland, Manichaeism understood existence to have two principles: Good and Evil. Equal in power and equally eternal, Good and Evil ruled over separate kingdoms. The principle of Good was ruled by the Father of Greatness, who had five dwellings (attributes): Sense, Reason, Thought, Imagination, and Intention. A vast host of angels served the wishes of the Father of Greatness. Ruled by the Prince of Darkness, the Kingdom of Evil consisted of five gulfs: Evil Smoke, Devouring Fire, Evil Air, Water, and Darkness. Within each gulf, a separate species (demons, quadrupeds, birds, fish, serpents) resided, and within each gulf, a ruler (demon, lion, eagle, fish, serpent) governed. These two kingdoms existed entirely separate from each other until the Prince of Darkness invaded the Kingdom of Light for the purpose of total conquest. Thus began a long war between the Father of Greatness and the Prince of Darkness, each creating beings to combat one another for dominance.[211] For Manichaeism, the eschatological culmination did not involve the ultimate judgment and punishment of evil, but merely the separation of evil from the world. Though this does not sound appealing to Christians, the separation of Light and Darkness for Manichaeism would be permanent, with Darkness never able again to invade the Kingdom of Light.[212]

Manichaeism's mythology depicts a cosmic conflict between good and evil. While differing radically from Christian theology, Manicheism did correctly understand that there is a spiritual reality that human beings are unable to see. The Bible refers to such a reality, not only with regard to God's existence, but also the presence of angels, Satan, and demons. Christians often reserve their polemical defenses primarily for disciplines in the fields of Theology Proper, Christology, and Soteriology, but with little concern for Angelology. Yet, biblical Angelology has also been undermined through various denials and heretical distortions, as the unbiblical worldview of Manichaeism demonstrates. Therefore, it is beneficial to discuss the rationality of the doctrines of angelology.

---

211 Gerald Bonner, *St. Augustine of Hippo: Life and Controversies*, rev. ed. (Norwich: Canterbury, 1986), 162–4.

212 Ibid., 169–70.

Angelology:
Who are the Angels?

Derived from the Greek, *angelos* (meaning "messenger"), an angel is a created spiritual being that glorifies and serves God. Three major tasks are described in the Bible concerning angels. They serve as deliverers of God's message, worshippers of God, and agents of judgment from God. Typically, they are not named, with the exception of Gabriel and Michael; Michael is referred to as an "archangel" in Jude 9.

Compared to the fierce debates concerning doctrinal issues under the categories of the Doctrine of God, Christology, Pneumatology, and Soteriology, the subject of angels appears to be a relatively mild topic. Yet, the doctrine of angels has received its fair share of attacks, starting even before the birth of Christ, and have continued into the twenty-first century. Sadducees may have the distinction of being the first to have had issue with this doctrine, denying that angels actually existed. They claimed that the status of angels was not verified in the Torah, which the Sadducees regarded as the sole extent of God's written revelation.[213] In a similar manner, atheists and agnostics, in their denial of God's existence, reject the notion of angelic beings. More serious issues concerning the belief in the existence of angels relate to the distortion of the biblical concept. Apparently, the church in Colossae encountered the practice of the worship of angels, which Paul denounced (Col. 2:18). This was, sadly, not the last distortion. Over the centuries, some have claimed that angels were sent to present or announce belief systems that were completely contrary to God's Word. Muhammad (570 – 632) claimed that Gabriel presented the teachings that brought about Islam.[214] Joseph Smith (1805 – 1844) asserted that the angel Moroni provided the location of the golden plates, which he translated to produce the Book of Mormon.[215] Then there is the common misconception, often depicted in media and some art, that angels are deceased human beings transformed by God after their death. Emanuel Swedenborg espoused this belief, asserting that humans evolved into angels by spiritual development in the afterlife.[216]

---

213 Eduard Lohse, *The New Testament Environment*, 2d ed., trans. John E. Steely (Nashville: Abingdon, 1974), 75.

214 Shorrosh, *Islam Revealed*, 53–4.

215 Martin, *Kingdom of the Cults*, 228.

216 McDannell and Lang, *Heaven*, 189.

Thinking Rationally About Christian Theology
A Handbook on Polemics

Despite the insistence of the Sadducees and other early skeptics, the Torah did mention angels. An angel intervened to save the life of Hagar and her unborn son, Ishmael (Gen. 16:7-12). Two angels warned Lot that the Lord was soon to bring judgment upon Sodom and Gomorrah (Gen. 19:1-16). Jacob had several encounters with angels, including his dream of angels ascending and descending a staircase or ladder (Gen. 28:12). Jacob also received a message from an angel in a dream (Gen. 31:11-13), met angels while returning to Canaan (Gen. 32:1-2), and even wrestled with an angel (Gen. 32:22-32; Hos. 12:4; although this "angel" may be a theophany). It was an angel who caused a bush to burn but not be consumed to draw the attention of Moses (Exod. 3:2). God sent His angel to go before the Israelites for their protection after they left Egypt (Exod. 14:19; 23:23; Num. 20:16). An angel blocked the way of Balaam, who planned to curse the Israelites, and caused Balaam's donkey to talk (Num. 22:22-35). Further references to angels exist in the Old Testament, including pronouncing God's judgment because of Israel's disobedience (Judg. 2:1-4), calling Gideon to serve as a deliverer of Israel (Judg. 6:11-13, 20-22), announcing the coming birth of Samson (Judg. 13:3-6, 9-21), bringing a plague in judgment against Israel over David's sin (2 Sam. 24:15-16), encouraging Elijah to eat in order to strengthen him on his journey (1 Kgs. 19:5-7), commanding Elijah to proclaim God's message (2 Kgs. 1:3, 15), bringing God's judgment upon Sennacherib's army (2 Kgs. 19:35; Isa. 37:36), and explaining visions to Zechariah and delivering the Lord's message (Zech. 1:7-21; 4:1-6:8). In addition, several Psalms refer to the existence of angels and God's use of them (Ps. 8:5; 34:7; 35:5-6; 78:49; 91:11; 103:20; 104:4; 148:2). All of these concern angels that have the appearance of men, but the Old Testament names two other types of angelic creatures: seraphim, who participate in worship of the Lord (Isa. 6:2-3, 6-7), and cherubim, who serve as messengers and members of God's army (Gen. 3:24; Ezek. 10:1-22; 11:22).

Regarding the mention of angels, the New Testament contains many further passages that ask the reader to accept that angels serve as divine messengers and for judgment. Angels announce the upcoming births of John the Baptist and Jesus (Matt. 1:20-24; Luke 1:11-20, 26-38). At Jesus' birth, an angel informs the shepherds, and a multitude of angels rejoice (Luke 2:9-14). Angels minister to Jesus after His temptation by Satan in the wilderness (Matt. 4:11; Mark 1:13). During His teaching ministry, Jesus stated that angels would separate the righteous from the unrighteous to be eternally judged (Matt. 13:39, 41, 49; 16:27; 24:31; Mark 13:27). Before Jesus' arrest, an angel came to strengthen Him in preparation for His ordeal (Luke 22:43). At the resurrection of Jesus, it was an angel who rolled away the stone at the tomb's entrance (Matt. 28:2), and it was angels who informed Jesus' disciples that He was risen (Matt. 28:5-6; Mark 16:5-7; Luke 24:23; John 20:11-13). In the early days of the Church, an angel spoke to Cornelius the Roman centurion to seek out Peter in order to hear the Gospel (Acts 10:3-6). Peter was freed from prison by an angel after he was arrested on orders by Herod Agrippa I (Acts 12:1-10). According to John's vision, angels will administer God's judgment upon the earth during the tribulation (Rev. 8:6-9:16; 14:9-19; 15:1-16:18). John shows that they will war against Satan (Rev. 12:7-9) and will take Satan to the bottomless pit (or abyss), where he will reside during Christ's millennial reign (Rev. 20:1-3). With so many references to angels in the Bible, it would be impossible to divorce this belief from Scripture.

A tendency exists to see the work of angels and even angelic appearances everywhere and at a constant rate. This tendency often devolves to the veneration of angels as beings worthy of worship, a practice that God's angel specifically prohibit in Rev. 19:10 and 22:9. Although biblical Christianity acknowledges the existence and continued work of angels, it also understands God to work in many ways, such as His providence and through His people, and not exclusively through angels. Furthermore, when angels perform their duties, it is ultimately God who receives the credit, because they are simply fulfilling His commands.

By the standards set by the secular humanistic culture so predominant in the West, belief in the existence of angels borders on fantasy. However, the existence of angels makes sense in this universe, which functions by information. All beings must have some information to rely on, and humans especially must have a considerable amount of knowledge to survive. Information is received through communication. Communication can come through numerous sources, and the most valued communication is that of an authority. When an authority delivers information, that information is accepted and respected. A scientist sharing his findings that result from extensive research is regarded as factual and trustworthy. God communicates information that humanity needs to hear. Much of that comes from His Word, which is the Bible, but there are times when information must be immediate and directly communicated. Angels are the means by which God offers such communication. Being in the presence of God (Luke 1:19), angels have direct access to Him, and the messages they deliver can be fully trusted. Because this universe and its inhabitants rely on information, it is reasonable to believe that God sends trustworthy messengers to communicate information that He desires others to hear.

As agents acting in service to God, angels function in a like manner to human followers of God. Both act in service to the Lord; angels operate on a grander scale due to the knowlege they have that human beings do not. If one questions why God would use angels, one may also wonder why God created mankind and offers them the opportunity to serve Him. Most individuals find significance serving a cause greater than themselves and acknowledge it as the greatest possible fulfillment. God offering humanity and other created beings fulfillment through service to Him is consistent with His nature in His bestowal of the gift of life. It is generally accepted that life is a gift preferable to nonexistence. A gift that would make life even more meaningful is the opportunity to base one's life in service to the Creator of life. Therefore, angels exist to serve God and to communicate God's grace and favor.

Confronting distorted beliefs about angels will be an issue for many believers, due to the popular distortions concerning them. Unfortunately, even many Christians hold to unbiblical ideas regarding angels due to their reliance on popular cultural concepts rather than Scripture. Narratives that describe angelic revelations divulging unbiblical doctrines present difficulties for those who adhere to them. These narratives were presented to substantiate the teachings of groups whose beliefs do not adhere to Scripture. Muslims and the Latter-Day Saints have doctrines and worldviews radically different from the message of the Old and New Testament. The message of Scripture is to be trusted over the Qur'an and the Book of Mormon, first because Scripture predates the aforementioned writings and then because of the Bible's substantiated accuracy. Being servants of the Lord like the true prophets of old, angels would not proclaim messages that contradict God's revelation, as Paul has attested ((2 Cor. 11:14; Gal.1:8), and so it is logical to assume that the contrary testimonies of books of Islam and of Latter-Day Saints are simply false.

Recorded events in Scripture that detail the appearances and work of angels amaze those who read them. As servants of the Lord, angels are extensions of His justice and His vengeance, as well as of His mercy and His grace. Believing in them demonstrates an acceptance of the trustworthiness of Scripture and coincides with the nature of the universe in its reliance on information.

Angelology:
Satan and Demons

His official title is "the Satan" (Hebrew) or "the Adversary," as such opposing both God and humanity. He goes by other names, including the devil ("Slanderer"; Matt. 13:39; Acts 10:38), Beelzebub the ruler of demons (Mark 3:22; Luke 11:15), and the ruler of this world (John 12:31; 14:30; 16:11).[217] By nature a spiritual being, Satan engages in an unceasing war against the Lord and His creation. Part of that war involves drawing human beings away from God through temptation and deception. Assisting Satan are his demons, the angels that rebelled with him and have joined him in his war against God and the rest of His creation.

Like the doctrines of God and Christology, the biblical beliefs related to Satan have also faced distortion. In Marcion's version of Gnosticism, Satan was a creation of the Demiurge, the evil god who created material existence. So, Satan was not the chief adversary against good, but a servant of the chief adversary.[218] Another Gnostic, Tatian, had a developed demonology. He believed that demons were once angels who became demons when they alienated themselves from God. Once this alienation occurred, they became more material in existence, similar to fire or air. The devil, according to Tatian, was the first-born of the demons and the first angel to rebel against God and become a demon.[219] Lactantius (c. 250 – c. 325) used figurative language to describe Satan's relationship with God the Father and the Son. Metaphorically, Satan was the son that the Father hated since he represented evil, and Christ was the Son He loved because of His goodness. Jesus and Satan represented two principles: good and evil. The angels were created after God established the two principles, and those that followed the good principle remained in Heaven and served God, while

---

217 By typographical convention, the names "Satan" & "Beelzebub" are capitalized, whereas "devil" never is (ESV).

218 Jeffrey Burton Russell, *Satan: The Early Christian Tradition* (Ithaca: Cornell University, 1981), 57–58.

219 Ibid., 73–4.

those who followed evil became demons and were cast out of Heaven.[220] A popular legend related to Satan emerged in the early Middle Ages and was written down in Latin verse by the tenth century. It was the legend of Theophilus, who made a pact with the devil to surrender his soul so that he might become a bishop. According to the legend, when Theophilus sensed that his life was soon to end, he repented and called upon the Virgin Mary for help. Mary intervened and forced the devil to return the written pact.[221] Numerous variations of Theophilus' pact featuring stories of a "deal with the devil" have been told and written down for centuries. Meant to be cautionary tales, these legends later relegated Satan to making pacts to tempt the world and the Church to fall into sin. The Bogomils and the Carthari, during the High Middle Ages, placed Satan on an equal level with God, including the act of his role in creation. Some of the Cathari also believed that human souls were actually fallen angels who were condemned to inhabit human bodies as a means of penance.[222] When the Enlightenment of the eighteenth century began to have its impact, Satan and demonic beings were taken less seriously. Personified evil in the form of Satan and fallen angels made for good entertainment, but these were not taken as beings who could seriously be thought to tempt and lead individuals astray. In the modern period, Satan was often portrayed symbolically. Alphonse-Louis Constant (1810 – 1875), depicted Satan as a positive force for revolution and liberty.[223] By the twentieth century, Satan was treated in the West as superstition; fascinating as fiction, Satan was hardly thought to be a real being among moderns.[224]

As secular humanism continues to grow stronger in influence, belief in Satan, the devil, or the Prince of Darkness and his demonic host is increasingly seen as archaic, passé, and even naïve. Why would any rational person living in the twenty-first century believe in a powerful, malevolent being who wages war against God and tempts humans to sin? This attitude did not first rise out of secularism but found its origins with the advent of higher biblical criticism in the nineteenth century.

---

220 Russell, *Satan: The Early Christian Tradition*, 153–4.

221 Robert Muchembled, *A History of the Devil: From the Middle Ages to the Present*, trans. Jean Birrell (Cambridge: Polity, 2003), 114.

222 Pelikan, *Christian Tradition*, 239–41.

223 Muchembled, *A History of the Devil*, 199.

224 Ibid., 217.

Angelology

Adherents of this school of thought have stated that belief in Satan or the devil comes not from Hebrew thought, but a syncretistic adoption of Zoroastrian beliefs. The argument does not stand due to anachronism; the fact is that Zoroastrianism could not have impacted the Bible within the time frame when Judaism, during the Babylonian Exile and Early Persian Rule (605-538 BC), supposedly was influenced by this religion. Also, the comparisons between Jewish and Zoroastrian doctrines yield no real similarity.[225] Furthermore, as with all other doctrines, the existence of Satan and demons proves to be absolutely rational as a belief.

When developing a biblical doctrine of Satan and demons, Christians should consider that much that is perceived as the biblical view of Satan is not actually biblical. The popular depictions of the horned being with a tail and hooves who rules over hell as his kingdom is, in fact, based on superstition and famous descriptions in literature and media, stemming from images as old as the ancient Greek mythological creature, the satyr. Like the popular caricature of the devil, the satyr was portrayed as half-goat and half human, but this imagery is not found in any part of the Bible.[226] Other distortions occur with cults, including the Latter-Day Saints who argue that Satan is a divine being who is one of the many spirit offspring of God and is therefore a brother to Jesus Christ.[227] Due to a dualistic understanding of reality, popular Christian culture believes Satan and his kingdom to have more power than they actually have, being blamed for every known evil affecting mankind. Conversely, Satan and demons are depicted as beings so limited that human beings can combat them on their own strength and ability. These representations have little to do with the biblical description of Satan or fallen angels. No Christian should waste his time defending such misrepresentations. In addition, Christians should (but do not always) argue that if one already believes in Satan, then the best source to build one's doctrinal understanding of Satan is the Bible, which has proven itself historically and prophetically accurate.

---

225 Winfried Corduan, "The Date of Zoroaster: Some Apologetic Considerations" in *Presbyterion* 23:1 (1997), 40-2.

226 Henry Ansgar Kelley, *Satan: A Biography* (Cambridge: Cambridge University Press, 2006), 295.

227 Bruce R. McConkie, *Mormon Doctrine*, 2d ed. (Salt Lake City: Bookcraft, 1966), 192-3.

Thinking Rationally About Christian Theology
A Handbook on Polemics

Biblically, Satan is discussed in numerous passages throughout the New Testament and a few Old Testament passages as well. In the Old Testament, he is Job's tormentor (Job 1:6-12; 2:1-8) and Joshua the high priest's accuser (Zech. 3:1-2). In the Gospels, he is Jesus' tempter (Matt. 4:1-11; Mark 1:13; Luke 4:1-13), Judas' possessor (Luke 22:3; John 13:27), and the father of lies (John 8:44). In Paul's letters, the devil misleads the Church in proclaiming a false gospel (2 Cor. 11:13-15) and tempts believers (Eph. 4:27; 6:11; 1 Tim. 3:6-7; 2 Tim. 2:26). James exhorts readers of his letter to resist Satan (Jas. 4:7). Peter warns that Satan prowls over the earth like a lion wanting to ruin lives (1 Pet. 5:8). According to the vision John received, Satan is portrayed as a red dragon who wars against the Lord, His Son, Israel, and the saints of God (Rev. 12:1-17). By John's testimony, Satan will also face defeat (Rev. 12:7-9; 20:1-3, 7--9) and be cast into the lake of fire (Rev. 20:10).

In addition to the passages discussing Satan, far more passages found in the New Testament depict the activity of demons or evil spirits. Demonic activity in the Gospels is primarily devoted to their possession of individuals and their subsequent exorcising by Jesus (Matt. 4:24; 8:16, 28-33; 9:32-34; 12:22; 17:14-18; Mark 1:32-34; 5:1-20; 7:26-30; 16:9; Luke 4:33-35, 41; 7:21; 8:2, 26-36; 9:38-42;). The Early Church also encountered these fallen angels and, through the name of Jesus and the power of the Holy Spirit, freed many who were under their oppression (Acts 5:16; 8;7; 19:12). Paul warned of demons who ruled over the powers of darkness in the world (Eph. 6:12) and posed as gods (1 Cor. 10:20-21) and deceived those within the Church by unbiblical doctrines (1 Tim. 4:1). John described a host of demons led by Abaddon/Apollyon sent to torment unbelievers during the tribulation (Rev. 9:1-11) and demons working with Satan, the antichrist, and the false prophet (Rev. 16:13).

One of the most controversial topics in relation to Satan deals with his origins. How did Satan come into being? Did God create him as the evil adversary? Traditionally, two passages in the Old Testament are considered sources for the origins of Satan. Isaiah 14:12-15 and Ezekiel 28:11-19 warn the King of Babylon and the King of Tyre of impending judgment. The passages describe their pride and their impending fall due to God's judgment. Both accounts are designated as the origins of beliefs about Satan's character, and this designation goes back to the second and third centuries in their interpretations by Origen, who doubted that the description of the Lucifer of Babylon and the King of Tyre could be attributed to a mere human being and must be applied to an angelic being who became corrupted.[228] These passages have continued to be popular depictions of Satan's origins into the modern era among evangelicals, notably by H. A. Ironside (1876 - 1951)[229] and, more recently, by Donald Grey Barnhouse (1895 - 1960).[230] While the imagery of the claims made by the two monarchs suggests something more than what earthly kings can accomplish and can therefore be considered as a possible reference to Satan's original state and subsequent rebellion, they do not specifically name Satan, although Isaiah 14:12, 15 says that the king of Babylon, having fallen from heaven, was brought down to Sheol and to the far reaches of the pit. Stronger references are available in Scripture and may be used to build a foundation for how Satan came to be the adversary of God and man. Two such passages fit the needed requirements. They are 2 Peter 2:4 and Jude 6, which describe God's judgment upon angels who sinned and rebelled against Him. The fact that Jesus describes Satan as one who was a "murderer from the beginning" of human history and "the father of lies" indicates that Satan was not only a part of this rebellion, but actually led it (John 8:44).

Clearly, to dismiss all of the verses indicating Satan's existence and his activity would require a rejection of a large portion of the New Testament, primarily portions of the Gospels. As has been discussed previously, the Gospels have demonstrated consistent accuracy with regard to historical names, places, and events. Discounting passages discussing Satan and demonic activity because they are supernatural beings betrays an anti-supernatural bias. It is not unreasonable to approach passages describing Satan and demonic activity as reliable given the overall reliability of the Gospels.

In the twenty-first century, how can a Christian present a reasonable defense for the existence of Satan and demons? One can present a solid defense on the basis of free will. A degree of free will exists for human beings, as is evident in their decisions. While many circumstances happen that are beyond the control of humans, they make decisions that are entirely their own. If no free will existed, then every behavioral pattern

---

228 Origen, *First Principles*, 6.5, 50; 8.3, 70.

229 H.A. Ironside, *Expository Notes on the Prophet Isaiah* (New York: Loizeuax Brothers, 1952), 88–90.

230 Donald Grey Barnhouse, *The Invisible War: The Panorama of the Continuing Conflict between Good and Evil* (Grand Rapids: Zondervan, 1996).

of every human being would be completely predictable. Yet, humans continuously surprise one another with their actions. Employees suddenly quit their jobs after years of faithful service. Dedicated spouses leave their mates without warning in order to have affairs. To argue that these decisions were still predetermined is inconsistent with the universally accepted sense of justice in the world. When an immoral act is performed or a crime is committed, legal blame is always directed toward the person who committed the act. The decision ultimately is the responsibility of the individual. If human beings bear responsibility for their actions, human beings must then have a degree of free will. If angels exist, as has been argued earlier, then it is reasonable to believe that God gave angels a degree of free will similar to the free will He gave human beings. Similar to humans, angels had the opportunity to serve God or rebel against Him. According to Scripture, a portion of the angelic population did exercise their free will to disobey God and, according to Scripture, Satan was their leader in battle (Rev. 12:7).

An obvious argument for the existence of Satan and demons is the well-attested and accepted reality of moral evil in this world (see earlier discussion on sin as needing salvation). Much evil, specifically the unspeakable horrors of rape, incest, murder by torture, and genocide, has been attributed to human beings. Yet, while such actions must be blamed on those who committed them, one must wonder what inspired such evil. Examining the practices of human sacrifice to the Aztec gods and the ritual slayings of children in the name of the cultic worship of the Hindu goddess Kali cause most to recoil in repulsion, as did the child sacrifice to Molech in Leviticus 20:1–5. However, it is necessary to wonder how those types of beliefs and practices originated. Would humans wish for beings of this nature to exist and then form a mythology and ritual worship around them to then follow through with their depraved desires? Humans are evil, but the depths of their evil cannot be explained merely by an interior source; belief in supernatural evil provides a better grasp of why the world is so thoroughly corrupt.

In defending the existence and activity of fallen angels, one might attempt to utilize well-documented case studies of demonic possession chronicled from instances around the world in the last century. Such events may sway some, but most secularists will dismiss them by claiming them to be the symptoms of extreme cases of mental illness. However, what cannot be dismissed is the knowledge that such possessed victims

Angelology

share, knowledge that they could not have known by any human means. That kind of behavior and its common rationale suggests supernatural rather than psychological origin.

The existence of the devil and his fallen angels has always been accepted by those who believe in the Word of God. Skepticism's dominance in the twenty-first century does not remove Satan's or his demons' influence. To pretend that supernatural evil does not exist ignores the evidence of Scripture and the evidence of a depraved world and places one in grave peril.

Chapter 8

Eschatology

Historical Background:

In the northwestern portion of the Westphalia region in what is now known as the nation of Germany, there lies a town named Münster. During the early period of the Protestant Reformation, Münster came under the control of radical Anabaptists. They renamed the town, "New Jerusalem" and thoroughly reorganized the government, laws, and policies of what became an Anabaptist stronghold. An early attempt at communism was mandated for all citizens with the abolishment of private property and the monetary system. Jan van Leiden, one of the Anabaptist leaders in the town, was eventually proclaimed king. He believed his mission was to conquer the world in order to spread his form of Christendom to prepare it for Christ's return and the inauguration of the Millennial Reign. In addition to the abolition of private property, the policy of polygamy was introduced. Jan van Leiden himself took fifteen wives. After a prolonged siege, the town of Münster succumbed to forces led by the city's exiled Catholic bishop in 1535. Jan van Leiden and two other leaders, Bernhard Knipperdolling and Bernhard Krechting, were tortured and executed. Their bodies were placed in cages and hanged from the steeple of St. Lambert's Church in Münster as a deterrent against any further insurrections.[231]

To say that the Münster radicals were motivated by their eschatological beliefs would be an understatement, and they certainly

---

231 Hans Hillerbrand, ed. *The Reformation* (Grand Rapids: Baker, 1972), 253–66

earned the designation "radical." Certainly, the Münster Anabaptists took their interpretation of the Christ Second Coming to an extreme. However, twenty-first century Christians should not think themselves immune from errant beliefs concerning earth's final days and the eternal destination of humanity. Two common errors occur among Christians with regard to eschatology. First, they ignore the study of the Second Coming and last things out of fear or apathy. Secondly, they surmise that because eschatology is concerned with the future, they are free to develop their own beliefs with or without Scripture. The lackadaisical attitude towards God's plan for eternity opens the door to unbiblical beliefs concerning eschatology. Christians, then, must study what the Bible declares about the doctrine of last things and prepare themselves to respond to unbiblical ideas purporting to be sound eschatological teachings.

Eschatology:
The Second Coming of Christ

The day is coming when Christ will return. He will come in judgment against the antichristian beast and the false prophet and the armies that stand with them. After defeating the antichristian beast and Satan, Jesus will establish a millennial reign of perfect peace and unimaginable prosperity over the entire world. This has been the hope for believers from the beginning.

Jesus' return, while eagerly awaited by those who call Him "Lord," strikes atheists and agnostics as sheer fantasy. The end of the world for secularists will come five billion years in the future with the death of the sun, or due to the effects of human-induced climate change, or through devastating war. Some still have a positive hope for the future. Marxism, along with its calls for revolution, has utopian dreams for a future society, where there will be perfect justice and all of mankind will be free from oppression.[232] Liberation Theology moves from a literal understanding of the coming eschaton to an emphasis on the community of believers establishing justice and bringing about liberation for all of creation.

---

232 Muchembled, *A History of the Devil*, 218.

Eschatology

According to Liberation Theologians, this will not occur at a future for which believers must wait, but is their responsibility to inaugurate.[233] The New Age movement also proclaims an eschaton brought about by man, but through heightened spirituality. When mankind pursues enlightenment through the power of the universal energy or mana, the world will be transformed to become a heaven on Earth with the trials of the current world erased.[234]

Within Christendom, the spectrum of belief with regard to Christ's Second Coming is long and wide. Albert Schweitzer (1875 – 1965) held the unique position that Jesus' teachings were properly understood through an eschatological perspective, but that this perspective was not realized because of the finality of Jesus' death. Christians who interpret the book of Revelation from the preterist position view much of that book of the New Testament as having been fulfilled. Charles H. Dodd (1884 – 1973) claimed that Jesus completely ushered in the Kingdom of God during His ministry and that the eschaton has already been fulfilled. James Stuart Russell (1816 – 1895) had a slightly more moderate view, understanding that much of the prophecies of Daniel and of John in Revelation were fulfilled with the Roman Empire's destruction of Jerusalem and the burning of the Temple in 70 AD. However, Russell did hold to future and final fulfillment at a yet undesignated time.[235] Rudolf Bultmann (1884 – 1976), indebted to existentialism, emphasized the coming Kingdom of God ushered in by Christ as happening at the moment when a person decides to follow Jesus, rather than as a future event.[236]

Unquestionably, the Second Coming of Christ is a treasured belief in Christianity and rooted in Scripture. Numerous passages mention Christ's return. Jesus warned that His Second Coming would come at a time unexpected (Matt. 24:36–44; 25:1–13; Luke 21:34–36), as a thief in the night, a tradition with which John (Apoc. 16:15) also accords. In addition to the suddenness of His return, Jesus explained that His Second Coming would reveal Him in all of His power and majesty while descending

---

233 Muchembled, *A History of the Devil*, 81.

234 Kyle, *Religious Fringe*, 294.

235 R. C. Sproul, *The Last Days According to Jesus*, (Grand Rapids: Baker, 1998), 20–25.

236 John C. McDowell and Scott A. Kirkland, *Eschatology* (Grand Rapids: Eerdmans, 2018), 44–5.

from the clouds (Matt. 16:27; 24:30-31; Mark 8:38; 14:62; Luke 9:26). The Apostle Paul reiterated Jesus' declarations about His return, including its imminence and unexpectedness (1 Thess. 5:2) and the display of Christ in all His glory (1 Cor. 4:5; Col. 3:4; 1 Thess. 4:16-17; Titus 2:13). For most believers, the passages from the Apocalypse (Revelation) are the ones most readily remembered concerning the return of Christ. There, Jesus' Second Coming is depicted as revealing His majesty and power (Rev. 1:7; 19:11-16) and also the imminence of His return (Rev. 22:6-21). Revelation also informs its readers that when Jesus returns, He will defeat the enemies of God, namely Satan, the antichristian beast, the false prophet, and their followers, and set up His millennial reign (Rev. 19:11-21; 20:1-6; 22:5). When examining the passages concerning Christ's return, two aspects emerge: the sudden coming of the Son of God when it is least expected so that His servants should be watchful (John 14:3) and the appearance of the Son of God to claim and conquer the earth to rid it of evil (Acts 17:31). The distinctiveness and separate nature of these two aspects suggests that Christ will return to collect His saints at one point and then come in glory to establish His millennial reign at a later point.

For believers, the ultimate hope and expectation is for Christ's return. Any future destiny that omits or differs from Christ's return is not a biblical belief. Many movements, including social and political utopias, have adopted the rhetoric of ushering in a new era to the point that their prospective efforts will lead to some form of Messianic age. Christians know from the testimony of Scripture that humanity is thoroughly sinful and therefore cannot itself bring about any type of Messianic age (Rom. 1:18-32; Rev. 5:1-14). Thus, Christians must be careful not to be caught up in movements, political, social, or otherwise, or attach themselves to leaders that promise what only Christ can fulfill. Furthermore, it should be clear that an allegorical return of Christ in any shape or fashion cannot bring about lasting transformation. Only a literal return of Jesus will bring the world into the ideal state as God intends. Religious and political leaders have attempted to bring about true change, but have failed miserably. The sinless Savior and Son of God alone can fulfill a new age of godliness and obedience that will transform humanity (Rev. 20:4-6).

In addition to the strong Scriptural testimony, believers should be encouraged that Christ's return is a doctrine that is logical, a property founded on a proper, clear understanding of the past and the nature of history. Pantheistic worldviews such as Stoicism and segments of

Eschatology

Hinduism regard history from a cyclical standpoint: history will repeat itself over and over again. Secular humanism looks at history from a linear perspective. Events and circumstances move in one direction to a goal. Many secularists optimistically believe that mankind is evolving and will eventually achieve unimaginable scientific progress. Evidence for a linear perspective comes by way of examining technological and medical advancements and scientific discoveries in the last two centuries. Mankind does appear to have moved forward in some respects and seems to continue to move forward with new discoveries. Furthermore, the universe is aging, and there are no indicators that it will reverse the aging process and renew itself, as a cyclical history would suggest. A linear perspective presents itself as the more logical of the two options.

Like humanism, the Bible argues for a linear perspective of history. Unlike humanism, the end goal of history is solely achieved on the efforts of God alone (Rev. 19:11–21; 20:1–3; 21:1–8). How is the biblical end of human history superior? Humans cannot ignore the demand for justice. The innate sense of right and wrong exists within human beings. Outrage occurs when wrongs are committed and go unpunished. Justice demands an ultimate end to evil. Despite their achievements, mankind has not advanced morally. As the genocides by Nazi Germany, the Soviet Union, the Peoples Republic of China, and the Khmer Rouge multiply, and as the widespread acceptance of abortion and the normalization of homosexual marriage and transgenderism demonstrate, humanity has become increasingly immoral and evil in the last century. To make matters worse, there is no sign that humanity will correct itself. For millennia, mankind has established civilizations, each having unique social structures and governments. Yet, during all that time, no human solution has been discovered to rid the world of evil. The solution, therefore, must exist outside of mankind. That solution must come from One who has far superior resources to put an end to evil. Mankind cannot exist indefinitely while evil continues to exist and grow.

An examination of evil will demonstrate that it is always detrimental to its environment. Adultery, physical and sexual abuse, enslavement, and murder all have a destructive impact on a community, as is evident by the trauma experienced by the victims and their loved ones. Evil cannot exist indefinitely. Eventually, evil destroys everything that it corrupts: individuals, families, societies, governments, and civilizations. Historians, for example, admit that the Roman Empire fell largely due to corruption from within. Evil, if left unchecked, will ultimately destroy this world. If one is inclined to believe that a human solution exists to put an end to evil, one should recognize that evil is embedded in the world, because evil exists within human beings. No attempts of utopia have succeeded, because, despite the removal of the trappings of the modern world, every utopia contains people, and people are sinners, "deceitful and desperately sick" (Jer. 17:9 ESV). Therefore, only a being of supreme power and intelligence can accomplish this task. Only one worldview, the Christian one, properly conceives of victory over sin and evil. Some worldviews, such as Islam and Zoroastrianism, depict the final victory of their concept of God, but do not explain how God ultimately defeats sin. Only the New Testament supplies the intricate solution of personal salvation that leads to God's perfection in heaven, with its three stages of justification, sanctification, and glorification; only the global salvation of Christ can restore the world to perfection (Rom. 8:33; 1 Thess. 5:23; Rev. 20:4-6; 21:1-4; 22:14-15). Therefore, it is rational to believe that Jesus Christ will come and usher in a glorious millennial reign and ultimately transform the world into a perfect state.

Eschatology:
Heaven

When referring to "heaven," Christians are typically speaking of the abode of God and the place where believers depart to after death. However, heaven can also be used to describe that place, or all of the sky and the universe above humanity. Theologians refer to it as the "intermediate state" for believers, due to the fact that it does not represent the final stage for followers of Christ. Heaven's existence has been a comfort for Christians for two millennia and a treasured assurance for those who have lost family members and friends. Despite this fact, some dispute the possibility of heaven or its existence.

Early deniers of the afterlife were the Jewish sect, the Sadducees. Their acceptance of only the Torah as Scripture caused them to reject any notion of the afterlife (Matt. 22:23; Mark 12:18; Luke 20:27; Acts 23:8). Most denials of heaven came in the modern age, beginning with the nineteenth century. Ludwig Feuerbach (1804 - 1872) asserted that the concept of heaven resulted from fear of death. Human desires for immortality fostered the belief in a pleasant afterlife. Heaven, for Karl Marx (1818 - 1883), was the ultimate result of human socioeconomic alienation. The privations and sufferings of the present world lessened if there was a promise of a far better life at the end of the current miserable one. Sigmund Freud (1856 - 1939) saw heaven as an illusion created by the unsatisfied desires of the human heart. Religion itself developed from a longing for a perfect father which evolved into God, and heaven was an escapist fantasy for millions of people who yearn for the unmet wishes of their hearts to be fulfilled.[237]

The biblical testimony of eternal life for believers is quite strong. Though some have argued that heaven is only referred to in the New Testament, there are hints of life after death in the Old Testament, as Jesus Himself pointed out to the Sadducees in quoting Exodus 3:6 (Matt. 22:31-32; Mark 12:26-27; Luke 20:37-38). In the Old Testament, there are also passages that depict the scenes of God in His heavenly court (Job 1:6; 2:1; Isa. 6:1-8; Zech. 3:1-3).

While the Old Testament has several references to heaven, many more are found in the New Testament. During His ministry, Jesus repeatedly confirmed its existence. According to His teaching, His followers would receive eternal life (Matt. 19:29; 25:46; Mark 10:30; Luke 10:25; John 4:36; 6:54; 10:28; 12:25), and part of that eternal life would occur in Heaven (John 3:12-17; 14:1-6). In the story of the Rich Man and Lazarus recorded in the Gospel of Luke, Heaven's inhabitants enjoy peace, joy, and fellowship with other believers (Luke 16:22, 25). John experienced a descriptive journey to Heaven, where he witnessed the exultant and joyous worship of both God the Father and the Son (Rev. 4:1-11; 5:8-14; 7:9-17). One of the most celebratory depictions of Heaven is found in Revelation Chapter Nineteen, where all of God's people enjoy the Marriage Supper of the Lamb (Rev. 19:6-9). At this Supper, believers, as the Bride of Christ, will enjoy fellowship with one another in the presence of God. True followers of Christ will find encouragement in the pages of Scripture because many references to the reality and the joyous descriptions of Heaven exist in God's written revelation.

One objection to heaven is that if it is a real place, then where is it located and why has it not been found? This is not a strong argument

---

237 Alister E. McGrath, *A Brief History of Heaven*, (Oxford: Blackwell, 2003), 146-9.

against the existence of heaven, because humanity's knowledge of the universe is limited. There are many things beyond the reach of human discovery. So, one cannot argue that a lack of evidence proves positively that heaven does not exist. Historically, most Christians have considered heaven to be beyond the access of humans through their own efforts, because it is in a separate sphere of existence. This is what Jesus seems to imply through the words of Abraham in His story of the Rich Man and Lazarus (Luke 16:26). If heaven exists in a separate sphere, then no amount of state-of-the-art technology can find it.

For those who find heaven implausible, another common charge against it is that it is too good to be true. Heaven, they explain, is only rational for those who wish it to be so. However, this argument would only work if nothing good existed in the world. If the world was completely and utterly miserable, having nothing that provided pleasure, then one might make the case that nothing wonderful could come after death and that death itself was a blessed finality. Yet the world, despite the suffering contained in it, also has beauty, love, friendship, marriage, music, delicious foods, and laughter. These wonderful things demonstrate the possibility that something as wonderful as heaven could exist.

Deniers of heaven should also ask why so many traditions over the centuries and all over the world have some sort of doctrine of a peaceful afterlife. The Fields of Aaru of Egyptian mythology, Valhalla of Scandinavian mythology, Paradise of Zoroastrianism, and Jannah of Islam all depict a form of enjoyable and everlasting afterlife. While the common belief of an afterlife provides plausibility for any kind of version of the hereafter, the Christian can look to the multitude of instances of fulfilled prophecy in the Bible, particularly the coming of Jesus, to find assurance in the accuracy of the biblical descriptions of Heaven. If the Bible consistently and accurately predicted a number of events and occurrences, then one can expect the descriptions of Heaven to be equally accurate.

A word of caution should be issued to believers who take artistic liberties in describing Heaven. Over the years, a number of individuals, both from within the Church and without, have attempted to make Heaven more appealing through vivid descriptions. Oftentimes, this results in relegating Heaven to the ceaseless participation in favorite hobbies, particularly sports and leisure. Not a few have spoken fondly of Heaven as a place where individuals will continuously fish from a lake teaming with the largest fish or playing perfect games of baseball with some of the greatest names in the sport. One should not be discouraged from longing to be in the presence of God in Heaven, but he should remember that Heaven is first the abode of God. Every description of Heaven in the Bible depicts believers worshipping the Lord and not of persons leisurely left to their own devices. Therefore, every activity in Heaven focuses on God and on pleasing Him and not on our own earthly wish-fulfillments.

Heaven, the intermediate state, is an actual place, a place yearned for by believers and a place where followers of Christ will rejoin loved ones. Though often ridiculed as the product of pure sentimentality, Heaven represents a promise from the Savior of the World, who assured all those who believe in Him that they will one day see it with their own eyes. True believers are not ashamed to believe in Heaven; they look forward to the day when they will be there.

Eschatology:
Hell

Satan and his angels' final destination and the eternal destination for all those who reject the salvation provided by and through Jesus Christ is called by many names, e.g. "Gehenna" in the Old Testament and the Gospels. In the New Testament, it is referred to as "hell," described as a place of immeasurable and intense suffering. Those who must enter hell have no hope of escape or rest from its torments.

Of all the beliefs in Christian theology, the doctrine of Hell has the reputation for being the most maligned and the most misunderstood. Literature and popular portrayals in film and television have distorted the purpose of Hell. Milton's *Paradise Lost* depicts Hell as the Kingdom of Satan, where the Prince of Darkness reigns with an iron fist.[238] The twentieth century witnessed attempts to depict Hell humorously by portraying it, particularly in comics, as a place where demons have fun torturing their denizens in odd ways. Yet hell, according to the testimony of Scripture, is not Satan's current abode, nor a place of enjoyment for him or for his demons.

---

238 Milton, *Paradise Lost*, 1, 263, l. 1674 (URL https://www.poetryfoundation.org/poems/45718/paradise-lost-book-1-1674-version, accessed January 25, 2023): "Better to reign in Hell, than serve in Heav'n."

The first major heresy to reject the doctrine of Hell was Universalism. Origen's version of Universalism believed that Hell had the temporary purpose of purging sin and corruption from all living beings. Once this process was completed, all of Hell's residents would enter Heaven, including Satan himself. [239] Modern Universalism has no need for Hell, due to the fact that all individuals have no need for salvation or a spiritual purification process because they are saved already.[240] A doctrine accepted in the Medieval Church and still adhered to by many Roman Catholics today is that of purgatory. It originated from the text of Second Maccabees 12:39–45, where Judas Maccabee is recorded to have made a propitiation for Jewish soldiers who had been killed so that their sins could be forgiven after death.[241] Later developments built up an entire doctrine of a place where sinners could purify themselves of their sins so that they might enter Heaven, offering a second chance after death.[242] In more recent years, Hell's existence has become a popular excuse for skeptics to dismiss Christianity as a judgmental and narrow religion. John A. T. Robinson (1919 - 1983), in the attempt to maintain an urgency of the Gospel and yet embrace universalism, explained that from God's viewpoint, Hell does not exist. Yet, for unbelievers, hell functions as a means to draw them to Christ and believe in the Gospel.[243] Unlike Universalism, Annihilationism asserts that the wicked will be punished, but instead of eternal punishment, God will assign them to obliteration or eternal nonexistence.[244] Holding to a similar view of Origen's universalism, some evangelicals do not believe that hell is ultimately a place for the eternal suffering of unbelievers, but an opportunity for redemption, claiming that evangelism will occur in hell, according to Ephesians 4:8-10. Since much of the world did not have the opportunity to hear the Gospel, inhabitants of hell will be evangelized and be given the choice to follow Christ. More recently, N. T. Wright has

---

239 Origen, *First Principles*, 3.6, 250-251.

240 Olson, *World*, 38.

241 Jerry L. Walls, *Purgatory: The Logic of Total Transformation* (Oxford: Oxford University, 2012), 12.

242 Ibid., 23.

243 Allison, *Historical Theology*, 718.

244 David George Moore, *The Battle for Hell: A Survey and Evaluation of Evangelicals' Growing Attraction to the Doctrine of Annihilationism*, (Lanham: University Press of America, 1995), 2.

proposed a state of "eternal conscious limbo" as an alternative to hell. In this state, humans do not experience the joys of heaven, nor any of state of consciousness whatsoever, but neither do they suffer.[245]

Unbiblical beliefs regarding hell do not end with its outright denial. Some disregard Scriptural teaching on the kinds of individuals who reside there. In popular culture, only those who have committed truly evil acts, such as murder or rape, will suffer in hell, but the majority of the world's inhabitants, who are essentially good, will enter a delectable afterlife. This belief denies the seriousness of sin and the need for salvation, arguing that a large portion of Earth's population is innocent and undeserving of eternal punishment.

To deny hell's existence would be a repudiation or, at the very least, a glossing over of a significant portion of the New Testament, from the Gospels to Peter's second letter and the book of Revelation. Hell was a prominent topic in the eternal warnings of Jesus' sermons (Matt. 5:22, 29-30; 10:28; 18:9; 23:15, 33; Mark 9:43-47; Luke 12:5). Jesus' most vivid description occurs in the story of the Rich Man and Lazarus, where the rich man suffers intensely and unceasingly and wishes for a messenger to warn his brothers so that they would not suffer the same fate (Luke 16:22-28). Concerning hell, Jesus further seems to distinguish between the intermediate punishment before the final judgment and the final punishment, which is the lake of fire. Intermediate punishment is reserved for unbelievers before they await judgment (Matt. 5:29-30; Mark 9:43-47; Luke 12:5; 16:23-26). In the final punishment, unbelievers are cast into the lake of fire, where they must suffer into eternity (Matt. 13:41-42; 25:41-46). In the Gospel of Matthew, Jesus also referred to the final punishment as "Outer Darkness" (Matt. 8:12; 22:13; 25:30). Peter referenced hell as the place where a certain group of angels who disobeyed God were sent to await final judgment (2 Pet. 2:4). John also included a description of the lake of fire in Revelation as the place of final punishment for the antichristian beast, the false prophet, and eventually Satan (Rev. 19:20; 20:10). Tragically, it is also the eternal place of torment for those not found in the Lamb's book of life (Rev. 20:15; 21:8). Without any doubt, hell is a thoroughly biblical doctrine.

---

245 John Sanders, "Hell Yes! Hell No! Evangelical Debates on Eternal Punishment" in *Hell and its Afterlife: Historical and Contemporary Perspectives*, eds. Isabel Moreira and Margaret Toscano (Burlington: Ashgate, 2010), 142-4.

Eternal punishment finds the necessity of its existence in the innate sense of judgment that exists within every human being. Even those not well-versed in history can recall names of brutal despots, mass murderers, and infamous criminals who have never faced justice. How can one believe in the negative consequences of evil, if many, such as Ivan IV of Russia, Jack the Ripper, Idi Amin, and Kim Il-Sung go unpunished? Hell's existence logically presents a case for ultimate justice for all of humanity.

Surprisingly enough, the validity of hell is linked to human freewill. If there is only one destination in eternity for all of humanity, then there is hardly any choice involved, and no individual has the freedom to reject God and the salvation He offers. Theologians have pointed out that heaven would not be an enjoyable place for unbelievers who have rejected God their entire earthly lives. Rather, it would be a worse torture for unbelievers to exist in a place (heaven), where God is always worshiped, served, and obeyed, than to live in spiritual rebellion in hell.

While an unpopular doctrine, hell is very much a biblical one. In a world that understands and, at times, even cherishes justice, hell is not an archaic belief but a sensible one. This truth should serve as a motivation to evangelize all unbelievers, because no Christian should wish that anyone should enter hell, and must, via evangelism, do whatever is possible to prevent such a fate befalling those they know may perish.

Eschatology:
Final Judgment

After Satan's final rebellion is defeated and before God ushers in the New Heaven and the New Earth, God will sit as Judge. For those who have not accepted Christ's offer of salvation, this moment will be a tragic and horrific day. Unbelievers will stand before Him and, because their names are not found in God's book of life, will be cast into the lake of fire to suffer eternally.

As a belief, final judgment is not foreign to other world religions or worldviews. Islam, for instance, stipulates that everyone will be resurrected and judged. Not only are there competing conceptions of final judgment in various belief systems, but there exist speculative theories concerning this event. Zoroastrians also believe in a resurrection and future judgement.[246]

---

246 Clifford and Johnson, *The Cross is Not Enough*, 145.

Eschatology

Traditionally, most Christians accepted final judgment until liberalism began to cast doubt on orthodox beliefs. Friedrich Schleiermacher (1768 – 1834) dispensed with the biblical understanding of judgment, believing that it was not in God's nature. The theme of judgment, he argued, signified that God will ultimately free human beings from evil and bring them into fellowship with Him as they realize their need for Him. William Newton Clarke (1841 – 1912) declared that judgment as a public event is not to be found in Scripture, instead proposing that a private evaluation would transpire following an individual's death.[247] For some Liberation theologians, final judgment will occur, but not on the basis of salvation through Christ, but on one's acceptance or rejection of the poor, somewhat following the biblical story of Lazarus and the rich man and other parts of Luke.[248] One prevailing theory in popular culture discards any form of judgment, with individuals simply entering into an eternal blessed state. Inspired by modern Universalism, this doctrinal error ignores God's attribute of holiness and places God's mercy as His predominant characteristic, proposing that God must forgive with or without repentance.

The Bible has much to say of God's final judgment. During almost the entire history of the world, God has acted in the role of Judge, because sin has existed during most of the world's history (Gen. 3:6-19). Due to the reality of sin and its corruption upon the world, final judgment is demanded (John 16:8). In disputing the claim that unrighteous behavior is justified in that it glorifies God in His righteousness, Paul declares that this would make God's punishment of sin unjust and disqualify Him from judging the world (Rom. 3:6). Scripture names God, who is Righteous and Holy, as the only perfect Judge (Job 21:22; Ps. 7:11; 50:6; 58:11; 75:7; 82:1; Heb. 13:4). Indeed, testimony from believers praises the judgment of God (1 Sam. 2:25). Aside from these passages, there are verses that declare a coming judgment from God (Rom. 2:16; 1 Cor. 4:5; 2 Tim. 4:1). Several of the parables of Jesus found in the Gospel of Matthew function as vivid images of the Lord's final judgment of man, including the Parable of the wheat and the tares (or weeds, Matt. 13:24-30, 36-43), the Parable of the dragnet (Matt. 13:47-50), the Parable of the talents (Matt. 25:14-30;), and the Parable of the sheep and the goats (Matt. 25:31-46). In his

---

247 Allison, *Historical Theology*, 715-17.
248 McDowell and Kirkland, *Eschatology*, 82.

letter to the church in Thessalonica, Paul encouraged Christians to endure their current persecution, because one day Christ would return to bring judgment upon all who have rejected Him, and they will receive eternal punishment (2 Thess.1:3-10). The book of Revelation offers the most detailed description, providing the scene of the great white throne judgment, and explains the ultimate fate of unbelievers, who will face eternal torment in the lake of fire (Rev. 20:11-15). Despite this doctrine's unpopularity, it holds a secure place in Scripture.

Two major views on Final Judgment are held among Christians. The Dispensationalist position understands that there will be two separate judgments, one for believers and one for unbelievers. For believers, the Judgment Seat of Christ occurs in Heaven during a seven-year Tribulation, when disciples of Christ will be rewarded based on their service to their Master during their lifetimes. Unbelievers will face the great white throne Judgment, which will reveal that they have not repented from their sins and have not committed to Christ. Their fate is eternal suffering. The Historic Premillennial, Postmillennial, and Amillennial positions, on the other hand, hold to only one judgment, where believers and unbelievers will be judged together, each receiving reward and punishment respectively. While Christians have debated the number of judgments, all biblical Christians agree that final judgment(s) will occur.

Similar to the argument for hell's existence, the final judgment is a rational concept due to the human sense of morality. A long history of legal development and the establishment of justice systems all over the globe indicate that humans not only understand the concept of right and wrong but use morality as a platform for jurisprudence to prevent injustice and prosecute individuals when injustice occurs. As has been pointed out by Christian apologists, the human capacity to understand morality indicates a perfect Source of morality and ethics; such a perfect Source must be personal, possesses intelligence, and exhibit attributes. Court systems are imperfect models of the perfect Final Justice of God.

In addition to the innate sense of justice within each person, the Final Judgment presents its reasonableness in the consistency of God's nature. God, being holy and sinless, could not let injustice continue indefinitely. If He did, then God would not truly be holy or good. Nor would any human want to live in a world in which injustice continues indefinitely. Such a world would degenerate further and further into evil and moral chaos. Those who claim that a world that fits that description is actually appealing have not thought through all of the consequences of living in that kind of world. A continually degenerating world offers no security or safety. The only suitable world is a world in which evil will one day be completely eradicated. That will occur at the Final Judgment when all who are in rebellion against God will be cast into the lake of fire.

Readers of the Bible are warned in many passages of God's final judgment. It is an event that every living person on this earth should take seriously. One day, judgment will come, and unbelievers will find that for them it will be eternally too late.

Eschatology: The New Heaven and the New Earth

After the Final Judgement, God will create a new heaven and a new earth for all of His people. On a new earth, God will construct a holy city, the new Jerusalem, incomparable in its vastness. On a new earth, God's people will fellowship with their Lord in the fullness of His presence and serve and worship Him for all eternity.

Emanuel Swedenborg uniquely asserted that there would be no transformed world and that the future existence for mankind would be very much like their previous ones.[249] Marxism envisions a world of liberation with justice for everyone.[250] Adherents of the New Age Movement hope for an enlightened era of a heaven on Earth.[251] Unfortunately, Christians have errant conceptions of believers' final destiny. For many Christians, Heaven is the final destiny for all believers. Sadly, they are mistaken. To accept Heaven as the final destination would erase the rich promises declared by God in Scripture, particularly in the book of Revelation. The acceptance of Christo Platonism among Christians has misled believers into picturing their eternal future in the clouds as disembodied spirits. The influence of the dualism contrast between material and spiritual in Gnosticism and Manichaeism has also caused believers to look at a material existence as corrupt, or at the least deficient.[252] Contrary to this popularly misinformed belief, the New Testament depicts an eternity of physical existence.

---

249 McDannell and Lang, *Heaven*, 189.
250 Muchembled, *A History of the Devil*, 218.
251 Kyle, *Religious Fringe*, 294.
252 Alcorn, *Heaven*, 112–13.

Thinking Rationally About Christian Theology
A Handbook on Polemics

The eternal existence described in the New Testament begins with the Millennial Reign of Christ. The Millennial Reign will demonstrate Jesus Christ's perfect ability to reign over the Earth and provide each and every resident of the planet all that he would need or ever hope to need (Rev. 20:4-6). It will be an era that will find no equal since the fall of mankind. Despite its perfection, the Millennial Reign will come to an end with the Final Rebellion of Satan (Rev 20:7-10). A number of believers may find it hard to imagine that a vast army will answer Satan's call to rebel against Christ, but Revelation assures its readers that this will indeed happen (Rev. 20;7-8). Though Satan will be able to amass an impressive army, he will suffer a quick and utter defeat by God (Rev. 20:9). This fiery end to Satan's last rebellion brings an end to the world. The words of the Apostle John indicate that nothing will be left at the Final Judgment, as unbelievers face God on His throne (Rev. 20:11). After unbelievers receive their eternal punishment (Rev. 20:12-15), God will usher in a new heaven and a new earth (Rev. 21:1) where the new Jerusalem will reside, and within its walls, believers will live for all eternity in fellowship with the Lord (Rev. 21:2-4, 9-27). Living in a new heaven and a new earth, Christians will experience perfect joy and serve in perfect obedience to God (Rev. 21:3-4, 24). The life God has planned for His people will surpass the highest expectations and have no end (Rev. 22:3-5).

The culmination of the history of the world, brought about by a divine being or beings, is not unique to Christianity. One of the constants of existence is the fact that everything has a beginning and an end. Only a few would argue that the world will go on to exist indefinitely as it is. Most hold to some ultimate fate for the world. Therefore, the question is, "What sort of fate will the Earth have?" The alternate theories of the eschaton cannot be accepted, because they have no historical foundation to support them—they are based on teachings from religious founders and their successors who have posited statements about the future, but their statements about the past have not been historically verified. Many of the accounts about the founders are legendary, such as the life of Muhammad. The naturalist attempts to base the end of the earth on the projected timeline of the sun, but scientists will admit that the exact moment when this occurs is merely an estimate. As has been demonstrated, Scripture is inspired by the Being who is both the Creator of the universe and the One who will bring about the culmination of the world's destiny. Archeology and extra-biblical evidence have confirmed the historical accuracy of the Bible time and again. Verified fulfillment of prophetic predictions found in Scripture number at two thousand, with only five hundred yet to be fulfilled.

Christian eschatology has been subject to ridicule in the last century and labeled as a dream impossible to come to pass. Yet, a perfect world has been the dream of many from many different worldviews and belief systems. Since Thomas More (1478 – 1535), that perfect world has been referred to as "utopia,"[253] a word that, ironically, means an unknown place. Utopia, in its myriad of descriptions and humanistic attempts at description (such as "Erehwon," which is "nowhere" backwards) is the idea that human beings, by their own efforts, can bring about a near-perfect world. Usually, the impetus for utopia is either sweeping change through government policies or violent revolution. Many have advocated for some version of utopia, and many have attempted it, whether on a large scale, such as Mao Zedong's Cultural Revolution in China or Pol Pot's brutal regime in Cambodia or on a small scale of the likes of John Humphrey Noyes' Oneida Community or the Brook Farm near Boston in the 1800s. Why have there been so many characterizations of and attempts to create a utopia? The answer is simple: human beings long to live in a perfect world. That desire, which extends from many different cultures, points to the possibility of a perfect world. However, that possibility exists beyond the reach of humans, because humans are not perfect. Biblically, Christians understand that all humans are sinners (Isa. 64:6; Rom. 3:10, 3:23). Only a perfect Being can create a perfect world. What is missing from the descriptions of utopia is the One who can make a perfect world possible. Those who laugh at the future depicted in Revelation 21:1-22:5 would do well to look at two centuries worth of failed attempts to usher in a similar future. Man's longing for a perfect world suggests that the world itself is flawed and that the possibility of perfecting it exists.

Followers of Jesus Christ long for the day when they will walk along the streets of the holy city, the New Jerusalem, and live in perfect fellowship with their Lord and Savior. To believers, eternity with the Lord is not a mere hope, but a promise from their Savior that will one day be fulfilled. They know this because the accurate Word of God has informed them of their destiny.

---

253 Thomas More, *Utopia*, trans. Ralph Robinson (New York: Alfred A. Knopf, 1910), 57–77.

Chapter 9

Conclusion

Since its earliest days, the Church has encountered and combatted unbiblical beliefs, at times, not so successfully. In several eras of history, the Church allowed heresy to seep into its belief system to be regarded as biblical doctrine. Similar challenges exist today. Many proclaim themselves to be followers of Christ, but do not adhere to the biblically orthodox beliefs. Subjectivism and Deconstructionism have so dominated the landscape in relation to biblical interpretation and the study of theology that many who take the name, "Christian," think that their beliefs are not grounded in the revelation of the Written Word but in their own speculations. The Early Church had to deal with movements such as Gnosticism and Montanism. In the twenty-first century, each individual is a movement unto himself and desires to believe as he wishes, not knowing that his opinion has been shaped by movements and prejudices accepted by the culture at large, and veers far from the truths found in God's Word. Compounding the problem is the popularity of social media, a place where unbiblical teaching is often promoted and that many Christians consider to be a viable source for their theological beliefs. Worse still, many church leaders have found themselves caught up in the zeitgeist of the twenty-first century and see the Church as a vehicle for progressive theology and Marxist-inspired social justice, seeing it as their mission to make the members of their churches socialists rather than disciples of Jesus. The Church faces challenges today indeed.

How can the Church address the challenges of heresy in the shifting sands of belief in the twentieth century? The task begins with the local church pastor. Fifteen-minute devotionals that are delivered to congregants more for the purpose of entertainment than biblical instruction and guidance are insufficient. Christians encounter competing worldviews and unbiblical beliefs on a daily basis. They must be equipped to counter these beliefs, understanding both *that* they contradict Scripture and *how* they contradict Scripture. Furthermore, pastors must deliver theological messages explaining the doctrines of the faith as presented in Scripture. Most believers will not encounter sound doctrine except in the context of the local church, and churches that proclaim biblical theology are becoming a minority. So, it is imperative that the pastor function not only as an evangelist, a counselor, and a biblical interpreter, but a theologian as well. With that in mind, pastors must be aware of movements and trends popular in current society so that he can contradict them if they are teaching unbiblical beliefs. These popular movements and trends will be both outside and inside of the Church.

In addition to the pastor's responsibilities, every Christian should be encouraged to study the Bible. The greatest theological text ever written is the Word of God, containing the Old and New Testament. Several great systematic theologies have been published, but they cannot and do not equal the inerrant and infallible Word of God. Christians should be encouraged to move away from spending all of their time seeking entertainment and instead turn to carefully examining Scripture. This, more than anything else, will ground the believer in biblical doctrine. As such, small groups and Bible studies where Christians can study books of the Bible together with fellow believers is also a necessity. Doctrinal discussions will naturally arise in the context of small groups as they study the Bible, and Christians will grow as they study the Bible together.

Over the two millennia of Christian history, the followers of Jesus have been noted for their fervent Gospel proclamation, their strong convictions, their love for their neighbor, and a passion for biblical doctrine. Christians must regain this passion for biblical doctrine. Michael Sattler was willing to be tortured and burned to death over the doctrines he believed in. Disciples of Jesus must return to such fervency. The doctrines that compose Christian theology are incredible beliefs, beliefs concerning God's amazing nature, His revelation to man, His orchestration of eternal salvation, and the promise of a perfect future world. What is so amazing about these doctrines is that they are true. Heresy seeks to subvert and replace that truth. Christians must stand for the truth and defend it.

Appendix

A Brief Summary of Heresies

Adoptionism/Dynamic Monarchianism

An ancient heresy that began in the early third century at the latest, adoptionism holds that Jesus originated as a man who later received the Spirit of God. Upon receiving the Spirit of God, Jesus was adopted as the Son of God and henceforth became the Son of God, negating the Son's eternity and denying the eternal Triune Godhead.

Agnosticism

A term coined by Thomas Henry Huxley (1825-1895) that combines the Greek terms *a* and *gnosis*, meaning, "no knowledge," Agnosticism asserts that the information to prove that God exists or does not exist is inaccessible, or that if God exists, one cannot know Him or have a relationship with Him. Agnostics find many similarities with atheists and often make the same arguments against theism. The main distinction between the two beliefs concerns the certainty of God's non-existence.

Antinomianism

Antinomian is the combination of the Greek terms, *anti* and *nomos*, meaning "against law." For antinomians, God's grace and the work of the Holy Spirit within the believer exempt any Christian from having to obey the law. Various forms of this belief have surfaced over the centuries. Anne

Hutchinson (1591-1643) of the New England colonies is perhaps antinomianism's most famous adherent.

Apollinarianism

Advocated by Apollinarius, Apollinarianism denies the biblical affirmation that Jesus is fully God and fully man. Apollinarius believed in the full
divinity of Christ, but did not believe that He had a completely human
nature, arguing that Jesus' human body did not have a human soul. Thus,
according to Apollinarianism, the Incarnation was incomplete.

Arianism

Initiated by the Alexandrian presbyter, Arius (256 – 336), Arianism rejects the doctrine of Christ's eternality and His full divinity. Arius believed that God the Father always existed, but not the Son, whom the Father created. A time existed, therefore, when God the Son did not exist.
The Son, then, did not exist forever in eternity past, nor is He fully God
as is God the Father. Arianism's structure of the Godhead bears similarity to mythological pantheons in which gods possess some divinity
and receive adoration by worshippers, but owe their existence to other
deities or supernatural power.

Atheism

Atheism, a combination of the Greek words, *a* and *theos*, meaning "no
god" is the absolute rejection of the existence of God. According to atheism, all that exists originated from natural, scientific processes and the
only reason why human beings believed in the supernatural is due to the
fact that ancient humanity did not have access to scientific explanations
for the laws of nature. With the advent of scientific and technological
advances, atheists claim that there no longer exists a reason for civilized
humanity to hold to a belief in God.

Appendix: A Brief Summary of Heresies

Black Liberation Theology

Originating with James H. Cone, Black Liberation Theology stresses the condition of African Americans in the United States in particular. Because of the abuses against African Americans over the centuries and the indifference shown by many white theologians to their plight, Cone developed Black Liberation Theology, which stressed salvation as freedom from oppression and looked to Jesus as primarily a liberator and advocate of social justice rather than a spiritual Savior. Eternal salvation to Cone was an escapism developed by white theologians to placate the oppressed and keep their minds focused on future hopes rather than bringing positive change in the here and now.

Continuous Revelation (Continuing Revelation)

Continuous Revelation is the belief that God's manifestation of new revelational truth is ongoing. Thus, new information comes from God that has equal or similar authority to Scriptural truth. For the Latter-Day Saints, the President continues to make proclamations that possess divine authoritative weight, claiming to come from God. The Society of Friends (Quakers) believes that continuous revelation occurs by means of the "inner light" within each person and directs the ongoing revision of doctrine when the need arises.

Deconstructionism

Initiated by Jacques Derrida (1930 – 2004) in the 1960s, Deconstructionism is primarily a literary movement that focuses on the autonomy of the reader to interpret the text. Also called, "Death of the Author Movement," Deconstructionism discards the necessity of interpreting a text on the basis of the author's original intent or that any text has a fixed meaning. Deconstructionists such as Jean-Francois Lyotard (1924 – 1998) and Stanley Fish (1938 –) deny that objective truth exists. Texts instead are interpreted by communities or power structures who determine their own truth.

Deism

Originating in the seventeenth century, Deism acknowledges God as Creator of the Universe, but dispenses with the concept of God as Sustainer of Creation. Deists claim that after bringing about existence into being, God relegated Himself to the role of observer, watching the world run its course. Thus, He does not intervene in human history or provide the means for the eternal salvation of sinful man. For intellectuals living in the Age of Enlightenment, this denial of orthodox Theism presented a logically acceptable version of belief in God. With Deism, one has the explanation of how the world and the Universe came to be, but then, amazingly, man is left to his own devices, uninterrupted and merely observed by the God who created Him. A few of the more well-known Deists include Edward Herbert (1583-1648), Gotthold Ephraim Lessing (1729 – 1781), Voltaire (1694 – 1778), and Thomas Jefferson (1743 – 1825).

Docetism

From the Greek, *dokein*, meaning "to seem" or "to appear," Docetism was a key part of Gnostic teaching. Docetism claims that the incarnation of the Son of God never happened. Antagonistic towards the material world, Gnostics considered human flesh evil, including the notion of God the Son taking on a human body. This revulsion towards human flesh led to the belief that either the Son appeared as a human but did not actually take physical form, or that the Son possessed the man Jesus of Nazareth.

Donatism

More of a schism than a heresy, Donatism was a controversy in North African Christianity that occurred from the fourth to the sixth centuries. Named after Donatus of Casae Nigrae (d. 355), the Donatist schism occurred when protests erupted over the consecration of Cæcilianus as Bishop of Carthage, due to the fact that one of the consecrating bishops, Felix of Abthungi, was under suspicion of apostasy while under persecution. Because of this suspicion, of which Felix was later exonerated, the

Appendix: A Brief Summary of Heresies

Donatists declared the consecration of Cæcilianus invalid. The doctrinal issue with Donatism concerns the stress placed on the validity of the ordinances of the Church being dependent upon the holiness of the ordained leadership and not upon Christ the Head of the Church, who actually inaugurated the ordinances.

Gnosticism

With some elements of the movement beginning at the end of the first century, Gnosticism became the rival to biblical Christianity in the second century. A syncretistic blend of Christian terminology, Platonic dualism, Hellenistic Judaism, and pagan mythology, Gnosticism possessed a reverence for the invisible and spiritual and an aversion toward the material and physical. All that was spiritual was holy, and all that was material was evil. To explain how God created a material world, Gnostics claimed that God created a being only slightly less perfect and powerful than himself called an aeon. That aeon created another aeon less perfect than the first, and a progression of creations of aeons, until the God of the Old Testament, often called the Demiurge, was created. It was he that created the world, and because he was evil and corrupt, the world was evil and corrupt. Christ, a pure aeon who was not incarnated, served as an emissary from God to guide humanity out of the slavery of the Demiurge to be in the presence of God after death. For Gnostics, salvation came through obtaining *gnosis* or knowledge, to be used to circumvent the Demiurge's and other corrupt aeons' barriers to the eternal paradise meant for humanity. The major proponents of Gnosticism were Saturnilus (active 100 – 120), Basilides (active 113 – 138), Valentinus (c. 100 – c. 180), and Marcion of Sinope (c. 110 – 160).

Hebrew Roots Movement/Torahism

Signifying a movement within Protestantism, Torahism stresses the return to obedience to key laws in the Old Testament, namely the observance of the Sabbath, dietary laws, feasts, and circumcision. Although Hebrew Roots followers do not believe adherence to the law is necessary for salvation, they do believe that it is necessary to be in right-standing with God.

Hyper-Calvinism

Hyper-Calvinism negates any work whatsoever on the part of the believer concerning evangelism and regulates the Christian to a completely passive role with regard to salvation. Hyper-Calvinists believe that God, in a demonstration of His sovereignty, has chosen the individuals whom He wants to save and then regenerates them without them having the need to voluntarily convert. Converts realize their spiritual transformation when the Holy Spirit informs them that they have received their salvation.

Inclusivism

A middle position between Universalism and Exclusivism, Inclusivism believes that Jesus alone saves human beings, but His salvation extends beyond Christianity. Clark Pinnock, who stressed God's omnipresence, originated the view. Though Christ alone saves, through His sacrificial death and resurrection, Pinnock argued, God is at work all over the world to bring people to salvation who will never have the opportunity to hear the Gospel. Therefore, according to Inclusivism, individuals may come to faith in Christ, without having acknowledged the truthfulness of the content of the Gospel and without having prayed to receive Christ as Savior.

Liberalism (Theological)/Modernism

Theological Liberalism originated in Europe during the early nineteenth century, with the father of the movement being Fredrich Daniel Ernst Schleiermacher (1768 – 1834). Flourishing throughout the nineteenth century and losing influence at the close of the First World War, Liberalism abandoned traditional Christianity in the attempt to make the faith more appealing to the modern era. Regarding the Bible as no longer having absolute authority, Liberalism stressed the importance of religious experience over adherence to creeds or confessions and redeeming society through acts of compassion rather than proclaiming the message of eternal salvation through Jesus Christ. Additional proponents included Albrecht Ritschl (1822 – 1889), Adolf von Harnack (1851 – 1930), and Walter Rauschenbusch (1861 – 1918).

Appendix: A Brief Summary of Heresies

Liberation Theology

Developing in the middle of the twentieth century in Latin America, Liberation Theology was the response to the fatalistic theology of Roman Catholicism in Central and South America that was prevalent during the later nineteenth century and early twentieth century. Liberation theology portrays Jesus as a fighter against oppression rather than as a Savior. The Gospel, then, is the fight against oppression, the liberation of the poor, and the establishment of justice for all people. Notable Liberation Theologians include Gustavo Gutierrez (1928 –), Juan Luis Segundo (1925 – 1996), and Jon Sobrino (1938 –).

Logical Positivism (based on Empiricism and its predecessor, Logical Atomism)

A development of Modernism, Logical Positivism states that the only statements of value are those that can be verified by scientific observation or logical proof. While it diminished in popularity after the 1950s, logical positivism's effects can still be felt in the academy and among proponents of atheism and skepticism. Significant logical positivists included A. J. Ayer (1910 – 1989), Rudolf Carnap (1891 – 1970), and the other members of the Vienna Circle.

Modalism (Modalistic Monarchianism)

To avoid the error of tritheism and stress both the oneness of God and the deity of Christ, some within the Early Church proposed that the Three Persons are actually One Person who presents Himself as separate identities. Noetus of Smyrna (act. 230s) articulated the earliest version, which states that the persons of the Trinity are distinct only by name, but are essentially the same Person. Sabellius (fl. 215) identified the Godhead as a monad who presented itself in three different modes or operations. Unfortunately, modalism is sometimes considered an attractive way to understand the Trinity.

Montanism

A second century movement, Montanism received its name from Montanus, a new convert to Christianity. Claiming, along with his associates Prisca and Maximilla, to be voices of the Paraclete or Holy Spirit, Montanus announced the imminent return of Christ. To prepare for Christ's return, Montanus and his associates told Christians to observe fasting and to abstain from sin. Montanists forbade second marriages. Though not a major heretical movement, Montanism had a somewhat extreme view of revelation in that Montanus, Prisca, and Maximilla spoke in the first person as if the Holy Spirit had possessed them to speak through them. They also claimed to have ecstatic visions further supporting their authority as mouthpieces of the Holy Spirit.

Monophysitism (Eutychianism)

Coming from the Greek words *monos or* "single" and *physis* or "nature," Monophysitism claims that the incarnate Christ possessed only the divine nature contained in human flesh, denying the orthodox doctrine that Christ has two full natures of divine and human. Its major advocate was Eutyches (d. 454) and, because of his defense of the belief, Monophysitism is also called Eutychianism.

Monothelitism

Derived from the Greek words, *monos* or "single" and *thelein* or "to will," Monothelitism is the heresy that proposes that Christ possessed one divine will and not a human will. This belief was a seventh century development, an attempt at compromise in the Monophysite controversy. In the Third Council of Constantinople (681), the orthodox opinion declared that Christ had two wills: a divine will and a human will.

Appendix: A Brief Summary of Heresies

Moralistic Therapeutic Deism

A name first coined by sociologists Christian Smith and Melinda Lundquist Denton in their book *The Religious and Spiritual Lives of American Teenagers*, Moralistic Therapeutic Deism is a conception of God developed in the early twenty-first century. Those who adhere to it believe that God has little concern for the daily lives of human beings, but only desires that they live fairly moral lives, and He will intervene when they ask Him for help. According to this conception, God does not take the role of Lord and Savior but functions as a cosmic acquaintance who provides assistance when asked. Furthermore, the purpose of man is to enjoy life rather than worship and serve God.

Naturalism

Naturalism is a mid-twentieth-century movement advocated by John Dewey (1859 – 1952), Roy Wood Sellars (1880 – 1973), Ernest Nagel (1901 – 1985), and Sidney Hook (1902 – 1989). Connected to Secular Humanism, Atheism, and Agnosticism, Naturalism accepts only the natural processes of existence and categorically rejects any notion of the supernatural. Naturalism primarily accepts only that which can be explained and validated by modern scientific theory. Therefore, naturalists do not believe in the existence of God, miracles, angels, or the afterlife.

Nestorianism

Nestorius (c. 386 – c. 451), patriarch of Constantinople, rejected the title of *Theotokos* or "God-bearer" for Mary. He believed Mary only gave birth to the human nature of Christ. As he defended his position against several orthodox theologians, Nestorius also denied the hypostatic union of the two natures of Christ. Upon doing this, Nestorius was labeled a heretic and ultimately removed from his post as patriarch at the Council of Ephesus (431). The belief that is ascribed to his name proposes that Christ is not one person with two natures, but two persons: one human and one divine.

The New Age Movement

Arriving in the United States around 1970, the New Age Movement is a combination of Eastern Mysticism, Western Occultism, Holistic Medicine, and the Human Potential Movement. The New Age Movement is represented by a variety of beliefs and practices embraced by the West in the last fifty years, including pantheism, monism, reincarnation, transcendental meditation, yoga, acupuncture, astrology, tarot card readings, and belief in psychic phenomena. A number of individuals have identified as spokespersons of the movement, including Shirley MacLaine (1934 -), Deepak Chopra (1946 -), Eckhart Tolle (1948 -), and Marianne Williamson (1952 -).

Openness Theology (Open Theism)

Based on the insistence that humans possess complete free will, Openness Theology or Open Theism declares that God is omnipotent and has perfect knowledge of the past and present, but does not have knowledge of the future. God does not know what actions He will take in the future, nor does He know what actions humans will freely take in the future. Open Theists believe God's lack of knowledge of the future guarantees the free decisions and actions of humans. Prominent proponents of Open Theism are Clark Pinnock (1937 – 2010), Richard Rice (1944 -), and John Sanders (1956 -).

Patripassianism

A heretical teaching in the second century, Patripassianism asserts that God the Father died an atoning death by Roman crucifixion for the sins of the world rather than God the Son. This belief is connected to modalism and was articulated by Praxeus at the end of the second century.

Appendix: A Brief Summary of Heresies

Pelagianism

A contemporary of Augustine of Hippo (354-430), Pelagius (354-418) opposed the doctrine of original sin and did not believe that all of humanity fell due to Adam's sin. Rather, Adam provided a bad example, and humans had the choice to follow his example or live a sinless life, exemplified by Jesus Christ. Pelagius believed it was within every person to live an ascetic life in perfect piety. Pelagianism ultimately argued that it was within every person to save himself.

Pluralism

An aberration of Exclusivist biblical salvation, Pluralism stipulates that salvation and a pleasant afterlife can be attained not only through faith in Christ, but through a sincere observance within other religions as well. John Hick (1922 – 2012) was the major proponent of this view during the twentieth and early twenty-first centuries.

Process Theology/Panentheism

A.N. Whitehead (1861-1947), influenced by Baha'i thought, developed a theory concerning the nature of God. His philosophy was later adapted by Charles Hartshorne (1897-2000) and John Cobb (1925-) into a theology. In contradiction to the concept of the transcendent God of theism, Process Theology depicts God as being limited in that He does not have the power to force humans to commit an act against their will. By Process Theology standards, God also consists of two poles. The primordial pole is eternal, unchanging, and does not exist in the world, while the consequential pole is temporal, changing, and exists in the world. Process Theology is a complete departure from Classical Theism and rejects the biblical description of the noncommunicable attributes of God.

Progressive Christianity

Progressive Christianity is the twenty-first-century attempt to adapt biblical Christianity to the current secularistic and relativistic culture. Essentially a repackaging of the Emergent Movement in the early 2000s, Progressive Christianity distances itself from the doctrines associated with orthodox Christianity, such as biblical inerrancy, the sinlessness of Christ, and exclusive salvation through Christ alone. Likewise, Progressive Christians stand on the opposite position on several issues which Evangelicals have taken strong stances on, like pro-abortion, advocacy for homosexual marriage, support for transgenderism, and acceptance of Socialism/Marxism in the guise of "Social Justice." Some of the primary advocates of Progressive Christianity include Richard Rohr (1943 -), Brian McLaren (1956 -), David Gushee (1963 -), and Rachel Held Evans (1981 – 2019).

Prosperity Gospel

Originating in the nineteenth century under the influence of Protestant Pentecostalism, New Thought, and Pragmatism, the Prosperity Gospel argues that Christ's atonement not only conquered sin, but also poverty and even physical well-being. Thus, all believers who live obedience to God and have a devout faith in Him will enjoy economic prosperity and good health.

Relativism

Relativism denies the existence of absolute truth. Several branches of relativism exist, including moral relativism. Moral relativists claim that absolute morals do not exist. Relativism has become a hallmark of Postmodernism in the latter half of the twentieth century and into the twenty-first.

Appendix: A Brief Summary of Heresies

Secular Humanism

Coming from the Latin *saeculum*, ("world"), secular refers to being worldly or current with the present age. Pitted against the sacred segment of society, secularism refers to what is outside of the Church's jurisdiction. As a form of humanism, secular humanism looks to humanity as the answer to the problems of the world rather than viewing God as the means of ultimate salvation, and opposes any religious (particularly Christian) influence on the public and the State.

Semi-Pelagianism

Derived in part from Pelagianism, Semi-Pelagianism developed in the fifth century with Vitalis of Carthage and John Cassian, among others, who in disagreement with Augustine of Hippo, believed that humans possessed a degree of free will. Semi-Pelagians acknowledged that man was unable to achieve salvation on his own, but the free will available to him enabled him to choose God on his own. Salvation, then, was a joint effort between God and man.

Sinless Perfection

A concept that emerged during the time of the Early Church and continued into the eighteenth century with the ministries of John and Charles Wesley (1707 – 1788), sinless perfection or Christian perfection stipulates that a believer's union with God can reach such a point of intimacy and nearness to the Lord that the believer no longer sins.

Subordinationism

Subordinationism is a heresy that distorts the Trinity by claiming that one or two members of the Triune Godhead, while maintaining full divinity, takes a lesser position in authority to another member. Typically, this is applied to the relationship between God the Father and God the Son.

Tritheism

Tritheism is the belief that not only are the Three Persons of the Trinity separate Persons, but they are also three separate beings. Therefore, there are not three persons and one God in the godhead, but three gods. It is the accusation that many in Islam have leveled against Christianity's doctrine of the Trinity.

Unitarianism (Socinianism)

Unitarianism is the antitrinitarian belief that God is not Three Persons. Two major variations exist within this heresy. The earlier form, advocated by Faustus Socinus (1539 – 1604), viewed Jesus as a man later adopted by God the Father to be His Son. The later model, accepted in the United States, understood Jesus to be merely a man who exemplified godliness, God the Father being the only Person of the Trinity.

Universalism

A heresy that goes back to Origen of Alexandria (c. 185 – c. 253) in the early third century, Universalism states that all individuals will or already have received their spiritual salvation. Thus, all human beings will go to Heaven, and no conversion to Christ is necessary. For Origen, eternal salvation could require a long and severe process of punishment to purge persons from corruption and prepare them for life in the presence of God. Origen believed this process could take long periods of time after a person's death. Modern Universalism dispenses with uncomfortable notions of punishment and purging and asserts that humans will automatically enter Heaven after death.

Bibliography

Alcorn, Randy. *Heaven*. Carol Stream: Tyndale House, 2004.

Allison, Gregg R. *Historical Theology*. Grand Rapids: Zondervan, 2011.

Aquinas, Thomas. *Summa Theologica*, translated by Fathers of the English Dominican Province, (1947), 2.1.113, (accessed April 15, 2023), https://www.sacred-texts.com/chr/aquinas/summa/index.htm.

Archer, Gleason L. *Encyclopedia of Bible Difficulties*. Grand Rapids: Zondervan, 1982.

Arius et. al. *The Confession of the Arians, Addressed to Alexander of Alexandria* in *Christology of the Later Fathers*, ed. Edward R. Hardy, 332-334. Louisville: Westminster John Knox, 1954.

Ashby, Stephen M. "A Reformed Arminian View," in *Four Views on Eternal Security*, edited by J. Matthew Pinson, Counterpoints: Bible and Theology, edited by Stanley N. Gundry. Grand Rapids: Zondervan, 2002.

Atwater, P.M.H. *Near-Death Experiences: The Rest of the Story*. New York: MJF Books, 2011.

Augustine. *The Confessions*. Translated by Maria Boulding. New York: Vintage, 1997.

Augustine. *The Deeds of Pelagius* 6. 16-19 in *Answer to the Pelagians*, *The Works of Saint Augustine: A Translation for the 21st Century*, trans. Roland J. Teske, ed. John E. Rotelle. Hyde Park: New City, 1997.

Augustine, *On the Gift of Perseverance*, 1.3, ed. Philip Schaff, trans. Peter Holmes and Robert Ernest Wallis, *A Select Library of the Nicene and Post-Nicene Fathers of the Christian Church* Grand Rapids: William B. Eerdmans Publishing Company, 1971.

Baalen, Jan Karel Van. *The Chaos of the Cults: A Study in Present-Day Isms.* 4th ed. Grand Rapids: Eerdmans, 1962.

Bailey, Sarah Pulliam. "Gay, Christian and...celibate: The changing face of the homosexuality debate," in *Religion News Service*, August 4, 2014, (accessed April 15, 2023). https://religionnews.com/2014/08/04/gay-christian-celibate-changing-face-homosexuality-debate/.

Barth, Karl. *Church Dogmatics.* 2, 1. edited by T. H. L Parker, W.B. Johnston, Harold Knight, and J. L. M. Haire, translated by G. W. Bromiley and T. F. Torrance. Peabody: Hendrickson, 1957.

Bell, Rob. *Love Wins.* New York: HarperOne, 2011.

Benson, RoseAnn. "The Articles of Faith: Answering the Doctrinal Questions of the Second Great Awakening" in *Joseph Smith and the Doctrinal Restoration*, edited by W. Jeffrey Marsh. Provo: Brigham Young University, 2005 https://rsc.byu.edu/book/joseph-smith-doctrinal-restoration (accessed May 16, 2024).

Berkhof, Louis. *The History of Christian Doctrines.* Carlisle: Banner of Truth Trust, 1937.

Beverley, James. "Unification Church" in *A Guide to New Religious Movements* edited by Ronald Enroth. 60 – 77. Downers Grove: InterVarsity, 2005.

Blomberg, Craig L. *The Historical Reliability of the New Testament.* Nashville: Broadman & Holman, 2016.

Bonner, Gerald. *St Augustine of Hippo: Life and Controversies.* rev. Ed. Norwich: Canterbury, 1986.

Bock, Darrell L. *Studying the Historical Jesus.* Grand Rapids: Baker Academic, 2002.

Bibliography

Borg, Marcus J. *Meeting Jesus Again for the First Time*. San Francisco: HarperSanFrancisco, 1994.

Bratton, Rachel. "The American Church has Fallen: Shocking Poll Shows 'Fake Christianity' Has Supplanted Biblical Worldview," *The Western Journal*, (July 4, 2021) https://www.westernjournal.com/american-church-fallen-shocking-poll-shows-fake-christianity-supplanted-biblical-worldview/ (accessed January 31, 2023).

Brown, Harold O. J. *Heresies: Heresy and Orthodoxy in the History of the Church*. Peabody: Hendrickson, 1998.

Brown, Peter. *Augustine of Hippo: A Biography*, 2nd Edition. Berkeley: University of California Press, 2000.

Brownworth, Lars. *Lost to the West: The Forgotten Byzantine Empire that Rescued Western Civilization*. New York: Crown, 2009.

Bruce, F. F. *The Books and the Parchments*. Rev. ed. Westwood: Fleming M. Revell, 1963.

Calvin, John. *Institutes of the Christian Religion*, 2, 3, xi-xii, trans. Henry Beveridge. Peabody: Hendrickson, 2008.

Carnell, Edward John. *An Introduction to Christian Apologetics*. Grand Rapids: Eerdmans, 1948.

Cassian, John. *Conference Three: The Three Renunciations* in *John Cassian Conferences*, translated by Colm Luibheid, 81-100. New York: Paulist, 1985.

Castelo, Daniel. *Pneumatology: A Guide for the Perplexed*. London: Bloomsbury T. and T. Clark, 2015.

Chalke, Steve and Alan Mann. *The Lost Message of Jesus*. Grand Rapids: Zondervan, 2003.

Childers, Alisa. *Another Gospel: A Lifelong Christian Seeks Truth in Response to Progressive Christianity*. Carol Stream: Tyndale Momentum, 2020.

Chopra, Deepak. *The Third Jesus: The Christ We Cannot Ignore*. New York: Harmony Books, 2008.

Clifford, Ross and Philip Johnson. *The Cross is Not Enough: Living as Witnesses to the Resurrection*. Grand Rapids: Baker, 2012.

Cone, James H. *A Black Theology of Liberation*. 2d. ed. Maryknoll: Orbis, 1986.

Corduan, Winfried. "The Date of Zoroaster: Some Apologetic Considerations." *Presbyterion 23*, no. 1 (1997), 25-42.

Craig, William Lane. *Reasonable Faith*. 3d ed. Wheaton: Crossway, 2008.

Craig, William Lane. *The Son Rises: The Historical Evidence for the Resurrection of Jesus*. Chicago: Moody, 1981.

Craig, William Lane. "The Historical Adam," *First Things*, (October 2021) https://www.firstthings.com/article/2021/10/the-historical-adam   b(accessed January 27, 2023).

Crossan, John Dominic. *The Historical Jesus*. San Francisco: HarperSanFrancisco, 1991.

Daly, Mary. *Beyond God the Father: Toward a Philosophy of Women's Liberation*. Boston: Beacon Press, 1973.

Dawkins, Richard. *The God Delusion*. Boston: Houghton Mifflin, 2006.

Decret, François. *Early Christianity in North Africa*, translated by Edward L. Smither. Eugene: Cascade, 2009.

Dickens, Charles. *A Tale of Two Cities*, (Salt Lake City: Project Gutenberg, 1994), 55-67, https://www.gutenberg.org/files/98/old/2city12p.pdf, (accessed January 29, 2023).

Dulles, Avery. *Models of Revelation*. Maryknoll: Orbis, 1992.

Ehrman, Bart D. *Jesus: Apocalyptic Prophet of the New Millennium*. New York: Oxford University Press, 1999.

Engelsma, David J. *Hyper-Calvinism: The Call of the Gospel*. rev. ed. Grand Rapids: Reformed Free Publishing Association, 1994.

Epicurus. *Letter to Menoeceus*, in *Greek and Roman Philosophy After Aristotle*, ed., Jason L. Saunders, 49-52. New York: The Free Press, 1966.

Bibliography

Estep, William R. *The Anabaptist Story*. 3d ed. Grand Rapids: William B. Eerdmans, 1996.

Fields, Weston W. *Unformed and Unfilled*. Phillipsburg: Presbyterian and Reformed Publishing, 1976.

Garrett, James Leo. *Systematic Theology*. Vol. 1 and 2. Grand Rapids: Eerdmans, 1990.

Geisler, Norman L. "A Moderate Calvinist's View," in *Four Views on Eternal Security*, edited by J. Matthew Pinson. Counterpoints: Bible and Theology, edited by Stanley N. Gundry Grand Rapids: Zondervan, 2002.

Geisler, Norman L. and Abdul Saleeb, *Answering Islam: The Crescent in Light of the Cross*, 2d. ed. Grand Rapids: Baker, 2002.

Geisler, Norman L. *Christian Apologetics*, 2d ed. Grand Rapids: Baker Academic, 2013.

Geisler, Norman L. and William E. Nix. *A General Introduction to the Bible*. Chicago: Moody, 1968.

Geisler, Norman L. and Thomas Howe. *The Big Book of Bible Difficulties*. Grand Rapids: Baker, 1992.

Giatti, Ian M. "Nearly 40% of Gen Z adults believe Jesus wasn't sinless: Survey," *Christian Post* (May 18, 2022) URL https://www.christianpost.com/news/nearly-40-percent-generation-z-adults-believe-jesus-sinned-survey.html (accessed February 1, 2023).

Gonzalez, Justo L. *A History of Christian Thought in One Volume*, rev. ed. Nashville: Abingdon, 1987.

Gospel of Thomas 2, 114, in *The Nag Hammadi Library*, 3d ed. edited by James M. Robinson, 126-138. San Francisco: HarperSanFrancisco, 1988.

Graham, Lloyd M. *Deceptions and Myths of the Bible*. New York: Citadel, 1975.

Grant, Robert M. and David Tracy. *A Short History of the Interpretation of the Bible*. 2d ed. Minneapolis: Fortress, 1984.

Green, Joel B. and Mark D. Baker. *Recovering the Scandal of the Cross*. Downers Grove: InterVarsity, 2000.

Greeson, Kevin. "Effective Bridging and Contextualization," in *Discovering the Mission of God*, edited by Mike Barnett and Robin Martin., 420-434. Downers Grove: InterVarsity, 2012.

Grenz, Stanley J. and Roger E. Olson. *20th Century Theology*. Downers Grove: InterVarsity, 1992.

Grenz, Stanley J. and John R. Franke. *Beyond Foundationalism*. Louisville: Westminster John Knox, 2001.

Grillmeier, Aloys. *Christ in Christian Tradition*. 2d ed. Atlanta: John Knox, 1975. vol. 1.

Habermas, Gary R. *The Risen Jesus and Future Hope*. Lanham: Bowman and Littlefield, 2003.

Hamilton, Edith. *Mythology*. New York: Warner, 1942.

Hartshorne, Charles. *Creativity in American Philosophy*. Albany: State University of New York, 1984.

Henry, Carl F. H. *God, Revelation, and Authority*. Waco: Word Books, 1979. vol. 4.

Hexham, Irving. *Understanding World Religions*. Grand Rapids: Zondervan, 2011.

Hick, John. "A Pluralist View," in *Four Views on Salvation in a Pluralistic World*, edited by Dennis L. Okholm and Timothy R. Phillips, 29-59. Grand Rapids: Zondervan, 1996.

Hillerbrand, Hans. Editor. *The Reformation*. Grand Rapids: Baker, 1972.

Hodge, Charles. *Systematic Theology*, Vol. 1. Grand Rapids: William B. Eerdmans, 1981.

Hoekema, Anthony A. *Created in God's Image*. Grand Rapids: Eerdmans, 1986.

Hughes, Philip. *The Church in Crisis: A History of the General Councils 325 - 1870*. London: Burns and Oates, 1961.

Bibliography

Huxley, Julian. *Religion Without Revelation*. New York: Harper and Brothers, 1957.

Irenaeus. *Against Heresies* (Selections) in *Early Christian Fathers* edited by Cyril Richardson, Library of Christian Classics, 358-397. Philadelphia: Westminster, 1953.

Ironside, H. A. *Expository Notes on the Prophet Isaiah*. New York: Loizeuax Brothers, 1952.

Johnson, Luke T. *The Writings of the New Testament*. Philadelphia: Fortress, 1986.

Josephus. *The Antiquities of the Jews*, 18. 3. iii. in *The Works of Josephus*, 2d ed. translated by William Whiston. Peabody: Hendrickson, 1987.

Keathley, Kenneth. *Salvation and Sovereignty*. Nashville: Broadman and Holman, 2010.

Kelly, Henry Ansgar. *Satan: A Biography*. Cambridge: Cambridge University Press, 2006.

Kelly, J. N. D. *Early Christian Doctrines*, 5th ed. New York: Continuum, 1977.

Kyle, Richard. *The Religious Fringe: A History of Alternative Religions in America*. Downers Grove: InterVarsity, 1993.

Letham, Robert. *The Holy Trinity*. Phillipsburg: P&R Publishing, 2004.

Licona, Michael R. *The Resurrection of Jesus: A New Historiographical Approach*. Downers Grove: InterVarsity Press Academic, 2010.

Lohse, Eduard. *The New Testament Environment*. 2d ed. translated by John E. Steely Nashville: Abingdon, 1974.

Lorkowski, C. M. *Atheism Considered*. Basingstoke: Palgrave MacMillan, 2021.

Louw, Johannes P. and Eugene A. Nida, eds. *Greek English Lexicon of the New Testament*, 2d ed. New York: United Bible Societies, 1989.

Maguire, Jack. *Essential Buddhism*. New York: Pocket Books, 2001.

Marsden, George M. *Fundamentalism and American Culture*, 2d ed. Oxford: Oxford University Press, 2006.

Marshall, I. Howard. *Kept by the Power of God: A Study of Perseverance and Falling Away*. Minneapolis: Bethany Fellowship, 1969.

Martin, Walter. *The Kingdom of the Cults*, 6th ed. Minneapolis: Bethany House, 2019.

Marxsen, Willi. *The Resurrection of Jesus of Nazareth*, trans. by Margaret Kohl. London: SCM Press, 1970 (originally pub. as *Die Auferstehung Jesu von Nazareth* [Mohn: Gütersloher, 1968]).

McConkie, Bruce R. *Mormon Doctrine*. 2d ed. Salt Lake City: Bookcraft, 1966.

McCulloch, Donald W. *The Trivialization of God: The Dangerous Illusion of a Manageable Deity*. Colorado Springs: Navpress, 1995.

McDannell, Colleen and Bernhard Lang. *Heaven: A History*. New Haven: Yale University, 1988.

McDowell, John C. and Scott A. Kirkland. *Eschatology*. Grand Rapids: William B. Eerdmans, 2018.

McGrath, Alister E. *A Brief History of Heaven*. Oxford: Blackwell, 2003.

McKinney, George D. *The Theology of the Jehovah's Witnesses*. Grand Rapids: Zondervan, 1962.

McLaren, Brian D. *A New Kind of Christianity*. New York: HarperOne, 2010.

McQuilkin, Robertson. *An Introduction to Biblical Ethics*. Wheaton: Tyndale, 1989.

Metaxas, Eric. *Bonhoeffer: Pastor, Martyr, Prophet, Spy*. Nashville: Thomas Nelson, 2010.

Milton, John. *Paradise Lost*, 1, 263, 1674 https://www.poetryfoundation.org/poems/45718/paradise-lost-book-1-1674-version (accessed January 25, 2023).

Moltmann, Jürgen. *The Spirit of Life*. Minneapolis: Fortress, 1992.

Bibliography

Moore, David George. *The Battle For Hell: A Survey and Evaluation of Evangelicals' Growing Attraction to the Doctrine of Annihilationism*. Lanham: University Press of America, 1995.

More, Thomas. *Utopia*, translated by Ralph Robinson. New York: Alfred A. Knopf, 1910.

Moreland, J. P. *Scaling the Secular City*. Grand Rapids: Baker, 1987.

Morrison, John Douglas. *Has God Said?* Eugene: Pickwick, 2006.

Muchembled, Robert. *A History of the Devil: From the Middle Ages to the Present*, translated by Jean Birrell. Cambridge: Polity, 2003.

Narayanan, Vadsudha. "Hinduism," in *Eastern Religions*. Edited by Michael D. Coogan, 8-109. Oxford: Oxford University Press, 2005.

Newport, John P. *The New Age Movement and the Biblical Worldview*. Grand Rapids: Eerdmans, 1998.

Nichols, Aidan. *Discovering Aquinas: An Introduction to His Life, Work, and Influence*. Grand Rapids: Eerdmans, 2002.

Norman, R. Stanton. "Human Sinfulness" in *A Theology for the Church*. edited by Daniel L. Akin. 409-478. Nashville: Broadman and Holman, 2007.

Norwich, John Julius. *A Short History of Byzantium*. New York: Vintage Books, 1997.

O'Meara, John J. *The Young Augustine*. 2nd edition. New York: Alba House, 2001.

Olson, C. Gordon. *What in the World is God Doing?* Cedar Knolls: Global Gospel Publishers, 1994.

Olson, Roger E. *The Story of Christianity*. Downers Grove: InterVarsity, 1999.

Origen. *On First Principles*, 3, 6. G.W. Butterworth, trans. New York: Harper and Row, 1966.

Osborn, Eric. *Tertullian: First Theology of the West*. Cambridge: Cambridge University Press, 1997.

Pelagius, "Letter to Demetrias" in *The Letters of Pelagius and His Followers*, edited and translated by B. R. Rees, 29-70. Woodbridge: The Boydell Press, 1991.

Pelikan, Jaroslav. *The Christian Tradition: A History of the Development of Doctrine*. vol. 3. Chicago: University of Chicago, 1978.

Picirilli, Robert E. *Grace, Faith, Free Will, Contrasting Views of Salvation: Calvinism and Arminianism*. Nashville: Randall House, 2002.

Pinnock, Clark H. *A Wideness in God's Mercy*. Grand Rapids: Zondervan, 1992.

Poythress, Vern Sheridan. *Logic: A God-Centered Approach to the Foundation of Western Thought*. Wheaton: Crossway, 2013.

Radmacher, Earl D. *What the Church is All About*. Chicago: Moody, 1972.

Rinpoche, Lama Zopa. *The Four Noble Truths: A Guide to Everyday Life*, edited by Yeo Puay Huei, Somerville: Wisdom Publications, 2018.

Roberts, R. Philip. *Mormonism Unmasked*. Nashville: Broadman and Holman, 1998.

Rogers, Jack. "The Church Doctrine of Biblical Authority," in *Biblical Authority*, edited by Jack Rogers, 17-46. Waco: Word Books, 1977.

Rosenberg, Alex. *The Atheist's Guide to Reality*. New York: W.W. Norton and Company, 2011.

Rowe, William L. "The Problem of Evil & Some Varieties of Atheism," in *The Evidential Argument from Evil*, edited by Daniel Howard-Snyder. 1-11. Bloomington: Indiana University, 1996.

Russell, Jeffrey Burton. *Satan: The Early Christian Tradition*. Ithaca: Cornell University, 1981.

Sanders, John. "Hell Yes! Hell No! Evangelical Debates on Eternal Punishment," in *Hell and its Afterlife: Historical and Contemporary Perspectives*, eds. Isabel Moreira and Margaret Toscano. 138Burlington: Ashgate, 2010.

Bibliography

Sanders, John. *The God Who Risks: A Theology of Divine Providence*, 2d. ed. Downers Grove: InterVarsity, 2007.

Shelley, Mary Wollstonecraft and Percy Bysshe Shelley. *Frankenstein or the Modern Prometheus*, 2d ed. ed. Charles E. Robinson. New York: Vintage, 2008.

Shorrosh, Anis A. *Islam Revealed*. Nashville: Thomas Nelson, 1988.

Sire, James W. *The Universe Next Door*. 5th ed. Downers Grove: InterVarsity, 2009.

Skinner, B. F. *Beyond Freedom and Dignity*. New York: Alfred A. Knopf, 1972.

Smith, B. F. *Christian Baptism*. Nashville: Broadman, 1970.

Solberg, R. L. *Torahism*. Rev. ed. Franklin: Williamson College Press, 2022.

Solomon, Robert C. and Kathleen M. Higgins. *A Short History of Philosophy*. New York: Oxford University Press, 1996.

Sproul, R. C. *The Last Days According to Jesus*. Grand Rapids: Baker, 1998.

Strong, Augustus Hopkins. *Systematic Theology*, Vol. 1. Philadelphia: Judson, 1907.

Tacitus. *The Annales*, 15, 44, trans. Alfred John Church and William Jackson Brodribb (The Internet Classics Archive, 1994-2009) http://classics.mit.edu/Tacitus/annals.htm (accessed February 1, 2023).

Tallaferro, Charles. "William Paley: Apologetics of Design and for Culture," in *The History of Apologetics*, edited by Benjamin K. Forrest, Joshua D. Chatraw, and Alister E. McGrath. Grand Rapids: Zondervan, 2020, 344-354.

Talvacchia, Bette. *Raphael*. New York: Phaidon, 2007.

Tertullian, *Against Praxeas*, 11 https://www.newadvent.org/fathers/0317.htm (accessed January, 21, 2023).

Theophilus. *Ad Autolycum*, translated by Robert M. Grant. Oxford: Clarendon, 1970.

Thiessen, Henry C. *Lectures in Systematic Theology*. Grand Rapids: Eerdmans, 1949.

Vanhoozer, Kevin J. *Is There Meaning in This Text?: The Bible, the Reader, and the Morality of Literary Knowledge*. Grand Rapids: Zondervan, 1998.

Vertovsek, Nenad and Ivana Greurgic Knezevic, Philosophy and Consciousness in the Future: Cyborgs and Artificial Intelligence waiting for Immortality, *In Media Res* 9, no. 16 (2020) https://doi.org/10.46640/imr.9.16.3 (accessed January 14, 2023).

Walls, Jerry L. *Purgatory: The Logic of Total Transformation.* Oxford: Oxford University, 2012.

Webb, Robert C. *The Real Mormonism.* New York: Sturgis and Walton, 1916.

Wells, G. A. *Cutting Jesus Down to Size.* Chicago: Open Court, 2009.

Weir, Ralph Stefan. "Christian Physicalism and the Biblical Argument for Dualism" in *International Journal for Philosophy of Religion* 91(2022):115-38, at URL https://doi.org/10.1007/s11153-021-09811-0 (accessed January 10, 2023).

Wesley, John. *Thoughts on Christian Perfectionism* in *The Works of John Wesley* vol. 13, edited by Paul Wesley Chilcote and Kenneth J. Collins, 57-80. Nashville: Abingdon, 2013.

Wright, N. T. *The Resurrection of the Son of God.* Minneapolis: Fortress, 2003.